DATE DUE

GAYLORD   PRINTED IN U.S.A.

Valéry and Poe

Valéry and Poe

A Literary Legacy

LOIS DAVIS VINES

NEW YORK UNIVERSITY PRESS

NEW YORK AND LONDON

Library of Congress Cataloging-In-Publication Data
Vines, Lois.
    Valéry and Poe : a literary legacy / Lois Davis Vines.
      p.   c.m.
    Includes bibliographical references and index.
    ISBN 0-8147-8771-1 (alk. paper)
    1. Valéry, Paul, 1871–1945—Knowledge—Literature. 2. Poe, Edgar Allan,
1809–1849—Influence. 3. French poetry—American influences.
    I. Title
PQ2643.A26Z84 1992   91-44348
848'.91209—dc20   CIP

New York University Press books are printed on acid-free paper,
and their binding materials are chosen for strength and durability.

Manufactured in the United States of America

c 10 9 8 7 6 5 4 3 2 1

To Robert, Sandra, and Jennifer

Contents

Acknowledgments

I wish to thank Ursula Franklin and Eric Carlson for their helpful suggestions and encouragement throughout various stages of this book's development. For my early interest in Valéry I am indebted to Jean Bucher, whose seminars at Georgetown University stimulated my desire to plunge more deeply into the published works and notebooks of one of France's greatest writers. Professor Bucher introduced me to the late Valéry scholar Emilie Noulet, who read some of my work and encouraged me to pursue the Poe connection. I am grateful to Judith Robinson-Valéry for responding at length to a number of questions I had concerning Valéry and Poe. Her husband, the late Claude Valéry, kindly shared early recollections of his father talking to him about Poe and recommending that he read the tales. I also appreciate the help of Burton Pollin, whose detailed knowledge of the *Marginalia* enabled me to clarify a difficult point.

For permission to use material that originally appeared in *Poe and Our Times*, edited by Benjamin Franklin Fisher IV, I acknowledge with gratitude the Edgar Allan Poe Society. I would also like to thank the editors of *French Forum* for their permission to include a modified version of an article published earlier in their journal. I am obliged as well to my editors at New York University Press for the careful attention they have given to the manuscript.

Abbreviations

B   *Eureka: A Prose Poem.* Ed. Richard P. Benton. Hartford, CT: Transcendental Books, 1973.

C   Paul Valéry, *Cahiers.* 29 vols. Paris: Centre National de la Recherche Scientifique, 1957–61.

C W   *The Collected Works of Paul Valéry.* 15 vols. Ed. Jackson Mathews. Princeton, NJ: Princeton UP, 1956–75. Contents of each volume:

1. *Poems*
2. *Poems in the Rough*
3. *Plays*
4. *Dialogues*
5. *Idée Fixe*
6. *Monsieur Teste*
7. *The Art of Poetry*
8. *Leonardo, Poe, Mallarmé*
9. *Masters and Friends*
10. *History and Politics*
11. *Occasions*
12. *Degas, Manet, Morisot*
13. *Aesthetics*
14. *Analects*
15. *Moi*

H   *Baudelaire on Poe.* Ed. and trans. Lois Hyslop and Francis E. Hyslop, Jr. State College, PA: Bald Eagle Press, 1952.

M   *Collected Works of Edgar Allan Poe.* 3 vols. Ed. Thomas Ollive Mabbott. Cambridge, MA, and London: The Belknap Press of Harvard UP, 1969, 1978. Contents of each volume:

      1. *Poems*
      2. *Tales and Sketches, 1831–1842*
      3. *Tales and Sketches, 1843–1849*

O   Paul Valéry, *Oeuvres*. 2 vols. Ed. Jean Hytier, coll. Pléiade. Paris: Gallimard, 1957, 1960.

OP   *Oeuvres en prose d'Edgar Allan Poe.* Trans. Charles Baudelaire; Notes by Y.-G. le Dantec, coll. Pléiade. Paris: Gallimard, 1951.

T   *Edgar Allan Poe, Essays and Reviews.* Comp. G. R. Thompson. New York: Literary Classics of the United States, 1984.

Introduction

> There is nothing in the critical field that should be of greater philosophical interest or prove more rewarding to analysis than the progressive modification of one mind by the work of another.
>
> —Valéry (CW 8: 241; O 1: 634)

Paul Valéry's death in 1945 marks the end of the century-long Poe cult in France, initiated by Baudelaire in 1847 when he discovered Poe's stories and decided to devote himself to the task of translating them into French. Baudelaire's vow to make Poe known in France was carried out with missionary-like fervor by his successors Mallarmé and Valéry. No major French author since Valéry has taken up the banner for Poe, to whom three generations of French writers were devoutly attached.

Although Baudelaire and Mallarmé have both been the subject of extensive research relating their thought and work to Poe's, the influence of Poe on Valéry has not been examined in a comprehensive manner. The neglect is probably due to the fact that Valéry published relatively little on the American writer. Studies on the influence of Poe in France make only brief mention of Valéry.[1] The best essay on the subject is T. S. Eliot's article "From Poe to Valéry," published over forty years ago.[2] Eliot's appraisal of Poe's effect on Valéry makes two essential points. First, Valéry's concept of pure poetry derives from Poe's idea that "a poem should have nothing in view but itself." Second, he points out that Valéry's interest in observing himself writing a poem comes from his reading of *The Philosophy of Composition*. After Eliot's article appeared, twenty-nine volumes of Valéry's handwritten notebooks were reproduced (each containing some nine hundred pages) and three volumes of correspondence were published. This material brings to light additional aspects of Poe's influence on Valéry that were not included in earlier studies.

Baudelaire and Mallarmé both played a part in the influence of Poe on Valéry because of the intricate chain of relationships that existed among them. Although Poe's effect on Valéry was unique, the Frenchman did nevertheless share a certain image of the American poet handed down to him by his compatriots. This continuity of admiration is interesting in itself. Poe died in 1849, a year after Baudelaire's first translation of one of his tales appeared in France. That Baudelaire had never met or corresponded with Poe did not diminish his devotion to translating Poe's stories, his cosmological poem *Eureka*, and some of his essays. Mallarmé admired both Poe and Baudelaire and supposedly came to Paris to meet the author of *The Flowers of Evil* but did not have the courage to approach him at a bookstall. Mallarmé learned English, he said, in order to have a better understanding of Poe, whose poems he rendered into French, thus completing a difficult task Baudelaire had not attempted. With a sense of mission accomplished, Mallarmé dedicated the volume of poems to the memory of Baudelaire.

Valéry admired Poe, Baudelaire, and Mallarmé, and had a personal association for seven years with Mallarmé before the latter's death in 1898. Valéry's first contact with Poe's work was through Baudelaire's translations and the introductions that accompanied them. Baudelaire mentioned in his 1852 essay that he could not give an account of *Eureka* because it required a special article. Valéry wrote that special article, "On Poe's *Eureka*,"[3] as a preface to the 1923 edition of Baudelaire's translation of the cosmological poem. In an essay on Baudelaire, Valéry expressed most eloquently his own admiration for Poe.[4] Valéry also made a contribution to the French version of Poe by translating fragments from the *Marginalia*.[5] The text is particularly interesting because Valéry added his own marginal notes alongside those he was translating.

Poe played a significant role in the relationship between Valéry and Mallarmé. The younger poet's first letter to Mallarmé, written from Montpellier when he was only nineteen, mentions Poe in a rather name-dropping fashion. Knowing Mallarmé's fondness for Poe, Valéry introduced himself as a person who is "deeply imbued with the cunning doctrines of the great Edgar Allan Poe—perhaps the most subtle artist of this century!"[6] When Mallarmé and Valéry met a year later in Paris, Valéry recalled that the subject of Poe brought the two of them together in a close relationship. But they got an essentially different message from their common mentor. Impressed by Poe's devotion to the technique of writing verse, Mallarmé dreamed of perfecting the art of writing and of giving it a universal value to be realized in a Book. Poe's effect on Valéry was, in one sense, just the opposite. Although he too was intrigued by poetic technique, for him it was not a means to the same end. Valéry's ultimate goal was not to create a supreme work but rather to understand the mind, his own mind, during the act of artistic creation. This particular effect of extreme intellectual self-consciousness distinguishes Poe's influence on Valéry from the effect the American author had on Valéry's predecessors.

As a keen observer of his own mind, Valéry was particularly interested in how literary influence operates. He makes a distinction between "imitation," in which the borrowed elements can be easily identified, and "influence," which produces significant changes that lead to "extreme originality." Influence is a normal process that every writer experiences, observes Valéry, but the problem is to transform what one receives into something innovative, bearing little resemblance to the work that inspired it. Valéry summarizes this idea in his often-quoted analogy: "The lion is made of assimilated sheep" (CW 14: 10; O 2: 478). The effects of Poe's work on Valéry exemplify Valéry's own concept of how literary influence should operate. Although there are a few examples of imitation in Valéry's work, the more important evidence reveals that Poe's essays, poems, tales, and cosmological poem *Eureka* inspired original creative endeavors that bear little resemblance to Valéry's American mentor.

Early in his literary career Valéry was obsessed with reading Poe. Traces of this immersion are evident in three of his prose pieces composed between 1889 and 1895. His first literary essay submitted for publication at age nineteen, entitled "On Literary Technique," is a naive paraphrasing of *The Philosophy of Composition.*

Valéry begins by declaring that the most important consideration of the poet must be to create the maximum effect on the reader, an idea that comes straight from Poe. As the essay continues, other phrases also bear a striking resemblance to Poe's work. Valéry: "the poem's only aim is to prepare its denouement"; Poe: "with the denouement proper . . . the poem . . . may be said to have its completion"; Valéry: "a hundred lines at the most will make up its longest poems"; Poe: "I conceived the proper *length* for my intended poem—a length of about one hundred lines."[7] Valéry goes on to mention Poe by name, but there is no indication that the ideas he expresses in the first part of the essay come directly from the American author. The essay would have been published by the *Le Courrier libre* in Paris had the literary journal not gone out of business. The manuscript was found after Valéry's death and finally published more than half-a-century after it was written. Although the essay clearly lacks originality, it is interesting to our study because it shows that Valéry was indeed "penetrated," as he said, by the ideas of Poe.

Valéry's next attempt at writing an essay was very successful. His *Introduction to the Method of Leonardo da Vinci*, written at age twenty-three, is still considered to be one of his best prose pieces. The original approach to the subject was inspired by his reading of Poe. Having been invited to prepare an article on Leonardo, Valéry decided that instead of bringing together biographical details and descriptions of the artist's work, he would recreate the mind that engendered the work. Poe's description of how he wrote "The Raven" suggested to Valéry the possibility of a new critical method. Valéry was convinced that the only valid means of evaluating an artist's (or a writer's) work was to examine the relationship between what the mind was attempting to do and how well it succeeded.

Since Valéry's approach to the study of Leonardo was different from anything that had previously been done, he begins the essay by explaining his new method to the reader. Here again, part of his explanation seems to come directly from *The Philosophy of Composition*. In a paragraph beginning with the statement "Many an error that distorts our judgment of human achievements is due to a strange disregard of their genesis" (CW 8: 8; O 1: 1156–57),

Valéry repeats the premise on which *The Philosophy of Composition* is based. He goes on to explain that most authors do not have the courage to take a look at how a particular work was created; other writers, says Valéry, could not even understand the process. Like Poe, Valéry attributes this failure to the vanity of the author, who would prefer to give the impression that his work sprang forth on its own. As both authors point out, inspiration plays a role in the creative process, but conscious effort, chance, and decisions made at the last minute are also involved. Valéry was fascinated by the drama that takes place in the creative mind and believed that Poe was the first to describe it.

It was this "drama of the intellect," as Valéry called it, that intrigued him for a lifetime. His essay on Leonardo sets forth an approach to literary criticism that he was to use later to evaluate the work of other writers. Rejecting a biographical or historical approach, Valéry attempted to discover the elements of artistic creation and the laws that govern them in an effort to understand the work of art as a machine designed to have an effect on the individual mind. He believed that Poe placed the study of literature on an analytical basis, a goal to which he himself aspired. Valéry expresses this idea very clearly in one of his *Notebooks*: "Poe was the first to think of giving literary works a theoretical foundation. Mallarmé and myself. I think I was the first to try having no recourse at all to the old notions, but to make a fresh start on purely analytical bases" (CW 8: 356–57; C 12: 703). Inspired by his reading of Poe, Valéry remarks in his essay "On the Teaching of *Poetics*" that "it seems strange that the form of intellectual activity which engenders the works themselves should be studied hardly at all" (CW 13: 83; O 1: 1438). His own goal was to consider literature as a *"kind of extension and application of certain properties of language"* (CW 13: 85; O 1: 1440), thus initiating an approach that we now recognize as a precursor to modern literary criticism.

At about the same time that Valéry was preparing his study of Leonardo da Vinci (1894–95), he began working on another prose piece that would eventually be titled *The Evening with Monsieur Teste*. His *Notebooks* and letters show that during the same period he was reading Poe's tales, a fact that some critics have overlooked.[8] In the *Notebook* dated 1894, he makes reference to an idea for a literary project, calling it for the moment "The Life and Adventures of Ch. Auguste Dupin" (C 1: 50). The unpublished manuscript of an early draft of *The Evening with Monsieur Teste* bears the title "Memoirs of Chevalier Dupin."[9] A careful examination of *The Evening with Monsieur Teste* and "The Murders in the Rue Morgue" provides convincing evidence that Poe's story served as a model for Valéry when he created his own fictional character Edmond Teste.

Valéry saw in Dupin a mind capable of observing its own analytical faculties. Not only was Poe's detective able to think logically, he also took pleasure in retracing the mental processes by which he discovered a coherent pattern in supposedly unrelated events. Teste is portrayed as an intellectual superman who understands how his own mind functions. He never engages in spectacular feats of logic that characterize Dupin, thus bringing him fame. On the contrary, the only mystery Teste attempts to unravel is that of his own mind. He aspires to no practical application of his mental power and is absorbed by only one question, *"Que peut un homme?"*—What is a man capable of intellectually? Teste is in this sense a purified Dupin; he seeks intellectual self-comprehension for its own sake and makes no attempt to exhibit his superior mind in public.

Another of Poe's tales, "MS. Found in a Bottle," inspired Valéry's prose poem called "Manuscript Found in a Brain" before the author changed the title to "Agatha" and then abandoned the piece. Published by Valéry's daughter after his death, "Agatha" reveals several striking similarities with Poe's tale. Like "MS. Found in a Bottle," Valéry's prose poem is recounted in first-person narration, describes a solitary and mysterious sea voyage representing a sequence of mental states, makes use of similar images, and attempts to circumscribe and preserve the life of the mind through the self-conscious act of writing. Valéry imagined "Agatha" as the interior of Teste's night during which consciousness would be freed from the body and could thus seek pure self-comprehension.

The description of Leonardo's creative mind and Edmond Teste's analytical brain reveal Valéry's obsession with intellectual rigor and self-comprehension. After publishing the prose pieces on Leonardo and Teste and several poems, Valéry went through a twenty-year period (1897–1917) during which he devoted himself to observing his own mind. His main goal was no longer to try to publish, but rather to learn more about how his own brain came to grips with mathematics, the sciences, and the creative process of writing a poem. His *Notebooks* during those years contain many examples of mathematical equations interspersed with comments on literary problems. Looking back on this period in a letter to Albert Thibaudet, dated 1912, Valéry describes the role that Poe played in this shift of focus in his life:

> I was brought to feel [Mallarmé's] power most by a reading of Poe. I read in him what I wanted and caught that *fever of lucidity that he communicates.*
>
> *Consequence:* I gave up writing verse. That art, which became impossible for me from 1892, was already simply an exercise, or an application of researches that were more important. Why not develop within oneself that which alone, in the genesis of a poem, is of interest to oneself?[10]

These lines express one of the most important aspects of Poe's influence on Valéry. This "demon of lucidity," as Valéry called Poe, pointed him in the direction of solving the mystery of his own mind. Valéry never claimed to have succeeded, but he never lost sight of his goal. One of the last lines he scribbled before his death was "After all, I did what I could . . ."[11]

During the twenty-year period referred to above, Valéry did not actually stop writing. He continued to compose poems and to develop topics that interested him, but little of his writing appeared in print. Finally, in 1917 Valéry published a long poem entitled *The Young Fate* (*La Jeune Parque*) that brought him immediate recognition as an outstanding poet. Five years later he published a slender volume of shorter poems, *Charmes*, which also became a bestseller among poetic works. A constant theme represented symbolically in many of the poems is the drama of artistic creation. Valéry went one step farther than Poe. Not only did he observe himself while writing a poem, the creative process itself became a major theme in his poetry.

The admiration for Poe's poetic theory that Valéry expressed in his first literary essay did not diminish over the years. From 1937 until just a few months before his death, Valéry taught a course in poetics at the renowned Collège de France, where a chair had been established in his honor. Poe was often the subject of his lectures.[12] He explained *The Philosophy of Composition* and *The Poetic Principle* to his students while giving examples from his own experience gathered from many years of observing himself write. Like Poe, he believed that writing poetry is a conscious act calculated to arouse emotion in the reader. Valéry liked creating verse within the strict rules of classical French prosody. A sudden inspiration or a stroke of luck might play a role in the creation of a poem, but for the most part, poetic composition requires a conscious, analytical approach to language. Valéry believed that Poe was the first to recommend eliminating from poetry all subjects that can best be treated in prose, such as history, politics, and morality. This was an important point for Valéry, and much has been made of his concept of "pure poetry," which was reaffirmed by his reading of Poe.

Valéry's interest in Poe was not simply a youthful enthusiasm. Comments in his *Notebooks* show that he continued to read Poe and think about him for the rest of his life. A series of references in his *Notebooks* dated 1919–20 indicate that he intended to give a lecture on Poe. He refers to his favorite American author as "conscious consciousness" and "the engineer of the mind" (CW 8: 354; C 6: 767, 772). He mentions that he would have difficulty talking about Poe because he had read him so much. There are also several references to *Eureka*, which was to become the subject of Valéry's only published essay on Poe, written when he was fifty years old.

Valéry saw in *Eureka*, once again, a drama of the intellect. He believed that any cosmogony is a myth, but at the same time he admired the heroic effort of the human brain as it tries to grasp the very notion of a universe and a beginning. This history of thought, says Valéry, might be summarized in these words: *"It is absurd by what it seeks, great by what it finds"* (CW 8: 170; O 1: 862). He admired Poe for his leap of the imagination backed up by scientific explanations. Valéry did not like several features of *Eureka*. He was unimpressed by the pretensions of the author, did not care for the solemn tone of the preamble, and was disappointed that all the consequences were not deduced with precision. And, as a final criticism, Valéry says, "There is a God." Nonetheless, he was fascinated by the ideas developed in *Eureka*. Poe awakened in him an interest in science, which had been numbed by the dismal instructors of his school days. In Poe's discussion of the symmetrical and reciprocal relationship of matter, time, space, gravity, and light, Valéry recognized a similarity with the formal symmetry of Einstein's universe. In spite of his admiration for Poe's scientific affirmations, Valéry concludes that the universe escapes intuition and logic. He affirms, however, that "it is the glory of man to waste his powers on the void. Often such crack-brained researches lead to unforeseen discoveries" (CW 8: 170; O 1: 862). He was convinced that imagination plays an important role in science and that scientific analysis is involved in creative achievements. Valéry believed that Poe was the first writer to see these relationships.

Looking back on his literary career, Valéry remarked in 1933 that Leonardo, Poe, and Mallarmé had a deep influence on him.[13] He explained the particular way in which this influence operated in his case. Certain aspects of the works of these men caught his attention, and he would then imagine the mind that had produced the work. This mental image, a creation of his own mind, had the greatest effect on him. Valéry wrote several essays on Leonardo and Mallarmé, but since he published only one article on Poe, it has been necessary to sift through his letters and *Notebooks* in order to recreate his vision of Poe. There emerges from this material a striking portrait. Valéry's Poe was a literary genius, a logical thinker who attempted to place creative work on an analytical basis, and the first writer to explore the psychological aspects of literature.

When we apply Valéry's own concept of literary influence, we discover numerous examples of "assimilated Poe" in his work. Upon close examination, traces of Poe's tales become evident in *Monsieur Teste*, "Agatha," and the poem "Disaster," all original creations that bear only the most subtle resemblance to the works that inspired them. Valéry's essay on Leonardo da Vinci shows a direct connection with Poe's *Philosophy of Composition*, which also provided the basis of Valéry's critical approach. Certain aspects of Valéry's poetics seem to come from *The Poetic Principle*, in which Poe sets forth his aesthetic doctrine. But common to all the specific cases of Poe's influence on Valéry there is a unifying theme: the "drama of the intellect," an expression Valéry uses to refer to his obsession with understanding how the mind functions. He was convinced that Poe was the first poet to consider the direct connections between the writer's intellect and his creation. The American "engineer of the mind," as Valéry called Poe, intrigued him for a lifetime.

CHAPTER ONE

The Image of Poe Inherited from Baudelaire and Mallarmé

This from Baudelaire speaking of the same Poe: "that marvelous brain always on alert." This struck me like the sound of a horn, a signal that excited the whole of my intellect.
—Valéry (CW 8: 358; C 22: 489)

In his essay "The Place of Baudelaire," published in 1924, Valéry remarked that Poe "would today be completely forgotten if Baudelaire had not taken up the task of introducing him into European literature" (CW 8: 204; O 1: 607). Valéry's brief statement contains two ideas that are often repeated in studies on Poe published in France. First, there is the implication that Poe's talent as a writer went unrecognized or neglected by his fellow countrymen. Second, had it not been for Baudelaire's devotion to the task of translating Poe's work, the American writer would never have received the recognition he deserved. There is no denying that French writers have played a major role in creating Poe's reputation as a literary genius, a status British and American critics are reluctant to grant unconditionally.

Baudelaire's discovery of Poe is an interesting story that bears repeating, especially in light of the effect this literary revelation had on succeeding generations of French writers. Baudelaire scholars have pieced together the series of events that brought Poe's tales to the French writer's attention, although there is some disagreement on specific details. In a rather ironical turn of events, Poe's name was introduced to the French public by press reports of a lawsuit involving plagiarism, a charge brought against Poe himself on several occasions. According to Patrick Quinn,[1] citing Lemonnier as his source, Emile Forgues, a French journalist whose interest in literature inspired him to translate stories from British and American sources, published a version of "The Murders in the Rue Morgue" that had appeared earlier, unbeknownst to him, in the Paris daily *La Quotidienne*. Although this newspaper raised no objection, a rival paper, *La Presse*, which Forgues had once accused of plagiarism, brought suit against him. The publicity generated by the litigation made the name Edgar Poe known in France in late 1846.[2] Capitalizing on the curiosity about the American writer that resulted from the Forgues trial, other French newspapers began publishing translations of Poe's stories.

Bandy's more recent research points out that it was Forgues who filed suit against *La Presse* when the paper refused to publish a letter in which he contended that he had a right to borrow the translated story from its author. Thus, the suit was based on Forgues' legal right to response rather than the plagiarism issue. Bandy does not believe the trial was a *cause célèbre* worthy of bringing Poe's name to Baudelaire's attention:

The fact is that the trial created hardly a ripple in the newspapers of the time, which were forbidden, with few exceptions, to report court proceedings. Only a handful of accounts were published and they were concerned almost exclusively with the quarrel between Forgues and *La Presse* and with the application of the law guaranteeing right of response. It would have taken a sharp eye, indeed, to discover Poe's name in the mass of legal verbiage.[3]

According to Bandy, Baudelaire's first impression of Poe came when he discovered Isabelle Meunier's translation of "The Black Cat," published in *La Démocratie pacifique* on January 27, 1847.

More important than the plagiarism trial was Forgues' long article on Poe that had appeared a couple of months earlier. He wrote a critique of twelve tales included in the Wiley and Putnam edition, thus becoming the first critic to publish a review of Poe's work in a foreign language.[4] The twenty-page article, which appeared in the prestigious *Revue des deux Mondes* on October 15, 1846, is particularly significant because it recognized Poe as a "logician, a pursuer of abstract truths," and as a "lover of the most eccentric hypotheses and the most difficult calculations."[5] Although Forgues knew Poe only through his short stories, he launched his reputation in France as a serious writer by comparing Poe's ideas to those of Pascal and Laplace, thus placing emphasis on the intellectual qualities that were to have a great appeal to Valéry.

Forgues appreciated Poe's skill at making scientific (and in some cases pseudo-scientific) analyses a plausible ingredient in a captivating story. After recounting the events of Poe's tale "A Descent into the Maelstrom," in which an uneducated Norwegian fisherman being sucked into a whirlpool improvises a theory of gravity that saves his life, Forgues concludes that

if everything that is rigorously and strictly possible in the situation is conceived by the human mind, one must admit the possibility that extreme peril might induce in a man . . . a peculiar lucidity of intellect, a miraculous power of observation, and that is enough to make this story captivate you.[6]

It is this "lucidity of intellect" that attracted both Baudelaire and Valéry to Poe's fiction. Forgues also recognized in Poe's detective C. Auguste Dupin qualities that were to inspire Valéry's creation of Monsieur Teste. After giving a synopsis of "The Murders in the Rue Morgue," Forgues shows that Poe is concerned with probabilities, which he weighs by intuition rather than by rules. Having described Dupin's analytical feat, Forgues remarks:

Apply this astonishing perspicacity, the result of almost superhuman concentration of the mind and of a marvelous intuition, to a police operation and you have . . . an investigator whom nothing escapes. . . . Mr. Poe fastens upon this situation and with completely American tenacity develops the extraordinary events to their extreme limits.[7]

These brief excerpts from Forgues' article show the keen insight the first French critic of Poe's work brought to the reading public. Although Bandy maintains that Baudelaire probably did not see this review at the time of its publication, other critics, including Quinn, believe that Forgues' analyses of "The Black Cat" and "Mesmeric Revelation" caught Baudelaire's attention, thus initiating the century-long fascination with Poe in Europe.

Contrary to popular belief, Baudelaire was not the first translator of Poe's works. Bandy has identified four earlier translators, the first publishing an adaptation of a Poe tale in a French news-paper in 1844. It was Isabelle Meunier's translation of "The Black Cat" (1847), however, that captivated Baudelaire and inspired his decision to find more of the American writer's tales and translate them himself. In July 1848 the Republican paper *La Liberté de penser,* whose staff included one of Baudelaire's former school-mates, published Baudelaire's first translation of a Poe tale, "Mes-meric Revelation" ("Révélation magnétique"). Why he chose this particular story, not one of Poe's best, is unclear, although his interest could be explained by the fact that Mesmerism was a popu-lar subject in Europe and America in the nineteenth century.[8] The story is a rather dull account of the narrator who puts a Mr. Vankirk into a hypnotic trance and interrogates him on the hid-den realities of the invisible world, including the theory of mat-ter, the gradations of matter, and the hierarchy of beings. While in a mesmerized state, Mr. Vankirk grasps a relationship that must have brought comfort to Baudelaire:

All things are either good or bad by comparison. A sufficient analysis will show that pleasure, in all cases, is but the contrast of pain. *Positive* pleasure is a mere idea. To be happy at any one point we must have suffered at the same. Never to suffer would have been never to have been blessed. (M 3: 1039)

Although Vankirk's reasoning is not always easy to follow, a story recounting the perceptions of a man who has transcended reality appealed to Baudelaire. The fact that the translation attracted no critical attention in the press did not daunt Baudelaire's determi-nation to make Poe known in France. He decided to use every means possible to obtain American editions of Poe in order to con-tinue his work.

Baudelaire's interest in Poe was more than youthful enthusiasm that would quickly wane. He devoted the next sixteen years of his relatively short life (forty-five years) to the laborious task of trans-lating Poe's tales and several of his essays, thus sacrificing time and energy he could have spent on his own literary production. While translating Poe, Baudelaire perfected his English, an en-deavor that made the time-consuming work even more tedious. As a child he had acquired some English from his mother, who was born in England and spent most of her childhood there.[9] He had also studied the language in school but, by the time he began the Poe translations, he realized there was a great deal more to learn. Challenged by the task, he made every effort to obtain dictionaries of American English and sought out "Yankees," as he called them, whom he could interrogate on the meaning of certain phrases or words that baffled him. Although some of his early pieces have flaws, Baudelaire's French version of Poe's work is generally considered a masterpiece in the art of translation.

Baudelaire's dramatic reaction to Poe's life and work has become legend in literary history. At the age of twenty-six he discovered in Poe's family history uncanny parallels with his own life and in Poe's work ideas that he himself had already conceived. Baudelaire recounted his recollection of the discovery in a letter dated February 18, 1860, sent to literary critic Armand Fraisse in Lyon:

In 1846 or '47 I came across a few fragments by Edgar Poe. I experienced a singular shock. His complete works were not assembled into a single edition until after his death, so I had the patience to make contact with Americans living in Paris to borrow from them collections of newspapers edited by Poe. And then—believe me if you will—I found poems and short stories that I had thought of, but in a vague, confused, and disorderly way and that Poe had been able to bring together to perfection. It was that that lay behind my enthusiasm and my long years of patience.[10]

When Baudelaire experienced the singular excitement that led to his Poe obsession, he had just published two monographs, the *Salon of 1845* and the *Salon of 1846*, which brought him notoriety as an outstanding art critic. Although his first poems were published in late 1846, his reputation as a poet was far from established. Between 1848 and his premature death in 1867, Baudelaire published five volumes of Poe translations[11] while continuing to write articles, reviews, and poems that were later to make up the collection *The Flowers of Evil*, published in 1857.

Baudelaire's obsession with Poe inspired him to write a major article on the American author that appeared in the 1852 March and April issues of the *Revue de Paris*.[12] Entitled "Edgar Allan Poe,

His Life and Works," the essay is important for two reasons. First, with emotional verve, it brought details about Poe's life to the attention of French readers for the first time (Forgues' article did not include biographical information). Second, Baudelaire's analysis of Poe's work and the biographical material contained in the article became the source of information for future French authors. Another article by Baudelaire bearing a similar title, published in 1856,[13] is for the most part a revision of the 1852 essay.

Baudelaire's description of Poe's love of science and his analytical mind caught the attention of Valéry, whose interest in mathematics and science was reawakened by Baudelaire's essays and translations. Although Valéry inveighed against including biographical details in literary criticism, preferring instead to concentrate on the mind that engendered the work, Poe was an exception to this rule. In his lectures on poetics, Valéry, who normally did not attempt to move his audience by emotional evocations, recounted to his students poignant details of Poe's life, which he had learned from Baudelaire.[14]

The version of Poe's biography handed down from one generation of French poets to the next was for a long time based on Baudelaire's account, which, through no fault of his own, contained a few errors. Since so little had been published on Poe in France, Baudelaire had to rely on newspaper reports and conversations with Americans whom he managed to meet in Paris. In a totally fictitious account, Baudelaire relates that Poe ran away from home to participate in the Greek Revolution after a violent argument with his adoptive father over gambling debts. These details reinforce the image of the Byronic hero, a misunderstood genius who leaves his homeland to sacrifice himself in the name of the oppressed,[15] but in Poe's case the adventure was pure fancy. In the Baudelaire version, Poe survived the Greek experience and went on to Russia, where, after getting into trouble, he was saved from exile to Siberia by the American Consul's intervention.[16] Although this story makes good reading, Poe's foreign travel was limited to the five years he spent in England with his adoptive parents (1815–20).

In spite of these errors, Baudelaire's 1852 essay provided a great deal of information about Poe's life and work that contributed to the image of Poe as a creative genius whose talent was unappreciated in his own country.[17]   All of Baudelaire's references to America are scornful.   He was convinced that for Poe, "the United States was a vast cage, a great counting-house, and throughout his life he made grim efforts to escape the influence of this antipathetic atmosphere" (H: 39; OP: 1002).   Numerous references to Balzac connect Poe to one of France's best writers:

Some time before Balzac sank into the final abyss, uttering the noble cries of a hero who still had things to do, Edgar Poe, who resembles him in several ways, fell stricken by a frightful death.   France lost one of its greatest geniuses, and America lost a story-teller, a critic, a philosopher who was hardly made for her. (H: 41; OP: 1003)

By recounting moving details of Poe's life spent in a country that did not have the intellectual capacity to understand his genius, Baudelaire stirred his readers both emotionally and intellectually by implying that the French had the sensitivity and intelligence to give this writer the recognition he deserved.   This essay prepared the way for Baudelaire's first volume of Poe's tales, published in 1856.

Using Valéry's own method of placing himself in the mind of the reader of a work, we can try to imagine his response to Baudelaire's description of Poe.   A number of references to Poe's intellect no doubt made a strong impression on Valéry, who had a special interest in developing his own analytical faculties.   The quality that impressed him the most in the human intellect is its ability to combine artistic creation with scientific analysis.   In Poe he recognized this particular trait, which Baudelaire mentions several times in his essay:

[Poe] was an excellent student and made incredible progress in mathematics; he had an unusual aptitude for physics and natural science, which may be noted in passing, since in several of his works there appears a great preoccupation with science. (H: 47; OP: 1007)

Another passage describing Poe's mental concentration must have impressed Valéry for two reasons.   First, it mentions Poe's recounting *Eureka*, a work that particularly interested Valéry and which he recalled having read aloud to his boss, who had no background in science. Second, the passage describes Poe as being unconcerned by rules of society, a characteristic Valéry uses to depict the fictitious personality of Monsieur Teste. Here is Baudelaire's description of Poe:

He would sit down in a tavern, beside some dirty scapegrace, and would gravely explain to him the grand outlines of his terrible book *Eureka* with an implacable composure, as he would have dictated to a secretary, or argued with Kepler, Bacon or Swedenborg. That was a peculiar trait of his character. No man ever freed himself more completely from the rules of society, or bothered himself less about passersby. (H: 62; OP: 1016)

Even in Baudelaire's explanation of Poe's continual struggle with alcoholism, he takes care to emphasize that the disease had no effect on his intellect:

It is an astonishing fact, but one attested by all who knew him, that neither the purity nor the finish of his style, nor the clearness of his thought, nor his ardor for work and for difficult researches were altered by this terrible habit. (H: 63; OP: 1017)

The details of Poe's life that especially interested Valéry were those that recounted the survival of the intellect against all odds, certainly one of the most striking aspects of Poe's sad life.

The shock of recognition that inspired Baudelaire's obsession with Poe was much broader than Valéry's, encompassing both his personal history and his literary endeavors. Baudelaire's strong feelings of identity with Poe were based on a number of similarities. They had both lost their biological fathers at an early age and had to deal with surrogates, a stern stepfather, in Baudelaire's case, and a foster father in Poe's. As a consequence, their mothers played a major role in their lives, creating a source of both conflict and comfort. Although Poe had three mother figures, Elizabeth Arnold (his biological mother, whom he lost at age two), Mrs. Allan (his foster mother), and Mrs. Clemm (his aunt and mother-in-law), it was Mrs. Clemm whom Baudelaire idolized. He dedicated his volume of Poe translations to her with these words:

I owe this public homage to a mother whose greatness and goodness honor the World of Letters as much as the marvelous creations of her son. I should be inexpressibly happy if an errant ray of that benevolence which was the sun of his life could, across the sea that separates us, reach me, insignificant and obscure, and comfort me with its magnetic warmth. (H: 164; OP: 4)

Each writer sought his mother's approval and encouragement as he confronted a day-to-day existence that seemed resolutely hostile, or at least indifferent, to literary aspirations. Although he never met Mrs. Clemm, in Baudelaire's mind she represented the ideal mother for whom he yearned because of her confidence in Poe's talent as a writer.

Both poets were brought up in well-to-do families but were later condemned to live hand-to-mouth because of their determination to establish themselves as writers. They counted on family money to tide them over until they could earn an honorable living on the income from their creative efforts. Poe expected to receive an inheritance from Mr. Allan but was bitterly disappointed to find that his name was not even mentioned in the final will and testament. After the death of his first wife, Mr. Allan remarried late in life. He apparently felt a stronger responsibility toward his second family than toward the adopted son who had caused him so much grief. Baudelaire fared better, at least at first. At the age of twenty-one he received an inheritance of 100,000 francs from his father but managed to spend half of it on a lavish apartment, hashish, and other less harmful extravagances during the first eighteen months of his majority. To protect the rest of the money, a family lawyer was appointed to dole out monthly payments, which were never enough to cover past debts and living expenses. Consequently, both Poe and Baudelaire shared a common agony—keeping the bill collectors at bay while pursuing their creative endeavors.

Their unusual life-styles brought reprobation from family and society, especially in regard to abuses of alcohol and drugs. Even though the two men lived in different cultures, they shared the status of *personae non gratae*, a fate bestowed upon poets, in Baudelaire's opinion. The bond of sympathy these similarities inspired motivated Baudelaire's determination to establish Poe as a great writer and a literary prophet, whose voice was ridiculed or ignored in his own country.

However interesting the biographical similarities between the two writers, of greater importance to our study are the effects of Poe's literary works on Baudelaire and his successors. Valéry's essay on Baudelaire contains insights that point out the most basic elements of this case of influence. Valéry emphasizes the important role Baudelaire has played in European literature, an influence that is largely based on one small volume of poems, *The Flowers of Evil*, containing less than three hundred pages. Valéry poses two essential questions in regard to Baudelaire: "What explains this extraordinary importance?" and "How could a man who was so peculiar, so far from the average, engender so extensive a movement?" (CW 8: 194; O 1: 599). Valéry offers his own response:

[Baudelaire's] great posthumous reputation, his spiritual richness, his fame now reaching its highest period, must depend not only on his own value as a poet but also on exceptional circumstances. Critical intelligence allied to the gift of poetry is one such circumstance. To this rare combination Baudelaire owes a capital discovery. He was born sensuous and precise; his demanding sensibility led him to pursue the most refined experiments in form; but these gifts would doubtless have made him no more than a rival of Gautier, or an excellent Parnassian, had his curiosity of mind not earned him the good fortune of discovering in Edgar Allan Poe a new intellectual world. The daemon of lucidity; the genius of analysis; the inventor of the newest, most seductive combinations of logic and imagination, of calculation, and mystical fervor; the psychologist of the exceptional; the literary engineer who had studied and utilized all the resources of art: thus Poe stood revealed to him and filled him with wonder. So many original views and extraordinary promises bewitched him; his talent was transformed, his destiny splendidly changed. (CW 8: 194; O 1: 599)

This passage not only reveals the dramatic aspect of Baudelaire's discovery of Poe, it also expresses very eloquently Valéry's own admiration for the American writer. Valéry goes on to recognize in Poe "a lucidity such as had never to this degree been encountered in a head gifted for poetic invention" (CW 8: 202–3; O 1: 605–6). But, he adds, Poe was born "among a people that were wholly concerned with their material development" (CW 8: 202; O 1: 605), a phrase that echoes Baudelaire's description of Poe's native culture as "a greedy world, hungry for material things" (H: 123; OP: 1050).

Valéry divides Poe's effect on Baudelaire into two categories: imitation and influence. While some critics have focused on particular similarities between Poe's poems and Baudelaire's,[18] Valéry considers the importance of such examples "merely local." Nonetheless, these exact transpositions have been the subject of extensive research and are, in fact, quite interesting to examine, especially in light of Baudelaire's own amazement upon discovering the resemblances. In a letter to Théophile Thoré (June 20, 1864) defending the painter Manet, whom Thoré had accused of creating pastiches of Goya, Baudelaire argues that Manet had never seen Goya's paintings. He then compares this claim of imitation to accusations made by critics who believed he borrowed from Poe:

You doubt the truth of this? You doubt that such amazing geometrical parallels can exist in nature? Well, I myself am accused of imitating Edgar Poe! Do you know why I've translated Poe so patiently? Because he was like me. The first time I opened one of his books, I saw, with horror and delight, not only topics I'd dreamed of, but *sentences* I'd thought of, and that he had written twenty years before.[19]

The subject of the Poe imitations seems to have preyed on Baudelaire's mind toward the end of his life. On February 18, 1865, he mentions the accusations again in a letter to his friend Mme Paul Meurice:

I lost a great deal of time in translating Edgar Poe and the great benefit it brought me was to make some kindly souls say I'd borrowed *my* poems from Poe—poems I'd written ten years before I knew Poe's works.[20]

Examples of Baudelaire's imitations of Poe most often cited by critics are found in "Le Flambeau vivant" and Poe's "To Helen." The texts of the two poems are presented below with the numbers in parentheses in Poe's poem indicating the lines in Baudelaire's poem that appear to be imitations. Only the significant portions of the first poem are reprinted here.

To Helen

All—all expired save thee—save less than thou
Save only the divine light in thine eyes—
Save but the soul in thine uplifted eyes.
I was but them—they were the world to me.
(4)   . . . those cristalline, celestial spheres!
            . . . *Only thine eyes remained.*
They *would not* go—they never yet have gone.
Lighting my lonely pathway home that night,
They have not left me (as my hopes have) since.
(1)   They follow me—they lead me through the years.
(7)   They are my ministers—yet I their slave.
(2-4)   Their office is to illumine and enkindle—
(5)   My duty, to *be saved* by their bright light
And purified in their electric fire,
And sanctified in their elysian fire.
(6)   They fill my soul with Beauty (which is Hope),
And are far up in Heaven—the stars I kneel to
In the sad, silent watches of my night;
(9)   While even in the meridian glare of day
(14)   I see them still—two sweetly scintillant
Venuses, unextinguished by the sun!

Le Flambeau vivant

Ils marchent devant moi, ces Yeux pleins de lumières,
Qu'un Ange très-savant a sans doute aimantés;
Ils marchent, ces divins frères qui sont mes frères,
Secouant dans mes yeux leurs feux diamantés.

Me sauvant de tout piège et de tout péché grave,
Ils conduisent mes pas dans la route du Beau;
Ils sont mes serviteurs et je suis leur esclave;
Tout mon être obéit à ce vivant flambeau.

Charmants Yeux, vous brillez de la clarté mystique
Qu'ont les cierges brûlant en plein jour; le soleil
Rougit, mais n'éteint pas leur flamme fantastique;

Il célèbrent la Mort, vous chantez le Réveil;
Vous marchez en chantant le réveil de mon âme,
Astres dont nul soleil ne peut flétrir la flamme!

As Wetherill points out,[21] eight of the fourteen lines of Baudelaire's poem appear to be translations from Poe. Additional examples given by Wetherill reveal images and metaphors in Baudelaire's poems that can be traced to Poe's.

The striking similarities between numerous lines of poetry found in the works of the two writers pose an interesting question: Did Baudelaire incorporate lines from Poe into his own poems or, even more intriguing, did he find in Poe's work ideas and phrases that he had already conceived, as he claimed in the letter cited above. Charles Asselineau, Baudelaire's friend and biographer, insisted that the poet completed the poems in question before 1856. Ernest Prarond, another contemporary, recalled that Baudelaire constantly rewrote and corrected his poems, thus allowing the possibility of incorporating lines from Poe.[22] Although the question has never been put to rest and perhaps never will be, readers still experience amazement upon discovering the numerous similarities.

This type of literary research based on identifying exact imitations was of little consequence to Valéry for the very reason that it proves nothing more than simple imitation. In his mind, imitation is not really influence because it is so obvious. By his definition, influence engenders originality, a quality that goes beyond repetition to create a new element whose constituent parts are no longer recognizable. Valéry's concept of influence is expressed in his often-quoted analogy: "Nothing is more 'original,' nothing more 'oneself' than to feed on others. But one has to digest them. A lion is made of assimilated sheep" (CW 14: 10; O 2: 478). Thus, according to Valéry, identifying the "unassimilated parts" of Poe's work found in Baudelaire's poems does not necessarily lead to a better understanding of the overall effect of the American writer on the French poet.

More important to Valéry is the consequence of what he calls "counter-imitation." Placing himself in the mind of Baudelaire, Valéry imagines his predecessor posing the problem of becoming a writer in the follow terms: "How to be a great poet, but neither a Lamartine nor a Hugo nor a Musset." He is not suggesting that Baudelaire consciously formulated the question in this manner; nevertheless, he imagines Baudelaire's response to be "I shall therefore do otherwise," meaning that he would put himself in direct conflict with Romanticism. It is at this point that Valéry credits Poe for playing a major role in Baudelaire's development as a writer. Baudelaire found in Poe the principles he needed to define himself in opposition to the majors poets of his time. Long before writing his essay on Baudelaire, Valéry had reflected upon the importance of "counter-imitation" as a factor in literary influence. The following thoughts on the subject are from his *Notebook* dated 1916:

> Those who study imitation must not forget counter-imitation. The tendency to distinguish oneself from, to "contrast with," is a reaction that must be considered along with the tendency "to do like."
> Both have for *idem genus* a more general tendency to deduce one's thorght or one's act from the thought or act that already exists. I will do what you have done. I will do the contrary of what you have done. I will do it better than you. More intensely than you—I will be something more.[23]

The effect of "counter-imitation" that Poe inspired is far more significant in Valéry's thinking because it reoriented Baudelaire in new directions of creativity that brought out his potential genius as a poet.

What are the principles in Poe's work that were to have such a profound influence on Baudelaire by helping him break with his precursors? Valéry defines the essential points:

Before Poe the problem of literature had never been examined in its premises, reduced to a psychological problem, and approached by means of an analysis that deliberately used logic and the mechanics of effect. For the first time the relationship between the work and the reader was made clear and proposed as the actual foundation of art. His analysis—and this circumstance assures us of its value—can be applied and just as clearly verified in every kind of literary production. (CW 8: 203; O 1: 606)

These guiding principles derived from Poe's work are found in two essays Baudelaire translated, *The Philosophy of Composition* (given the French title *La Genèse d'un poème*) and *The Poetic Principle*. The latter piece is an example of Baudelaire's total intellectual merging with Poe—or plagiarism, depending on one's point of view. Baudelaire did not include *The Poetic Principle* as a separate essay in his translations. Instead, we find the piece almost verbatim without quotes or credit to the author embedded in his 1857 preface to the translation of Poe's tales. The unsuspecting reader would have no reason to believe the ideas expressed are other than Baudelaire's. Valéry recognized that Baudelaire had considered the Poe essay "his own property":

This plagiarism would be open to discussion if its author had not himself, as we shall see, drawn attention to it: in an article on Théophile Gautier he reproduced the whole passage in question, and prefaced it with these very clear and surprising lines: "It is on occasion permissible, I believe, to quote from one's own writings in order to avoid self-paraphrase. I shall therefore repeat . . ." The borrowed passage follows.[24] (CW 8: 206; O 1: 608–9)

Although Valéry points out this case of *double* plagiarism, he was more interested in the ideas that Baudelaire took as his own than dwelling on the obvious deception.

In *The Poetic Principle* Baudelaire was particularly impressed by what he considered the psychological conditions of a poem, meaning that the poet consciously determines the effects the poem will have on the reader. In order to create a calculated effect, the poet must keep in mind the length of the poem, which must be short. But most important, both Baudelaire and Valéry credited Poe with the idea of eliminating from poetry subjects that can best be treated in prose, such as history, science, and morality. According to Valéry, Baudelaire received from Poe's essays an essential message that was to change his destiny:

Poe saw that modern poetry was destined to conform to the tendency of an age which has witnessed an increasingly sharp distinction between the modes and provinces of human activity; and that it could now entertain claim to attain its true object and produce itself, as it were, in a *pure state.*

Thus, having analyzed the conditions for poetic enjoyment, and defined *pure poetry* by way of *elimination,* Poe was opening up a way, teaching a very strict and deeply alluring doctrine, in which a kind of mathematics and a kind of mysticism became one. . . . (CW 8: 207; O 1: 609)

This "doctrine," as Valéry calls it, was to have a profound influence on three generations of French poets.

In *The Philosophy of Composition* Poe attempts to show the direct connection between his poetics and the actual composition of his poem "The Raven." While Anglo-Saxon critics generally do not take the essay very seriously, some calling it a hoax, Baudelaire saw in it a lesson for both poets and readers. Even for a genius such as Poe, explains Baudelaire in his short introduction to the essay, inspiration and enthusiasm do not produce a poem. Every step of the poem's creation requires conscious effort and calculation. Poe also gives the reader, according to Baudelaire, a glimpse of "the benefits that art can gain from deliberation" and a more precise idea of "the labor that this luxury called Poetry demands" (H: 156; OP: 979). For Baudelaire and his successors, it was of little importance whether Poe, in truth, composed "The Raven" the way he described; they were excited by the hypothesis expounded in *The Philosophy of Composition*, one that presented a new dimension to the art of writing poetry. Baudelaire found in Poe's essay confirmation of his own aesthetic doctrine, published in the *Salon of 1846* before he had even read Poe's work:

Chance has no more place in art than in mechanics. A felicitous detail is the simple result of good reasoning, in which the intermediate deductions are sometimes skipped, just as something wrong is the result of a false principle. A painting is a machine in which all the systems are evident to a practiced eye. If the painting is a good one, everything in it has a reason for being there.[25]

In *The Philosophy of Composition* Baudelaire saw these same ideas applied to the creation of poetry. In the case of Valéry, Poe's essay inspired a method of literary criticism and the basic concepts of his poetics.

Valéry remarked that "Baudelaire and Edgar Allan Poe exchanged values" (CW 8: 204; O 1: 607), a statement that might seem paradoxical at first, if we apply it literally. The two writers never met nor corresponded; Poe died in 1849, just two years after Baudelaire began working on his translations. But, says Valéry, "Baudelaire gave Poe's thought an infinite expanse. He offered it to future generations" (CW 8: 204; O 1: 607). Baudelaire's legacy includes translations of over half of Poe's tales, *Eureka*, and several of his essays. Through prefaces and articles that describe Poe as a literary genius, "that marvelous brain always on alert," Baudelaire accomplished his mission of establishing Poe as a great writer in

France and Europe. A question that bothers Anglo-Saxon critics is whether this fame is deserved.

In an attempt to respond to the question "Is the Poe honored in France only a mythical construction of the French imagination?" American scholar Patrick Quinn set out to find an answer:

With an entirely lukewarm appreciation of Poe's writings, I began my investigation into Poe's immense reputation in France. I thought that my inquiry would take me back to the origins and up through the history of a great misunderstanding, or even a hoax. Frankly, I had it in mind to write a kind of exposé, and I suspected that the villain of the piece would be Baudelaire, the man who, on the subject of Poe, had led France and most of Europe up the garden. Only get to the bottom of the matter, I told myself, and it should not be too difficult to explain how and why Poe came to be so mistakenly overrated in France. Such were my thoughts at the outset of this inquiry, and I went to France with the expectations of developing them. But now, some years later, I have rather different proposals to make.[26]

Quinn immersed himself in Baudelaire's translations, compared them with the English originals, and participated intellectually in the French response to Poe. This was, indeed, an interesting experiment, which produced three hundred pages of observations and a few conclusions.

Baudelaire's acumen as a literary critic, notes Quinn, paid off in his judicious selection of forty-five tales out of the seventy-one titles Poe published. The stories Baudelaire chose to translate are generally recognized as among Poe's best and have withstood the test of time. In addition, Baudelaire had a keen sense of marketing. As he mentions in a letter to the critic Sainte-Beuve, he organized the stories into two volumes, the first of which "was designed as bait for the public: tricks, divination, leg-pulls, etc . . . the second volume is of a loftier kind of fantastic: hallucinations, mental illness, pure grotesque, supernaturalism, etc."[27] The plan was successful; his version of Poe's tales enjoyed a wide readership and inspired numerous critical studies in France.

A judgment on the quality of Baudelaire's translations is presented in Quinn's chapter "The Poet as Translator," which would be of particular interest to readers with some experience in this difficult art. Using precise examples too numerous to cite here,

Quinn shows that in specific cases Baudelaire's French improved or even corrected Poe's faulty syntax and vocabulary; in other cases, Baudelaire mistranslated certain expressions that are particularly obscure for a non-Anglophone. Although the translations are not flawless, Baudelaire accomplished an amazing feat, considering the fact that he had so little contact with the English language other than a dictionary. After careful examination of the evidence, Quinn comes to the following conclusion:

> This or that detail may have been overlooked, or improved, or weakened in translation. But there is no full-scale transmutation. Baudelaire did not melt down these stories, remove their dross, and recast them in the pure gold of his French. He could have done so, perhaps. But his admiration for Poe's work was too intense, his identification with the man too complete, to allow him even to contemplate such an experiment in literary metallurgy.[28]

The fact remains, however, that Poe's tales were translated into French by one of France's greatest writers. Had an author of lesser talent attempted such an ambitious undertaking, perhaps Poe's fate would have been different.

Baudelaire's essays on Poe set forth the qualities that have long been admired by French critics. In general, scholars in France focus on the psychological and analytical aspects of the tales rather than on the grotesque or sordid details that have offended English-language critics. While the French response to Poe's works has been overwhelmingly positive, mainly because of the great respect accorded the opinions of Baudelaire, Mallarmé, and Valéry, there have been a few discordant notes. Baudelaire was particularly annoyed by the opinions of two of his own contemporaries, Charles Augustin Sainte-Beuve and Jules Barbey d'Aurevilly. The major literary critic of his time, Sainte-Beuve remained strangely silent on the subject of Poe, even after Baudelaire wrote to him on several occasions urging him to write an article on the tales. "You who love to show your prowess at all depths," wrote Baudelaire to Sainte-Beuve in June 1858, "won't you make a journey into the depths of Poe?"[29] The total lack of response to his request must have vexed Baudelaire but probably angered him less than the 1858 review by Barbey d'Aurevilly, which had a strongly negative effect on Poe's reputation.

While praising Baudelaire's skill as a translator, Barbey d'Aurevilly saw in Poe a writer devoid of the essential concerns of humanity: God, society, and family. After the incessant praise and adoration that characterize Baudelaire's essays, Barbey d'Aurevilly's language shocks the reader's sensitivity. Poe, says the critic, born in "that whirlpool of dust that is called, by a mockery of history, the United States" was the "finest literary product of that cream of the scum of the world."[30] He condemns Poe for his lack of moral education, his mind, "which never has more than two convulsive movements—curiosity and fear," and his lack of willpower to overcome a penchant for alcohol. Nor did the critic think much of Poe's poetic talent, remarking that "the poet—the poet, that divine self-sparker—expires in the frightful exhibitions of the American charlatan and laborer." Barbey d'Aurevilly concludes his article by noting that the most one can say about Poe is that he is "the most beautiful corpse in literary Bohemia."

Needless to say, Baudelaire was devastated by such a vicious attach on his idol, but his protests were in vain, the damage done. He himself had been branded as satanic and immoral during his trial for obscenity following the 1857 publication of *The Flowers of Evil*. Barbey d'Aurevilly's article, Baudelaire's trial, his poor health, and subsequent death in 1867 all contributed to a decline in Poe's reputation in France during the next decade. But on the horizon was a new poetic movement whose most illustrious adherent, Mallarmé, would elevate Poe's renown to even greater heights.

Stéphane Mallarmé was twenty-five years old when Baudelaire died. Born in Paris, where his father worked in a government office, Mallarmé earned his *baccalauréat* at the *lycée* of Sens. The following year, 1861, he met Emmanuel des Essarts, a young teacher who shared his love of poetry and introduced him to Baudelaire's poems and the Poe translations. These works were to have a profound effect on Mallarmé's life and literary orientation. At first, Baudelaire's poetry had the attraction of forbidden fruit. Mallarmé was forced to hide *The Flowers of Evil* from his father and stepmother, who had confiscated two earlier copies in their son's possession. Judges at Baudelaire's trial had found the poet guilty of offending public morality and banned six poems from his collection. A writer whose work had been condemned for moral reasons was not approved reading in Mallarmé's bourgeois milieu.

Baudelaire's Poe translations inspired Mallarmé to break with his family and head for London to perfect his understanding of English in order to read Poe in the original. Accompanying him on the trip was Marie-Christina Gerhard, a German woman seven years his senior with whom he had fallen in love. After a stormy relationship and a return to France, they were finally married in London, where Mallarmé completed his English studies. Critic Léon Lemonnier remarked that Poe's greatest influence on Mallarmé was giving him a livelihood.[31] Mallarmé did, in fact, earn a teaching certificate in English while translating Poe in London, but the latter's influence is certainly not limited to such a narrow interpretation.

After returning from Great Britain in 1863, Mallarmé was appointed to the post of English teacher in the *lycée* at Tournon (in the Rhône Valley), thus launching a thirty-year career teaching the language of Poe to recalcitrant high school students. Eight of these years were particularly painful because they were spent in the provinces, far from the literary and intellectual center of the country. Mallarmé's love for the English language and his fascination with Poe's works did not translate into good teaching in spite of a great deal of time and effort put into creating his own pedagogical materials. One of his more interesting didactic creations is a volume called *English Themes* (*Thèmes anglais*) in which he sets forth one hundred grammar rules each followed by ten English sayings or proverbs illustrating the same grammar point, all to be memorized by the students. The successful student would thus be able to converse in English using such phrases as "A pin a day is a groat for a year" and "Knit my dog a pair of breeches and my cat a codpiece," just two among the one thousand recommended. This curious volume was published posthumously in 1937 with a preface by Valéry,[32] who mentions that Mallarmé was bored to death by his teaching and sought refuge in his own poetic universe.

Mallarmé's drab, bourgeois existence as husband, father of two children, and high school teacher presents a sharp contrast to Baudelaire's life-style of Paris dandy, Bohemian, and *poète maudit.*

But these differences are purely external; intellectually and aesthetically Mallarmé discovered close ties with Baudelaire. Wallace Fowlie gives an excellent description of these similarities, not apparent on the surface:

The dandyism of Baudelaire, which was infinitely more profound than a mere pose or attitude, was bequeathed to Mallarmé in a somewhat altered, but still recognizable, form. In its spiritual sense, Baudelaire's dandyism was the artist's heroism of concentration, the almost fatal need to adorn himself in so special and personal a way that he will be separated from all other men. The artist must be unique, or he has failed. . . . Mallarmé went even farther than Baudelaire. There is something of the dandy in Mallarmé's composed and serene manner; in his speech . . . in his general attitude of sage and high priest and martyr . . . Mallarmé became the dandy as artist.[33]

Around 1880 the famous Tuesday evening gatherings began at Mallarmé's apartment on the rue de Rome. Surrounded by writers and artists who would become celebrities of the next generation, Mallarmé held forth as the High Priest of Poetry. For Valéry, who frequented these gatherings in the 1890s, Mallarmé "was both so profound and so gracious . . . the purest and most authentic example of the intellectual virtues" (CW 8: 271; O 1: 680).

Although both Baudelaire and Poe became his literary idols, Mallarmé reserves the title "mon grand maître" (my great master) for Poe. In a letter of 1864 to his friend Henri Cazalis concerning the creation of his poem "L'Azur," Mallarmé pays homage to the American writer:

The more I work, the more I will be faithful to the strict ideas that my great master Edgar Poe bequeathed to me. The remarkable poem "The Raven" was created according to his ideas. And the soul of the reader responds absolutely as the poet intended. The reaction of the reader is none other than that which he had counted on.[34]

Mallarmé goes on to point out other lessons he learned from Poe. Convinced that writing poetry demands a conscious effort rather than sudden inspiration, Mallarmé emphasizes to his friend that each word of his own poem cost him "several hours of research" and "the first word serves to prepare the last." Recalling Poe's sentence from *The Philosophy of Composition*, "I designate Beauty as the province of the poem," Mallarmé mimics with the phrase "There is only Beauty;—and it has only one perfect expression—Poetry."[35] Poe was Mallarmé's guiding light as the French poet plodded along on his own poems, driven by a sense of perfection and limited by the time he could spend during breaks from his teaching career. In reference to the writing of "Hérodiade" Mallarmé commented in another letter to Cazalis dated April 1866: "It will take me at least four more winters to complete this work, but I will finally have written a poem which I hope will be worthy of Poe and whose own poems will not surpass."[36]

While pursuing his own poetic aspirations Mallarmé was also devoting a great deal of effort to translating thirty-six of Poe's poems selected from fifty that had been published. Baudelaire had translated only four poems: "The Raven," rendered in French prose in his version of *The Philosophy of Composition*, "To My Mother," a sonnet serving as a dedication to *Histoires Extraordinaires*, "The Conqueror Worm" included in the tale *Ligeia*, and "The Haunted Palace," in his translation of "The Fall of the House of Usher." Mallarmé felt inspired to continue Baudelaire's task and judged his own time well spent because each poem was, in his opinion, a *chef-d'oeuvre*. Of "Ulalume" he remarked: "It is perhaps the most original and the most strangely suggestive of all"; "For Annie" was "a poetic miracle"; and "The Bells" had an "impalpable richness" but was a "demon for the translator."[37]

Mallarmé's translations of Poe's poems were published together as a volume in 1888 and then again in the Vanier edition in 1889 with the following dedication:

To the memory of Baudelaire, whose death alone prevented him from completing, by translating all of these poems, the magnificent and fraternal monument dedicated by his genius to Edgar Poe.[38]

Mallarmé never met Baudelaire, although, as already mentioned, he spotted him once at a bookstall but could not muster the courage to approach him. By translating the poems, Mallarmé was able to make a contribution to the literary endeavors of both his idols.

Here again the question arises as to whether the French translation of Poe's work enhances the original. T. S. Eliot, who knew

French writers and their works very well, addresses this question in his article "From Poe to Valéry." After pointing out the basic weaknesses of several of Poe's poems, Eliot observes that while Mallarmé's translations are an improvement over the originals, "the rhythms, in which we find so much of the originality of Poe, are lost." He goes on to conclude:

The evidence that the French overrated Poe because of their imperfect knowledge of English remains accordingly purely negative: we can venture no farther than saying that they were not disturbed by weaknesses of which we are very much aware. It does not account for their high opinion of Poe's *thought,* for the value which they attached to his philosophical and critical exercises.[39]

It was indeed Poe's thought, expressed in three short essays, that made a deep impression on Baudelaire, Mallarmé, and Valéry.

Poe's views on the relationship between poetry and music, set forth in the following passage from *The Poetic Principle,* were basic concepts for the French poets:

Contenting myself with the certainty that Music, in its various modes of metre, rhythm, and rhyme, is of so vast a moment in Poetry as never to be wisely rejected—is so vitally important an adjunct, that he is simply silly who declines its assistance, I will not now pause to maintain its absolute essentiality. It is in Music, perhaps, that the soul most nearly attains the great end for which, when inspired by the Poetic Sentiment, it struggles—the creation of supernal Beauty. It *may* be, indeed, that here this sublime end is, now and then, attained *in fact.* We are often made to feel, with a shivering delight, that from an earthly harp are stricken notes which *cannot* have been unfamiliar to the angels. And thus there can be little doubt that in the union of Poetry with Music in its popular sense, we shall find the widest field for the Poetic development. (T: 77–78)

A similar idea is found in "Letter to B——," an essay Baudelaire did not translate but which Mallarmé read in English:

A poem, in my opinion, is opposed to a work of science by having, for its *immediate* object, pleasure, not truth; to romance, by having, for its object, an *indefinite* instead of a *definite* pleasure, being a poem only so far as this object is attained; . . . Music, when combined with a pleasurable idea, is poetry;

music without the idea is simply music; the idea without the music is prose, from its very definitiveness. (T: 11)

Although both Poe and Mallarmé use the term "music" to describe their poetics, Joseph Chiari points out that "the difference between Poe's attitude and that of Mallarmé towards music is fundamental, and is the very measure of the gap which separates their poetry."[40] For Poe, music is an "adjunct," a term he uses in the passage quoted above, or, as Chiari states "the music of the words is merely an external attribute conferred upon the poem for a purpose."[41] In Mallarmé's poetry, concludes Chiari:

The words are connected not as intrinsic carriers of meaning but as the links of a chain or the notes of a musical composition; they do not aim at creating a state, they aim at being for the creative mind of the reader an act of transcendence, a flickering imitation of the passage from nothingness to being—the nothingness of the white page to the poem.[42]

Chiari finds Poe guilty of abusing the use of music to create an effect, which "at times is so blatant that it falls into the vulgarity castigated by Aldous Huxley in his essay on 'Vulgarity in Literature.'"[43]

Baudelaire's translation of Poe's *The Poetic Principle* contains the vital word "correspondence" that took on such important meaning in symbolist poetry. The first of the two passages that follow is Hyslop's translation from Baudelaire, the second, Poe's original version:

It is this admirable, this immortal instinct of the beautiful which makes us consider the earth and its spectacles as a revelation, as something in correspondence with Heaven. The insatiable thirst for everything that lies beyond, and that life reveals, is the most living proof of our immortality.

It is at the same time by poetry and *through* poetry, by and *through* music that the soul glimpses the splendors beyond the tomb; and when an exquisite poem brings us to the verge of tears, those tears are not the proof of excessive pleasure; they are rather evidence of an aroused melancholy, of a condition of nerves, of a nature which has been exiled amid the imperfect and which would like to take possession immediately, on this very earth, of a revealed paradise. (H: 140–41)

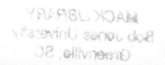

An immortal instinct, deep within the spirit of man, is thus, plainly, a sense of the Beautiful. This it is which administers to his delight in the manifold forms, and sounds, and odours, and sentiments amid which he exists. . . . We have still a thirst unquenchable, to allay which he has not shown us the crystal springs. . . . And thus when by Poetry—or when by Music, the most entrancing of the Poetic moods—we find ourselves melted to tears—we weep then—not as the Abbaté Gravina supposes—through excess of pleasure, but through a certain, petulant, impatient sorrow at our inability to grasp *now*, wholly, here on earth, at once and forever, those divine and rapturous joys, of which *through* the poem, or *through* the music, we attain but brief and indeterminate glimpses. (T: 76–77)

The word "correspondence" cannot be found in Poe's text, although the idea of transcending the physical world and discovering a spiritual realm revealed through the senses is explicitly stated.

While Mallarmé admired the emphasis Poe placed on the calculated use of language in poetry, his own aesthetics went far beyond Poe's goal of creating a state of pleasure. Mallarmé envisioned a poetic language that would be purified of everyday meaning through the creation of new usage, rhythms, rhymes, and even the positioning of the words on the page, as we see in his poem "Dice Thrown Never Will Annul Chance" ("Un Coup de dés n'abolira jamais le hasard"). Valéry remarked that "Mallarmé never ceased thinking of the nature and possibilities of language with the lucidity of a scientist and the conviction of a poet" (CW 8: 270; O 1: 679). He goes on to describe Mallarmé's ultimate goal:

He would say that the world had only been made so as to end in a beautiful book, and that it could and must perish once its mystery had been represented, and its expression found. He could see, in the existence of all things, no other explanation and no other excuse. (CW 8: 270; O 1: 679)

Creating the ultimate book was certainly not Valéry's ambition as a poet and writer, but he admired the intellectual process by which Mallarmé hoped to realize his ideal. In Mallarmé's poem "Hérodiade" Valéry recognized a glimpse of this state of perfection and a resemblance to Poe:

As for "Hérodiade," this poem produced on me an effect of incomparable beauty. It was a marvelous union of a rather external kind of art—the art of the Parnassians—but of a most refined kind, and a *spirituality* whose origin can be found in the works of Edgar Allan Poe. (CW 8: 263; O 1: 674)

While Poe inspired in Mallarmé a desire for perfection through the constant refinement of language, Valéry, on the contrary, saw his own literary efforts in a different light:

I was no longer disposed to grant more value to the act of writing than that of a pure *exercise*, founded on the properties of language as redefined for the purpose and generalized with precision: a game that should tend to make us extremely free and sure in the use of language, while detaching us from the illusions created by its use—though literature is nourished by those illusions, and men as well. (CW 8: 252; O 1: 643)

Mallarmé and Valéry each received a different message from their common mentor. Valéry was more interested in observing the mental process that goes on during the creation of a poem than in the final product of that action. In *The Philosophy of Composition* he recognized the efforts of a poet to understand this process.

The image of Poe that Mallarmé bequeathed to his successors is best summed up in his poem "The Tomb of Edgar Poe," written in 1876 to honor the twenty-fifth anniversary of the poet's death.[44] The sonnet is presented below with the English translation by Mary Ann Caws:[45]

LE TOMBEAU D'EDGAR POE
Tel qu'en Lui-même enfin l'éternité le change,
Le Poëte susite avec un glaive nu
Son siècle épouvanté de n'avoir pas connu
Que la Mort triomphait dans cette voix étrange!

Eux, comme un vil sursaut d'hydre oyant jadis l'ange
Donner un sens plus pur aux mots de la tribu
Proclamèrent très haut le sortilège bu
Dans le flot sans honneur de quelque noir mélange.

Du sol et de la nue hostiles, ô grief!
Si notre idée avec ne sculpte un bas-relief
Dont la tombe de Poe éblouissante s'orne,

Calme bloc ici-bas chu d'un désastre obscur,

Que ce granit du moins montre à jamais sa borne
Aux noirs vols du Blasphème épars dans le futur.

THE TOMB OF EDGAR POE
As into Himself at last eternity changes him
The Poet wakens with a naked sword
His century dismayed not to have known
That death was triumphant in this strange voice!

Like a Hydra's vile spasm once hearing the angel
Give a purer sense to the words of the tribe
They proclaimed with loud cries the sortilege drunk
From the dishonored depths of some black brew.

From hostile soil and cloud, alas,
If our concept does not sculpt a bas-relief
To ornament the dazzling tomb of Poe,

Calm block here fallen from a dark disaster,
Let this granite at least mark bounds forever
To the dark flights of Blasphemy dispersed in the future.

The opening line of the first quatrain, "As into Himself at last eternity changes him," is one of the most often quoted from Mallarmé's poems because of its beauty and its succinct statement on the poet's fate in the universal sense.   Misunderstood in his own time, the poet must wait for future generations to discover his superiority, which went unnoticed because his contemporaries preferred a mediocre voice that recounted what was familiar to them. Fowlie sees in the first quatrain Mallarmé's central philosophy or doctrine on the poet:

An absolute statement in itself, it might serve as an introduction to all the poems of Mallarmé and to the work of all the poets. It is almost the condensation of one hundred years' thinking about the poet, about the strange alchemy of time, which ends by revealing the true stature of a poet and which illumines the images of his poetry. The poet himself, during his own lifetime, could not behold that luminosity, which is always future.[46]

Valéry saw in this line the particular relationship between Baudelaire and Poe: "That transcendence which changes the poet into himself, as in Mallarmé's great line, that was what

Baudelaire's action, his translations, his prefaces, assured for the miserable shade of Edgar Allan Poe" (CW 8: 204; O 1: 607).

The second line of the second quatrain, "Give a purer sense to the words of the tribe,"[47] is perhaps equally well known and served as an inspiration to Valéry. For both Mallarmé and Valéry, the aspiration of the poet is to give a more refined meaning to words that are already part of the language. Because Poe's fellow countrymen did not understand this purer meaning, they attributed the power of his words to the drunken magic of a "black brew."

The two tercets are an expression of grievance and hope for the future. The personal tragedy of the poet's life and art must be transcended; the granite stone will serve as a reminder of the blasphemy against the creative spirit, which now takes on a life of its own that will never know the bounds of cold stone. The sonnet begins with the word "eternity" in the first line and ends with the word "future." The fate of the truly creative writer is to be misunderstood by his own generation and appreciated by those who come after him. Thus, in a most eloquent homage, Mallarmé fixes the image of Poe that would have greatly pleased Baudelaire, that of the misunderstood genius whose hostile surroundings prevented him from becoming a great poet in his own time, a fate Baudelaire himself had to endure.

The Poe cult that French poets handed down from one generation to another can best be understood in the context of the development of the Symbolist movement. Looking back on this period of literary history, Valéry points out that Symbolism was not a school nor did it profess a common aesthetic. The poets whom we call "Symbolists" did not know themselves by this label. Nonetheless, he continues, poets such as Verlaine, Rimbaud, Villiers de l'Isle-Adam, Mockel, Mallarmé, and others did have something in common. Valéry sets forth the traits that unite these writers:

We arrive at this paradox: an event in aesthetic history that cannot be defined in aesthetic terms. The secret of their cohesion lies somewhere else. I offer one hypothesis. I suggest that in all their diversity the Symbolists were united by some negation, and by one that was independent of their temperaments and their function as artists. This negation was all they had in common, but it was essentially marked in each of them. However different they were, they recognized themselves to be identically separated from the other writers and artists of their time. No matter how much they differed . . . they continued to agree on one point which is foreign to aesthetics. *They agreed in a common determination to reject the appeal to a majority*: they disdained to conquer the public at large. (CW 8: 220; O 1: 690–91)

Valéry goes on to emphasize that these writers did not set out to solicit a large reading public or seek the praise of established critics. They rejected public honors, preferring to exalt their own heroes and martyrs, all of whom had suffered, says Valéry: "Edgar Poe, dying penniless; Baudelaire, haled into court by a public prosecutor; Wagner, hissed down at the Opéra; Verlaine and Rimbaud, suspicious vagrants; Mallarmé ridiculed by the lowest journalist" (CW 8: 220–21; O 1: 691). By going against the established literary norms, these writers were forced to create their own reading public. One of the essential features of Symbolism, remarks Valéry, was to demand an active intellectual cooperation from the reader, who would in turn experience unexpected effects from such an effort. Needless to say, winning "readers of superior merit" was a slow process the success of which some of the poets did not live long enough to enjoy.

Renouncing any appeal to public preference gave the Symbolist writers the freedom to experiment with new forms, thus breaking away from the precepts of Romanticism and the fashionable rhymes of the Parnassians. These experiments went in many directions, from *Vers Libre* to *Instrumentisme*, which kept the classical alexandrine but added other qualities such as a table of correspondences between the sounds of the alphabet and the tones of orchestral instruments. The devotion to pure art rejected any obligation to treat political, social, or moral subjects. Valéry recalls his own impression of the period between 1896 and 1900:

At no other time did the powers of art, beauty, and form, or the virtue of poetry, come so close to providing a number of persons with the substance of an inner life that might well be called "mystical," since it proved to be sufficient in itself, and since it satisfied and sustained more than one heart *as effectively as a formal creed.* There is no doubt that some few depended on this sort of religious faith to furnish constant nourishment of their thoughts, the guiding principle of their conduct, and the strength to resist temptation; or that, in the most difficult circumstances, it inspired them to pursue projects that had as little chance of being carried out as they had of being understood if by any chance they were ever completed. (CW 8: 224–25; O 1: 694).

By extending the analogy between Symbolism and religious faith, we can appreciate the role Poe played as spiritual leader and prophet, whose voice went unheeded in his own land. Poe's writing went against the grain of the accepted norm, thus he had to create his own readership. He was an iconoclast who attempted to establish poetry as a pure art that exists for its own sake. He believed that the poet is capable of instilling a sense of mystery that transcends reality. Poe believed in the power of music, which became a major preoccupation for the Symbolist poets. And last, but not least, French poets admired Poe's sense of discipline and devotion to form. Although the Symbolists cast aside the conventions of the day, they were highly disciplined in the art of poetic technique. Valéry points this out as being a common characteristic:

I cannot undertake to expound the various theories advanced at the time, but I note as a characteristic feature of Symbolism the long theoretical discussions, often developed in a scholarly manner, that accompanied or contributed to the artistic production of the period. (CW 8: 235; O 1: 703)

As Valéry is careful to recognize, the poets whom we classify as part of the Symbolist movement were each different one from the other. At the same time, they shared traits that link them to Poe, who served as a literary idol for the movement. Mallarmé's sonnet consecrated Poe as the holy martyr by the use of the uppercase letter, "As into Himself at last eternity changes him"; the religious symbolism in the stone of the tomb and the reminder of blasphemy complete the literary Christ-figure image that was handed down to the next generation of French poets.

Valéry inherited a concept of Poe that had been cast by major French writers during a period of forty years. He understood the relationship that existed among them:

As for Stéphane Mallarmé, whose earliest poems might be confused with the most condensed and beautiful compositions of *Les Fleurs du mal,* he pursued to their most intricate and ingenious consequences the formal and technical experiments of which Poe's analyses and Baudelaire's essays and commentaries had conveyed to him the passion and taught him the importance. While Verlaine and Rimbaud have continued from Baudelaire in the way of feeling and sensuousness, Mallarmé extended his influence in the realm of perfection and poetic purity. (CW 8: 211; O 1: 612–13)

Valéry continued in the lineage of Mallarmé by making perfection and poetic purity the subject of his own meditations. While his goal was not to create the supreme work that Mallarmé envisioned, he was nonetheless captivated by his own attempt to understand the mechanism of the mind capable of producing artistic perfection.

Valéry's reaction to Poe can best be seen in contrast to the position of Rémy de Gourmont. In his "Marginalia on Edgar Poe and Baudelaire" de Gourmont argues that Poe's recounting of how he wrote "The Raven," a deliberate act that involved the careful selection of sounds and their effects, was simply a paradox that Poe created for amusement. De Gourmont goes on to say that Poe's

method, like all others, will remain forever unknown to us. We scarcely understand how we ourselves work, how our ideas came to us, how we carry them out; if we understood too well, we would no longer be able to work at all. Those are questions that a writer ought to avoid exploring. Besides, it is extremely dangerous to think too much about one's acts or life: the "Know thyself" is perhaps the most harmful nonsense ever uttered.[48]

This statement represents the complete antithesis of Valéry's reaction to Poe and the formulation of his own goals. For Valéry, Poe was the first writer to suggest the *possibility* of examining the intellectual process by which a creative work is accomplished. He did not believe that this method would be forever unknown to us. On the contrary, Valéry was convinced that the human intellect is capable of understanding how its own mechanism works. Instead of avoiding such questions, as de Gourmont recommends, Valéry devoted a lifetime to seeking the answer. He believed that an understanding of how ideas come to us and how we render them comprehensible can lead to the discovery of a universal method applicable to both artistic creation and science. Valéry's goal was as fundamental as it was impossible: the pure conquest of his mind.

Baudelaire and Mallarmé bequeathed to their successor excellent translations of Poe's tales, literary essays, and poems through which Valéry first became acquainted with the American writer. Baudelaire's articles depicting Poe as the martyred artist, the outcast in a world devoted to materialism, inspired admiration in Valéry, for whom the survival of a great intellect assailed by devastating circumstances was the most moving aspect of Poe's biography. But more important to Valéry were the works themselves, particularly the literary essays and tales. In *The Poetic Principle* and Baudelaire's commentary on the essay, Valéry discovered the basis on which to build his own aesthetic doctrine, namely, that Beauty is the province of poetry, which must have no other reason for existing. Valéry's obsession with the creation of "pure poetry" was inspired by Poe's insistence that all non-poetical elements be eliminated from poetry. Mallarmé carried this doctrine even further by making poetry and the creation of poetic language the subject of his poems. Valéry advanced this ideal to its limit by making the creative process itself the focus of his poetry.

Although Valéry did not share Mallarmé's enthusiasm for Poe's poems, he enjoyed discussions on Poe's ideas concerning poetic technique. *The Philosophy of Composition* held particular interest for Valéry because it revealed to him the possibility of understanding the creative process involved in writing a poem. While Mallarmé developed Poe's ideas in the direction of poetic purity and perfection, Valéry became fascinated by the intellectual process itself. It is this particular trait that distinguishes Poe's influence on Valéry from that of his predecessors and brings out his own originality.

CHAPTER TWO

Valéry's Views on Influence

> Nothing is more "original," nothing more "oneself" than to feed
> on others. But one has to digest them. A lion is made of assimi-
> lated sheep.
>
> —Valéry (CW 14: 10; O 2: 478)

Valéry's keen sense of intellectual self-observation takes into account the effects of outside factors on his thinking and literary production. The modification of the mind by its own thought processes as well as by the works of others interested him a great deal.
His reflections on the effects of influence and imitation show a
preoccupation with the subject throughout his lifetime. In his studies of literary works he examines the affinities between the authors and their predecessors, as we have seen in the case of
Baudelaire and Poe. Valéry's views on influence, expressed in several essays and in his *Notebooks,* provide valuable insights on
which to base our own study of Poe's effect on Valéry.

In his "Letter about Mallarmé," written thirty years after the
elder poet's death, Valéry reflects upon the effects Mallarmé had
on him as a young writer. Before describing the meaning of this
relationship, Valéry clarifies his own ideas on influence. He begins with the following caveat: "No word comes easier or oftener
to the critic's pen than the word *influence,* and no vaguer notion can
be found among all the vague notions that compose the phantom
armory of aesthetics" (CW 8: 241; O 1: 634). The warning is not
meant to discourage such inquiry or diminish its importance. On
the contrary, Valéry emphasizes that "there is nothing in the crit-

ical field that should be of greater philosophical interest or prove more rewarding to analysis than the progressive modification of one mind by the work of another" (CW 8: 241; O 1: 634). Valéry sets forth in this statement the premise on which his definition is based: true influence produces significant changes rather than simply inspiring repetition.

The effects of this modification, continues Valéry, must lead to "active consequences that are impossible to foresee" (CW 8: 241; O 1: 634). He adds a footnote to this assertion in order to specify that influence differs from imitation by the very fact that the former produces unexpected results while imitation can be predicted and easily recognized. Influence is much more difficult to analyze than imitation and in many cases it is impossible to ascertain. The careful observer, says Valéry, can discover in an author's so-called originality subtle effects of influence:

> We say that an author is *original* when we cannot trace the hidden trans-formations that others underwent in his mind; we mean to say that the de-pendence of *what he does* on *what others have done* is excessively complex and irregular. There are works in the likeness of others, and works that are the reverse of others, but there are also works of which the relation with earlier productions is so intricate that we become confused and attribute them to the direct intervention of the gods. (CW 8: 241; O 1: 634–35)

Influence, in Valéry's mind, is a normal process which has the potential to produce unexpected consequences. He was convinced that this process operates in all fields of intellectual endeavor:

> What we do know is that this derived activity is essential to intellectual production of all types. Whether in science or the arts, if we look for the source of an achievement we can observe that *what a man does* either repeats or refutes *what someone else has done*—repeats it in other tones, refines or amplifies or simplifies it, loads or overloads it with meaning; or else rebuts, overturns, destroys and denies it, but thereby assumes it and has invisibly used it. Opposites are born from opposites. (CW 8: 241; O 1: 634)

Valéry's essay on Baudelaire offers a specific example of this definition of influence. Valéry points out that in relation to what had been done before him, Baudelaire came into "increasingly direct conflict with the system, or lack of system, called Romanticism"

(CW 8: 196; O 1: 600). Thus, the denial, the desire to do the opposite played a key role in Baudelaire's developing his own poetic genius. On the positive side, Baudelaire discovered in Poe certain basic concepts that he was able to refine and "overload with meaning," such as the use of symbols and music which he perfected in his poems, thus going far beyond the mere concepts. Valéry affirms in this essay his own belief that influence is not necessarily a dependence on one's predecessors for ideas but rather a catalyst for discovering one's own originality.

The process by which influence is transformed into originality preoccupied Valéry throughout his own career as a writer. Determined to preserve his intellectual autonomy but conscious of the effect of other works on his thinking, he almost developed a complex concerning the problem of originality in his creative endeavors. Suzanne Nash emphasizes this point in her study of Valéry's early poetry:

> There are countless examples of Valéry's preoccupation with originality registered throughout his notebooks and private writings . . . he was really never free of anxiety concerning the impingement of the past on the originality of his thought.[1]

Although Valéry perceives influence as inevitable, the problem of the writer is to transform what he receives into something innovative and unrecognizable. As he so aptly summarizes this idea, "the lion is made of assimilated sheep" (CW 14: 10; O 2: 478).

Concluding his remarks on influence in the Mallarmé essay, Valéry makes a point that is fundamental to our analysis of Poe's effect on his thought and work:

> It is when a book or an author's collected work acts on someone not with all its qualities, but with one or a few of them, that influence assumes its most remarkable values. The development of a single quality of one person by the full talent of another seldom fails to produce results marked by an *extreme originality*. (CW 8: 242; O 2: 635)

Although Valéry read Poe's works over and over throughout his lifetime, one quality struck him above all, whether it was found in a tale or an essay: Poe's intellectual self-observation, his desire to know how the mind functions. Valéry succeeded in developing this quality in his work to the point of "extreme originality," as he puts it, where traces of Poe are barely recognizable, thus fulfilling his own definition of authentic influence. At critical points in his life, Valéry mentions that Poe played a pivotal role. This influence must be seen in the context of other determining factors such as contacts with his contemporaries—Pierre Louÿs, André Gide, and Mallarmé, his crisis of 1892, and the day-to-day reality of existence.

The lush, clear landscape of the Mediterranean coast inspired many images in Valéry's poetry and essays. Born in 1871 in the port of Sète (spelled Cette at that time), Valéry was the son of a civil servant of Corsican blood and a mother who was descended from an old Italian family. His early childhood was a happy time spent close to the beaches and the many human activities typical of a small seaport. In a charming essay titled "Mediterranean Inspirations," first given as a speech, Valéry describes the importance of this early period, mentioning at the same time his distrust of the term "influence":

> Now I would like to try to tell you about a profounder action of the sea on my mind. It is difficult to be precise about these matters. I am not fond of the word *influence,* which indicates ignorance or a hypothesis and plays a great and convenient role in criticism. But I will tell you what is evident to me.
>
> Certainly nothing so formed me, permeated me, instructed—or constructed—me as those hours stolen from study, hours seemingly idle but really given over to the unconscious worship of three or four undeniable gods: the Sea, the Sky, the Sun. Without knowing it, I recaptured something of the wonder and exaltation of primitive man. I do not know what book could match or what writer incite communion, as I experienced in my early years. (CW 15: 27–28; O 1: 1091–92)

The sounds, smells, colors, shapes, and landmarks of Valéry's birthplace were the source of many images in his poetry as well as the setting for his most well-known poem, "The Graveyard by the Sea" ("Le Cimetière marin"). Part of his originality as a poet can be attributed to his skill at celebrating certain intellectual joys through sensuous images engraved on his mind from early childhood.

This idyllic existence came to an end when Valéry graduated from the Collège of Sète at age thirteen. In 1884 the family moved inland to Montpellier, where Valéry's father died three years later, leaving the elder son Jules in charge. Valéry recalls his school years as a drab, endless routine, an experience he was forced to endure. To overcome the boredom, he developed an island in his mind, discovered authors on his own that interested him, and wrote poetry in his school notebooks.

After passing his *baccalauréat* exams in July 1888, he entered law school at the University of Montpellier. From the fall of 1888 to the spring of 1892 Valéry's life seemed to run on parallel tracks. He was obliged to fulfill his duty: legal studies (following in his brother's footsteps), military service, and completion of the law degree. Alongside the obligations demanded by family and state, his literary interests were developing through his writing and through the personal connections he managed to make while living in the provinces.

Two references to Poe in Valéry's brief autobiographical pieces indicate that he was reading the American author while in law school. His formal studies suffered because of his interest in subjects unrelated to law, such as architecture and Edgar Poe:

> I read a great deal of Poe, in whom I found a scientific bent, a taste for precision, rigor, and reasoning that joined forces with my own love of Architecture.
>
> I felt developing in me a sort of will toward an *intellectual* art, premeditated works requiring the presence of all the faculties of the mind. I posed to myself many questions about aesthetics, and gave great importance to reflections on *Ornament.* (CW 15: 6)[2]

Pierre Féline, a close friend of Valéry's during his law school days, remembers that the subjects of his regular intellectual conversations with Valéry, which they referred to as their *"amicales,"* were most often mathematics, Mallarmé, and Poe. The format of the conversations was very serious as Féline recalls: "Each *amicale* allowed us to confront two opposing theories, and to go from one to the other, accentuating their difference" (CW 15: 363).[3] To relieve the solemn tone of the meetings, Féline attempted to trick his older companion: "Before Paul arrived I would amuse myself by writing in chalk at the two ends of the blackboard some fragment from Mallarmé or Poe . . . playing the trick of changing it slightly by omitting or adding a word" (CW 15: 362). Féline took pleasure in these friendly jousts but felt overwhelmed by what he calls the "unbalanced dialogue." Although his superior skills in mathematics made him the teacher, his knowledge of Mallarmé and Poe lagged far behind Valéry's, thus his enthusiasm began to wane. These early references to Valéry's interest in Poe and mathematics reveal the beginning of his preoccupation with analytical skills and their application to the study of literature.

In May 1890 Valéry made the acquaintance of Pierre Louÿs, a young poet and founder of the literary review *La Conque.* This "capital event," as Valéry called their chance meeting, took place during another capital event, the celebration of the six-hundredth anniversary of the University of Montpellier. At a banquet concluding the festivities, Valéry happened to sit beside a young man who was to play a major role in his life:

Fate had taken on the features of this delightful table companion. We exchanged a few words. He was from Paris. An album I had placed on the table plunged us into the arts. Sacred or yet unknown names were murmured between us. We were in raptures. (CW 15: 39)[4]

It was this chance acquaintance with Pierre Louÿs that led to Valéry's publishing one of his poems in Paris and to his introduction to Mallarmé.

The following September Valéry sent an autobiographical sketch to Louÿs in which he expressed his likes and dislikes, an interesting record of his strong sentiments at the age of nineteen. He does not fail to mention Poe and, apparently, prefers to think about the American writer rather than about women (Valéry refers to himself in the third person):

Women are for him graceful little animals who have the perverse ability to draw the attention of too many minds. They are placed on the summit of the altars of art, and our elegant psychologists know better, alas, how to note their bitchy sulking and their catlike clawing than to analyze the difficult brain of an Ampère, a Delacroix, or an Edgar Poe. (CW 15: 14; O 2: 1431)

The total meeting of minds and confidence he felt in his relationship with Pierre Louÿs inspired Valéry to submit his poem
"Narcissus Speaks" ("Narcisse parle") for publication in *La Conque*.
The poem enjoyed a success that astonished Valéry and encouraged
him to continue writing poems while in law school.

During this same period he met André Gide, who sent him
Mallarmé's poems, which were very difficult to find in the provinces. Valéry mentions 1889 as the year he first became aware of
the name of Mallarmé, whose poetry had been ridiculed in various
publications (CW 8: 257; O 1: 662–63). He learned more about
Mallarmé from short quotations included in J.-K. Huysmans' novel
Against the Grain (*A Rebours*), which cited a few lines from Mallarmé's poems "Hérodiade" and "Afternoon of a Faun."[5] Struck by
the clarity and the difficulty of Mallarmé's poems, Valéry was
convinced that they "demanded an activity, an energy, a strength
of mind that were rare and absolutely incompatible with the
mental state of a madman" (CW 8: 259; O 1: 667). Through his
friendships with Pierre Louÿs and André Gide, Valéry was able to
gain information about the person and the life of Mallarmé,
which led to the discovery that he shared Mallarmé's interest in
Poe.

The year 1889 is significant in Valéry's intellectual development for another reason: he attempted to publish his first article,
entitled "On Literary Technique." He submitted it to a publication
called *Le Courrier libre*, which went out of business before the piece
was printed. The manuscript, found after the author's death, is of
particular interest to our study because it shows that as early as age
eighteen Valéry discovered in Poe's work ideas that he adopted as
his own. His reading of Baudelaire's Poe translations inspired
him to write the essay, which turned out to be simply a rehash of
Poe's *Philosophy of Composition*.

In the first part of the article Valéry sets forth what appear to be
his own ideas on poetics. His opening line declares that "literature is the art of playing upon the mind of others" (CW 7: 315; O 1:
1809).[6] He goes on to explain that the primary concern of the poet
is to create an effect upon the listener which is calculated from the
beginning. The means by which the artist accomplishes such an
effect is by careful attention to form. The modern poet, says Valéry,

does not compose in a frenzy nor does he complete a poem during one feverish night. On the contrary, the poet is "a cool scientist, almost an algebraist, in the service of a subtle dreamer" (CW 7: 315; O 1: 1809). Emphasizing this conscious effort, Valéry spells out the creative process in even more specific terms. Everything the poet "has imagined, felt, dreamed, and planned will be passed through a sieve, weighed, filtered, subjected to *form*, and condensed as much as possible so as to gain in power what it loses in length" (CW 7: 315, 317; O 1: 1809). The ideal length is one hundred lines, says Valéry, repeating Poe's recommendation.

After pointing out the importance of symbols and citing Baudelaire as his source, Valéry concludes the first part of his essay by stressing the importance of the poem's dénouement. In strikingly Poesque terms Valéry describes how the climax should be reached:

We cannot find a better comparison than the stair to a magnificent altar with steps of porphyry surmounted by the Tabernacle. The ornaments, the candles, the golden vessels, the clouds of incense—everything rises towards and is arranged to draw one's attention to the monstrance, to the last line! The composition that lacks this progression has a fatally monotonous appearance, however rich and cunningly wrought it may be. (CW 7: 317; O 1: 1810)

Stating again that the poem should be limited to a hundred lines, Valéry recommends that the artist concentrate his attention on the "last, decisive flash" ("l'éclat dernier et décisif") (CW 7: 319; O 1: 1810). At this point, halfway through an essay that repeats Poe's ideas, Valéry remarks rather naively: "This leads me to speak of the extremely original poetic theory of Edgar Poe" (CW 7: 319; O 1: 1810).

The connections between the ideas Valéry expresses in the first part of his essay and those in Poe's *Philosophy of Composition* are so obvious that Valéry himself would no doubt categorize them as imitations, the pieces being easily recognizable. In the original French version of Valéry's opening line cited above ("la littérature est l'art de se jouer de l'âme des autres") the word *âme* meaning "soul" is used instead of "mind," thus revealing a closer similarity to Poe's comment: "It is needless to demonstrate that a poem is such, only inasmuch as it intensely excites, by elevating, the soul" (T: 15). The role of the poet is to create an effect, which must be consciously contrived. Poe remarks that "most writers—poets in especial—prefer having it understood that they compose by a species of fine frenzy—an ecstatic intuition—" (T: 14). Valéry's version of this idea reads: "He [the poet] is no longer the disheveled madman who writes a whole poem in the course of one feverish night" (CW 7: 315; O 1: 1809). Recalling how he wrote "The Raven," Poe states:

It is my design to render it manifest that no one point in its composition is referrible either to accident or intuition—that the work proceeded, step by step, to its completion with the precision and rigid consequence of a mathematical problem. (T: 14–15)

Poe also uses mathematical analogy to describe the extent and effect of his poem:

Within this limit, the extent of a poem may be made to bear mathematical relation to its merit—in other words, to the excitement or elevation—again, in other words, to the degree of the true poetical effect which it is capable of inducing; for it is clear that the brevity must be in direct ratio of the intensity of the intended effect. (T: 15)

Poe then states that he calculates the intended length of his poem to be about one hundred lines. Each of these lines is carefully planned to prepare the dénouement, which, says Poe, must be brought about "as rapidly and as *directly* as possible" (T: 23), a point Valéry makes very clearly in his essay.

To repeat Valéry's comment in reference to Baudelaire's plagiarizing Poe, the importance of these obvious imitations in his own article is "merely local"; of greater significance is the overall effect of one writer's work on the mind of another. Reading Poe at the age of seventeen or eighteen helped Valéry formulate his idea of the poet and the role of literature. He ruled out the concept of poet as transcriber of the Muse; inspiration must pass the same rigorous analysis as consciously formulated verse. Working within the restrictions of a finite form the poet must create a magical effect that is infinite. The primary purpose of literature is not to serve as a vehicle for the release of the writer's passion but rather to trigger an effect on the reader. Valéry's idea of a poem, first formulated in his literary article of 1889, did not change over the next fifty years. In a lecture delivered at Oxford University in 1939 he repeated a definition similar to the one found in his early manifesto: "A poem is really a kind of machine for producing the poetic state of mind by means of words. The effect of this machine is uncertain, for nothing is certain about action on other minds"[7] (CW 7: 79; O 1: 1337). Valéry recognized in Poe the first writer to analyze the relationship between the work produced and its effect on the reader.

In the second half of his 1889 article Valéry recounts Poe's description of how he wrote "The Raven." Judging from Valéry's comment introducing the subject, there is no reason to believe that he considered the essay a hoax:[8]

Edgar Allan Poe, mathematician, philosopher, and great writer, clearly demonstrates in his curious little work *The Philosophy of Composition* the mechanics of poetic creation as he understands and practices it.

None of his works contains more acute analysis or a more strictly logical development of the principles discovered by observation. (CW 7: 319; O 1: 1810)

Again, Valéry expresses his admiration for Poe the literary scientist. He praises him for applying an *a posteriori* technique "based on the psychology of the *listener,* on the knowledge of the different notes that must be sounded in another's soul" (CW 7: 319; O 1: 1810).

Valéry's reference to the original version of "The Raven" indicates that he was familiar with Poe's poem in English, although he had no doubt also read Baudelaire's translation. Since he knew so little about Mallarmé at the time, it is unlikely that he would have acquired Mallarmé's translations of Poe's poems, which had just been published in a single volume. Even without having read Mallarmé's comments on Poe's description of how he wrote "The Raven," Valéry expresses similar views in his 1889 article. Mallarmé was not convinced that *The Philosophy of Composition* was a hoax, and in his mind it was not a question worth debating.[9] Of greater importance to him were the ideas on conscious poetic creation and the modern concept of the poet set forth in Poe's essay.

Like Mallarmé, Valéry admired specific qualities in "The Raven," which they both felt were unique. Particularly impressed by Poe's effective use of repetition within a line ("And the Raven, never flitting, still sitting, still sitting") and the repetition of the word "nevermore" at the end of each stanza throughout the last half of the poem, Valéry remarks that judicious use of a refrain has not been made in French poetry. He goes on to imagine a poem in which several monotonic refrains would flow together in a "melodic torrent" giving the effect of a *Leitmotiv,* the basis of Wagnerian musical theory.

Concluding his essay, Valéry advocates a literary world in which diverse approaches are appreciated, from the brutality of life's struggle in Zola's novels to the elegance of the rarest pleasures found in poetry. He sees the literary art of his own age tending toward the "complicated and *artificial,* too vibrant, too tense, too musical, and all the more as it becomes more mysterious, narrower, more inaccessible to the crowd" (CW 7: 323; O 1: 1811). But for Valéry this is the right direction. The last line of the essay expresses Valéry's lifelong preoccupation with perfection and poetic purity. "What does it matter," he remarks with youthful pride, if art "is inaccessible to the crowd, if it remains the luxury of a small number, provided that it reaches a few worthy readers for whom it is the divine kingdom, the highest degree of splendor and purity!" (CW 7: 323; O 1: 1811). He sees the literary perfection Poe envisioned as the antithesis of the "barbarous grandeur of the industrial world" (CW 7: 323; O 1: 1811).

Valéry attempted to apply his *art poétique* to his own poems, which he had been writing since the age of thirteen. During a year of military service (1889–90), he wrote over eighty poems. Although a few of his pieces had appeared in small reviews in Paris and in the provinces, it was through his relationship with Pierre Louÿs that Valéry made his *entrée* into the literary world and, most important, made contact with Mallarmé in Paris. It was Louÿs who encouraged Valéry to write to his idol and send along some of his poems. This first letter from Valéry to Mallarmé is touching to read because of its humble tone and the way in which the author presents himself as a disciple of the "great Edgar Poe." The complete text of the letter (dated October 1890) is presented here to convey the feeling of Valéry's respect for Mallarmé and his admiration for Poe (again Valéry refers to himself in the third person):

Dear Master,

A young man who, though lost in the provinces, has been enabled—thanks to a few rare fragments discovered here and there in reviews—to divine and to love the secret splendor of your works, now takes the liberty of presenting himself.

His conviction is that art can now no longer be other than a city of narrow confines where beauty reigns solitary. He longs, with his private dream, to be among the few lovers of aesthetic purity.

One of these, M. P. Louis,[10] has already mentioned the writer to you, a fact which decided him to send you these lines and these verses.

To make himself known in a few words he ought to say that he prefers poems short, concentrated toward a final impact, in which the rhythms are like the marmoreal steps to the altar, crowning the final line! It is simply that he is deeply imbued with the cunning doctrines of the great Edgar Allan Poe—perhaps the most subtle artist of this century!

That name alone will suffice to reveal the nature of his Poetics. So let him stop at this point, and yield place to the poems here submitted to you, in the hope of counsels written by that same hand which, in *Hérodiade,* created dazzlement and despair. (CW 8: 406–7; O 1: 1581–82)

Mallarmé replied promptly in a letter dated October 24, 1890, beginning with the complimentary salutation "My Dear Poet." Although his remarks were brief, they were encouraging: "The gift of subtle analysis with a music befitting it, this you certainly possess, which is all that matters . . . As for counsels, only solitude can give you these" (O 1: 18).

Six months later Valéry wrote a second letter to his mentor in which he expresses a certain discouragement and confusion as he tries to reconcile his lofty poetics with the experience of writing poems. He reaffirms his devotion to Poe but appears to be seeking reassurance that his own ideals are not illusory. The second letter is twice as long as the first; key paragraphs are cited below to show the importance of Valéry's preoccupation with defining his poetics, which appear to come straight from Poe.

Dear Master,

For the second time I am seeking your advice, in the desire to know whether certain aesthetic meditations which I have stored up this past winter, far away in the provinces, are not altogether wild and illusory.

A poem entitled "Narcisse Parle," which appeared in *La Conque,* throws some light on them, but as often happens, experience has made a mock of theory, and left me perplexed and at a standstill.

Poetry it seems to me is a delicate and beautiful explication of the World, contained within a peculiar and sustained music. Where the art of Metaphysics sees the Universe made up of abstract and absolute ideas, and painting sees it in colors, the art of poetry has to view it clothed in syllables, organized in sentences.

Considered in its naked and magical splendor, the word can be raised to the elemental power of a musical note, a color, or the keystone of an arch. A line of verse takes form like a chord which involves the meeting of two modes, in which the mysterious and sacred epithet, mirror of submerged suggestion, operates like a hushed accompaniment.

A very special devotion to the work of Poe has led me to assign to the poet the kingdom of analogy. He defines the mysterious echo of things, and that secret harmony of theirs which is as real and certain as a mathematical equation to all artist minds, which means to all who are vehement idealists. (CW 8: 407–8; O 1: 1740–41)

The ideas Valéry expresses in this letter could be presented as a definition of Symbolism. In Poe he discovered what he believed to be the power to produce a magical effect with the certainty of a mathematical equation, the basis on which Valéry formed his own poetics.

Mallarmé replied to the second letter by saying "Your 'Narcisse Parle' charms me . . . keep this rare tone." A few months later, on October 10, 1891, during a visit to Paris, Valéry was introduced to Mallarmé by Pierre Louÿs. Valéry recalls the momentous occasion: "Nine o'clock: at Mallarmé's. He opens the door himself. Small. The impression of a quiet, tired bourgeois of forty-nine . . . There is quiet at first . . . Then the conversation gets underway" (CW 8: 409; O 1: 1741). The visit was repeated many times during the next seven years until Mallarmé's death in 1898. Every Tuesday evening Mallarmé received a coterie of aspiring poets and artists who came to listen to the master proposing in his soft low voice a literary idealism that none would ever achieve. Looking back on these magical evenings, Valéry remembered that among the many things he talked about with Mallarmé, it was the subject of Poe that brought them close together:

One evening, a conversation on Poe, growing more and more concentrated, transformed the admirable host into a supreme, fatherly friend. What an evening for me, as centrally important as the stretto of a fugue—when the gropings of a dialogue growing more and more condensed arrive at a sense of pure unanimity—what a scholastic might call a dream—at the very source of individuation. As though, in the strange movements of two involved opponents who foresee less and less their own actions, a threshold had been crossed, almost that very one which speech itself forbids to talkers-in-general. (CW 8: 421–22; O 1: 1749)

A few days after his first visit with Mallarmé in Paris, Valéry had to return to Montpellier to complete his law degree, which was conferred in the summer of 1892. The modest success he had achieved by publishing a few poems, and his budding personal relationship with Mallarmé seemed to be the auspicious beginning of a promising literary career. But just the opposite happened. In the fall of 1892, Valéry experienced an intellectual crisis that resulted in the rejection of poetry and reoriented his thinking toward science and the effort to understand how his own mind functioned. Literature became "suspect," as he put it, and he was no longer willing to allow it to dominate his intellectual life. Poe played an important role in this dramatic transformation that determined Valéry's commitment to pursue intellectual self-comprehension.

The traumatic event in question has become known in Valéry biographies as the "Night of Genoa" that led to the "Great Silence." In September 1892 Valéry accompanied his family to Genoa to visit his mother's relatives. Earlier visits to the Italian port had always been pleasant, offering a relaxing break from his intense university studies and literary endeavors. On this occasion, during a violent storm the night of October 4–5, Valéry came face to face with himself and his aspirations. As he recalled later, it was "a frightful night—spent on my bed—the storm everywhere—my room dazzlingly bright with each lightning flash—and my whole fate was being decided in my head. I was between myself and myself" (O 1: 20). In a letter to Guy de Pourtalès he gave an even more dramatic description:

As for Genoa . . . I nearly became mad there in 1892. A certain *white* night—white with lightning—which I spent sitting up, and hoping that a bolt would strike me . . . It was a question of decomposing for myself all my first ideas and idols, and breaking off from a me who couldn't do what he wanted and didn't want to do what he could.[11]

What is the explanation for such a dramatic turn around and what did it all mean?

Critics and biographers speculate on the cause, taking into account fleeting references to the event found in Valéry's *Notebooks* and letters. There seems to be general agreement that the young poet was reacting, in part, to a sentimental crisis. During the summer of 1892, he had fallen in love with a certain Madame de "Rov" to whom he had never even spoken, much less made a declaration of love. Nevertheless, the beautiful woman of Catalan origin caused him a long period of suffering that fifty years later inspired a brief reference in his *Notebook* to "that absurd affair" (C 23: 589–90).

However devastating, an unrequited infatuation with a strange woman does not seem to justify giving up a promising literary career. For Valéry the experience was one of losing control, of being overwhelmed by his emotional feelings. He remarked many years later that "this crisis set me against my 'sensibility' insofar as it worked against the freedom of my mind" (CW 15: 294; O 2: 1511). The sentimental crisis probably served as a catalyst that resulted in profound changes already in the making.

There are several possible contributing factors that could have provoked Valéry's moment of truth. Francis Scarfe suggests that the twenty-one-year-old law school graduate had to face the question of what he was going to do with his life, a decision that traditionally causes mental and emotional anguish. Scarfe goes on to point out that

such crises as the "Night of Genoa" are by no means rare among men of intelligence and sensibility: we recall that Mallarmé suffered such a dark experience at Tournon, while the "dream" of Descartes and the "season in hell" of Rimbaud are classic examples of such a reorientation at critical stages in life.[12]

Anxiety concerning how he would earn a living was perhaps a contributing factor to the crisis, but a more fundamental conflict tormented Valéry. After writing some three hundred poems, he faced a crisis of originality. He felt a need to reject the influence of his predecessors, Baudelaire, Heredia, and Hugo, while at the same time feeling discouraged by the perfection envisioned by his idol Mallarmé. Among the recollections Valéry expresses concerning this turning point in his intellectual development, the following text is most revealing:

> But in my twentieth year I had been as if transformed by various torments of soul and mind, or rather by the extreme effort to overcome them—for nothing alters or transfigures us more profoundly than the struggle against those of our powers that have turned against us. Finally, I was led by I know not what daemon to set consciousness of my thought in opposition to its products, and thoughtful action against spontaneous formations (even when beautiful), against chance (even when lucky)—in a word, in opposition to all that can be attributed to automatism. (CW 15: 350–51; O 2: 1602)

From this point on the conscious effort involved in artistic creation became the focal point for Valéry rather than the poem produced by such effort. He expresses this idea very succinctly in a letter to his friend Albert Thibaudet: "The question was, not to be a poet, but to be able to be one" (CW 8: 419; O 1: 1748).

Poe played a major role in Valéry's decision to renounce a literary career, a fact that the author himself mentions on several occasions. In another letter to Thibaudet, also dated 1912, Valéry describes his relationship with Mallarmé and makes reference to his own dramatic change:

> I was brought to feel his power most by a reading of Poe. I read in him what I wanted and caught that fever of lucidity which he communicates.
> *Consequence:* I gave up writing verse. That art, which became impossible for me from 1892, was already simply an exercise, or an application of researches that were more important. Why not develop within oneself that which alone, in the genesis of a poem, is of interest to oneself? (All this is sheer history, not a thesis or an argument.)
> My last poems—very inferior Mallarmé—were a part of this mental gymnastics. (CW 8: 421; O 1: 1749)

Two important factors are evident in this passage: Valéry seems to have reached an impasse in his own poetic development and, secondly, he had become more interested in how the mind creates a poem than in the poem itself. We have seen in his first article on poetic technique and in his letters to Mallarmé that he was "penetrated" by the ideas he found in *The Philosophy of Composition.* Poe's essay had the double effect on Valéry of inspiring an interest in the art of writing poetry and, at the same time, causing him to reject literature in order to understand how the mind functions. The theme of *consciousness*, which became the major preoccupation in his poetry and prose, began to dominate his thinking and writing in 1892. Valéry was convinced that Poe reoriented his view of literature. A remark in his *Notebook* (1917) reflects this conviction: "Poe was the first to consider the mental mechanism as the producer of works. No one followed him" (CW 8: 354; C 6: 717). Valéry carried Poe's interest in the "mental mechanism" to its ultimate possibilities by making the Intellect his idol.

Poe's cosmological poem *Eureka* also played an important role in Valéry's intellectual crisis. The best description of Valéry's mental state during the period 1891–92 was written by the author himself in the introduction to his essay "On Poe's *Eureka.*" He describes his state of mind so that the reader can appreciate the full impact the reading of *Eureka* had on his thinking:

I was twenty and believed in the might of human thought. I found it a strange torment to be, and not to be. At times I felt I had infinite forces within me. They collapsed when faced with problems, and the weakness of my effective powers filled me with despair . . .

I had ceased writing verse and almost given up reading. Novels and poems, in my opinion, were only impure and half-unconscious applications of a few properties inherent in the great secrets I hoped some day to discover, basing this hope on the unremitting assurance that they must necessarily exist. As for the philosophers, I had read little of their work and was irritated by that little, because they never answered any of the questions that tormented me.

I had dipped into a few mystics. One can hardly speak ill of them, for what one finds in their work is only what one brings to it.

This was the point I had reached when *Eureka* fell into my hands. (CW 8: 161–62; O 1: 854–55)

Valéry goes on to state that Poe was the first to open his eyes to the power of scientific thought. His study of science, which in his school days had been pure boredom and drudgery, was suddenly turned into a passion by his reading of Poe. Through scientific analysis he hoped to discover the limitations of his own intellectual powers. The study of mathematics provided a model of the mind's functioning which required controlled thought processes and rigorous language. In science he admired the verification process required to substantiate theories, which themselves sometimes came about through leaps of the imagination. His renewed interest in mathematics and science was to last a lifetime; pages in his notebooks scribbled with formulas and scientific inquiries alongside references to literary problems bear witness to Valéry's efforts to reconcile concrete analysis and creative power.

In the passage cited above Valéry mentions that he gave up reading novels, a genre that interested him very little because, as he put it, these works "offer so little resistance" to his mind. The facility of the genre bothered him most: "The novel is possible because the *true* costs *nothing*, and is in *no way* distinct from the spontaneous creation of a barely disguised memory" (CW 15: 302; O 2: 1515). Nevertheless, he did read Poe's tales, a fact that some critics have overlooked. One of the first scholars to recognize the theme of intellectual self-consciousness in Valéry's poetry and prose was Emilie Noulet, whose study inspired a rare note from Valéry congratulating her on the keen sense of perception she brought to his work.[13] He did not mention, however, a misconception in Noulet's five-page chapter dealing with Poe's influence. Noulet assumed that Valéry had never bothered to read Poe's short stories, stating that had he done so, he would have found "a logic of the unreal and a rigor of the absurd."[14] She goes on to say that "Valéry, anti-narrative, read Poe in his most abstract work, in *Eureka*. Moreover, like Mallarmé, he proclaimed his debt."[15] The long prose poem *Eureka* is in fact the subject of Valéry's only essay devoted entirely to Poe, but his debt to the American author does not stop there. Evidence that Valéry did indeed read Poe's tales is found in his *Notebooks* and correspondence, documents that were not available to Noulet at the time she was preparing her study.

Valéry's earliest reference to one of Poe's short stories is found
in a letter to Gide dated 1891 in which he declares enthusiasti-
cally: "I insist, 'The Fall of the House of Usher' is the masterpiece
of all the past centuries."[16] A few months later in another letter to
Gide he mentions his admiration for two other Poe stories,
"Morella" and "Mesmeric Revelation,"[17] the first tale that Baudelaire translated. But the story that stuck in Valéry's mind for the
rest of his life was "The Domain of Arnheim." In a *Notebook* reference dated 1940 Valéry recalls the effect of one sentence on his
mind:

> *Arnheim.* Poe.
> In this fantasy of Poe's, there is one of those sentences that had so much
> . . . thematic influence on me at nineteen.
> A sentence on the possibilities of perfection. It said that man is very far
> from having attained what he could, etc.
> The idea of perfection possessed me. It soon changed into will-to-power,
> or the possession of power without using it. (CW 8: 359; C 23: 188)

The relationship between this sentence from Poe's tale and
Valéry's intellectual crisis of 1892 is evident. He envisioned perfecting his mental powers to the highest level possible without any
intention of practical application. Writing for publication represented a "sacrifice of the intellect" (CW 15: 298; O 2: 1513). Valéry's goal was to develop his intellectual mechanism in its purest
form.

Even after the specific tale faded from his memory, Valéry recalls the same sentence from Poe and one from Baudelaire describing Poe:

> Guiding themes and types.
> Ego.
> I no longer know where, nor in which of his works, Poe says that man is
> far from having realized, in any genre, the perfection he could attain, etc.
> (Perhaps in *Arnheim.*) But this remark has had the greatest "influence" on
> me. And this from Baudelaire, speaking of the same Poe: "*That marvelous
> brain always on alert.*" This struck me like the sound of a horn, a signal that
> excited the whole of my intellect. (CW 8: 358; C 22: 489)

The importance of the phrase "the highest degree of perfection" in Valéry's intellectual development can be seen in the repetition of the idea in his *Notebooks* and in the span of years between the initial reading of the tale (1890–91) and his recollection of its effect. In 1939 he emphasizes once again the significance of two sentences:

If I should write my memoirs, which would be those of a mind with no memory of events, I should have to include the phrase-motif which greatly excited me when I was nineteen and twenty. Like those of Baudelaire on Poe: "that marvelous brain always on the alert." That is what I envied—and not some "regular" career, a career . . . abroad!

Or again that phrase from the "Domain of Arnheim" on the highest degree of perfection that man . . . etc. That is what decided my direction. (CW 8: 358; C 22: 702)

Valéry's description of the effect of one sentence from Poe's work is a striking example of his own observation on influence: "It is when a book or an author's collected work acts on someone not with all its qualities, but with one or a few of them, that influence assumes its most remarkable values" (CW 8: 242; O 1: 635).

In addition to the sentence Valéry cites in his references, there is another one in "The Domain of Arnheim" that was to have a significant effect on his work. First, a brief synopsis of the tale will establish the context. A gentleman by the name of Mr. Ellison inherited four hundred and fifty million dollars from a distant relative, who had bequeathed the fortune to him a hundred years earlier. After considering the most frivolous means of disposing of such wealth, the narrator describes a unique personal quality in Mr. Ellison that will inspire him to spend the money in an unusual way: he comprehends "the true character, the august aims, the supreme majesty and dignity of the poetic sentiment" (M 3: 1271; OP: 945). Although Mr. Ellison has the potential to be a poet, musician, or an artist, he prefers an original medium for the expression of his concept of physical loveliness, the landscape garden, on which he will spend his fortune. The narrator goes on to describe two more unusual personal traits in Mr. Ellison that were certainly not lost on the young Valéry: a contempt of ambition and an obsession with perfection. Poe's sentence that made such a strong impression on Valéry is the narrator's comment in reference to Mr. Ellison:

I believe that the world has never seen—and that, unless through some series of accidents goading the noblest order of mind into distasteful exertion, the world will never see—that full extent of triumphant execution, in the richer domains of art, of which the human nature is absolutely capable. (M 3: 1271; OP: 944)

Baudelaire inserts two important words into the sentence that are not in the original version. After "distasteful exertion" (translated correctly as "efforts répugnants") Baudelaire adds "of practical application," ("efforts répugnants de l'application pratique") (OP: 944). Since Valéry's recollection of the sentence was in French from Baudelaire's translation, the idea of the mind's "repugnant efforts of practical application" and the goal of perfection oriented his thinking at a time when he decided to renounce writing for publication and to cultivate his mind for its own sake.

Another sentence that must have held particular significance for Valéry precedes the one just cited. The narrator asks rhetorically:

Is it not indeed, possible that, while a high order of genius is necessarily ambitious, the highest is above that which is termed ambition? And may it not thus happen that many far greater than Milton have contentedly remained "mute and inglorious?" (M 3: 1271; OP: 944)

In the hierarchy of geniuses, those who do not manifest their superiority through literary works hold higher rank. By renouncing literature and other outward manifestations of ambition in order to develop his intellectual powers, Valéry would place himself in the lofty sphere of unknown minds who choose to remain "mute and inglorious." Although the rejection of ambition and notoriety seems to be tinged with the sin of excess pride, writing for publication, which, in Valéry's mind, represented a "sacrifice of the intellect," was no longer a viable alternative after his crisis of 1892. In Poe's tale of a man who seeks to realize his aesthetic ideals in the form of a landscape garden Valéry discovered a couple of sentences that were to give him direction and bring out his own originality.

Two other Poe tales made a strong impression on Valéry. "MS. Found in a Bottle" inspired the title of a story Valéry was working on called "Manuscript Found in a Brain," a project he described to Pierre Louÿs, who chided him for borrowing straight from Poe:

> "Manuscript Found in a Brain," excellent title. Why is it directly connected to Poe, almost word for word? Divide it.
> The good part is "Found in a Brain;" that's entirely yours. Then why do you stamp it with the import label "Made in U.S.A." by the useless word "Manuscript."[18]

Taking his friend's advice, Valéry changed the title of the manuscript, calling it "Agatha" before abandoning it. Another idea bearing a Poe title began to gestate in Valéry's mind, "The Life and Adventures of Ch. Auguste Dupin," whom he calls the "Cazanova of the Mind" (C 1: 50). Poe's famous detective Dupin, the main character in three of his tales, served as a model for Valéry when he created his first fictitious personality, Monsieur Teste. In Teste Valéry brought to life the "mute and inglorious" genius whom Poe had only postulated. "Agatha" and *The Evening with Monsieur Teste* require an extensive analysis, which will be presented in the next chapter.

Evidence from Valéry's own comments prove beyond any doubt that he did indeed read Poe's tales, and they had a special effect on him. He focused on specific intellectual qualities that he was searching for during his formative years. In "The Domain of Arnheim" he found the reaffirmation of his desire for perfection and renunciation of ambition in the traditional sense (fame as a writer and financial wealth); in Dupin he recognized a human thinking-machine that could be purged of its outward manifestation of mental power, thus becoming pure intellectual potential, Valéry's own goal.

The lasting effects of the "Night of Genoa" are well documented. Valéry returned to Montpellier, where he got rid of most of his books, except for Poe's, which he read all the more intensively. He entered a period of his life that has become known as the "Great Silence," a misnomer because he did continue to write and publish occasionally. As we will see in subsequent chapters of this study,

Valéry produced more works of prose than poetry during the period 1892–1917. The fact that he wrote less is partly due to preoccupations of a practical nature, such as leaving Montpellier, finding a job, and getting married.

Visits to his brother in Paris resulted in Valéry's decision to settle there permanently in 1894, although it was not until three years later that he began a full-time job. His austere hotel room, furnished with a bed, chair, writing table, and blackboard (often covered with equations), satisfied his ascetic life-style. It was in 1894 that he began his lifetime habit of rising between 4 and 5 a.m. to reflect and write for several hours in his notebooks. This intellectual chronicle had nothing to do with day-to-day events, as Valéry points out:

> I do not keep, I have never kept a record of my days. I jot down my ideas. What do I care about my biography? What do my used-up days matter to me? Nothing of the past should be retained but the true wealth, the bounty snatched from time, which increases our power to act and which necessarily loses at the same time its attachment to its source. (CW 15: 287; O 2: 1506)

And what a bounty indeed! Valéry's meditations, filling 261 notebooks, provide a wealth of material that contribute to a deeper appreciation of his own thought processes. Although originally not intended for publication, after Valéry's death the notebooks were photocopied and bound in twenty-nine quarto volumes each containing between nine hundred and nine hundred fifty pages.[19] The contents of the *Notebooks* are stunning because of the breadth and profundity of the subjects, which range from brief notes to rough drafts of essays, from formulas jotted down in a couple of lines to pages almost filled with mathematical equations. Valéry was fond of drawing sketches and painting small watercolor scenes in his notebooks, which are also reproduced in the photocopies. His interest in English is evident in the titles of the earliest notebooks: "Logbook" and "Self Book." Since Valéry published very little on Poe, his *Notebooks* are a valuable source for thoughts that reveal the effects of the American writer at various stages of his intellectual development. When Valéry began publishing again after 1917, his notebooks provided material for many articles and speeches on subjects as varied as poetics and history.

Valéry's life in Paris during this early period was certainly not one of a recluse. Known as a brilliant conversationalist, he counted among his close friends André Gide and Pierre Louÿs, who had introduced him to Henri de Régnier, Marcel Schwob, Paul Léautaud, and Francis Vielé-Griffin, all of whom were regulars at Mallarmé's Tuesday evening gatherings at his apartment on the rue de Rome. Before settling permanently in Paris in 1894, Valéry had known Mallarmé only through a small number of poems, a few letters, and the brief visit with the poet in 1891. From 1894 until Mallarmé's death in 1898, Valéry's relationship with the elder poet became that of father and son, master and disciple.

As Valéry mentions, the subject of Poe brought the two together in a close relationship. Valéry's descriptions of Mallarmé reveal characteristics that portray him as a living Poe,[20] in whom he recognizes a synthesis of the qualities of a mathematician and a literary artist. This is a quality Valéry very much admires: "Mallarmé never ceases thinking of the nature and possibilities of language with the lucidity of a scientist and the conviction of a poet" (CW 8: 270; O 1: 679). In Mallarmé he saw the creative consciousness Poe describes embodied in a man whose ambition was to dominate the entire system of verbal expression. Valéry pointed out this quality in a conversation with Mallarmé: "I said to him one day [that] he closely approached the attitude of the algebraists who vastly extended the science of forms and the symbolic aspect of their mathematical art" (CW 8: 291; O 1: 658). The results of Mallarmé's conscious efforts, as Valéry describes them, are reminiscent of the goal Poe envisioned: "the very essence of his work requires that the creator of beauty and fantasy should exert himself to provide the public with pleasures that demand no exertion" (CW 8: 247; O 1: 639).

Mallarmé reconfirmed in Valéry a belief in other concepts they both admired in Poe: distrust of inspiration, importance of conscious effort, elimination of non-poetical elements from poems, "the Rythmical creation of Beauty" as the sole purpose of poetry, and the scientific approach to creative endeavors. Valéry credits Mallarmé for introducing into art "the necessity of making an intellectual effort" (CW 8: 247; O 1: 639), a quality he also admires in

Poe. Through his reading of Poe and his many conversations with Mallarmé, Valéry arrived at a resolution he intended to apply to himself:

If I am to write, I should infinitely prefer writing something feeble that was produced in full consciousness and utter lucidity, rather than being carried out of myself to give birth in a trance to one of the greatest masterpieces in literature. (CW 8: 249; O 1: 640)

The qualities in Mallarmé that most impressed Valéry were his extreme intellectual self-consciousness, his total commitment to perfection, and his disdain for notoriety, qualities mentioned in the sentence from "The Domain of Arnheim" that stuck in Valéry's mind for a lifetime. Concluding his essay "Stéphane Mallarmé," Valéry refers to the elder poet as "the purest and most authentic example of the intellectual virtues." Valéry's final sentence, "I do not believe anything like it has ever been witnessed in the realm of letters" (CW 8: 271; O 1: 680) recalls the sentence from "The Domain of Arnheim": "I believe the world has never seen . . . that full extent of triumphant execution, in the richer domains of art, of which the human nature is absolutely capable" (M 3: 1271; OP: 944).

While Valéry recognizes that Mallarmé's influence on him was to a great extent a reaffirmation of ideas and goals he had formulated before arriving in Paris, he also emphasizes the element of *refusal,* which is an important part of influence in Valéry's mind. Again, his reading of Poe played a role in Valéry's setting off in a different direction. Mallarmé's dream was, as Valéry describes it, to give the art of writing "a *universal meaning,* a universal value, and to acknowledge that the supreme object of the world and the justification of its existence . . . was and could only be a *Book*" (CW 8: 244; O 1: 637). At this point Mallarmé and Valéry no longer share a common goal. Inspired by Poe's description of how he wrote "The Raven," Valéry envisioned the possibility of understanding how the creative mechanism functions. His goal was not to produce literature in its purest state, but rather to comprehend how the mind operates in its attempt to do so. He even formulates this ambition into a statement of conviction:

It is not the finished work or the impression it makes on the world that can develop or complete us, but only the manner in which the work was performed . . .
In that respect I withdrew some degree of importance from the *work* and transferred it to the will and purposes of the *agent.* (CW 8: 249; O 1: 640–41)

In this statement Valéry realizes there is both a danger and a contradiction. The idea is dangerous to literature because it negates the *raison d'être* of most writers. The contradiction lies in the fact that Valéry admires a man who, in his words, "reached a point nothing short of deifying the written word" (CW 8: 249; O 1: 641). Valéry refuses Mallarmé's deification of the written word, preferring instead his own deification of the process that creates the written word. While Valéry enjoyed and admired Mallarmé's poems, what fascinated him most was the mind capable of creating such a high degree of perfection. Thus, as Valéry points out, Mallarmé exercised both a positive and a negative influence on him, negative in the sense that he refused Mallarmé's ultimate goal, which was no longer his own. Valéry's intellectual self-analysis, reaffirmed by his reading of Poe, demanded rigorous training and refinement that writing poetry no longer satisfied.

Interest in Poe shared with Mallarmé encouraged Valéry to develop his proficiency in English, a subject that had been rendered as boring as science in his school days. Mallarmé's descriptions of his adventures in London in his early twenties inspired Valéry to set off for the British capital, which for French artists and writers had the same exotic attraction as Paris did for their Anglophone counterparts. It is interesting to note that neither Baudelaire, Mallarmé, nor Valéry had the desire, and certainly not the means, to visit the United States. The closest they came to learning the language of Poe was a familiarity with British English, the standard "correct" version at the time. Valéry recalls that his first trip to England at the age of seven made no linguistic impression at all; his only memories were those of being seasick during the crossing and experiencing a terrible fright while visiting Mme Tussaud's Museum (CW 15: 41).[21]

The second trip to the British Isles sixteen years later in the summer of 1894 was an exciting and stimulating visit. Valéry met several young men of letters with whom he shared an interest in

Symbolist poetry. Thanks to a letter of introduction written by Marcel Schwob, Valéry met George Meredith, an important writer and Francophile who spoke fluent French. Valéry's return trip to London in early 1896 was prompted by a letter from Meredith and by an offer for a job in the press department of the Chartered Company, an agency in charge of overseeing British interests in Africa. Valéry gives a charming description of the bewilderment of his first day on the job in his article "My Early Days in England," in which he also mentions that had it not been for the intervention of Fate, in the form of a case of influenza bad enough to send him home, he might have remained in England to earn a livelihood (CW 15: 50–51). After reading descriptions of London recounted by Mallarmé, Verlaine, and Rimbaud, Valéry experienced for himself "London intellectual intoxication," as he calls it. Among the many pleasant recollections of his sojourns across the Channel, Valéry expresses one regret: "I have only retained one bitter thought, and that is the hateful sensation of a kind of impotency, which I have never been able to overcome, in expressing myself in English or understanding it as it is spoken" (CW 15: 54). All the sensitivity he brought to the sounds and nuances of his native language did not enable him to acquire aural proficiency in English, a source of frustration that was to plague him for many years. T. S. Eliot recalls that his conversations with Valéry were always in French and that he never heard the French poet speak English, even in Great Britain.[22]

Valéry's weakness in spoken English did not daunt his determination to learn the written language. Translating works from one language to another was an intellectual exercise he enjoyed. Although the foreign language he knew best was Italian, he translated Thomas Hardy, Einstein, and Poe from English to French.[23] Valéry does not describe the circumstances that inspired him to make a contribution to the body of Poe translations, but one can imagine his dilemma upon choosing a text. Baudelaire had translated most of Poe's tales and critical works, and Mallarmé had rendered his poems into rythmic prose. Poe's correspondence, the *Literati,* and the *Marginalia* offered possible texts for the French translator. The *Literati* held little interest for Valéry because the pieces dealt with lesser-known figures in American literature who would have no importance or appeal in France. The *Marginalia* also contained sections that did not interest him, such as those on Thomas Moore and Thomas Carlyle, but he decided to pick and choose, selecting only parts that caught his attention, thus calling his translation "Some Fragments from the *Marginalia*" ("Quelques Fragments des *Marginalia*").[24]

If Valéry had simply translated these fragments, there would be no need for further discussion. The interest in this text lies in the commentary Valéry added alongside his translation. While translating Poe, his mind was reacting to the thoughts expressed in the *Marginalia,* which are themselves Poe's reflections on various subjects. Valéry's marginal notes express major themes that his reading of Poe's novels and essays had already reaffirmed. In accordance with his own conviction of how literary influence works, Valéry reacts to specific qualities in Poe that were to bring out his own originality. These themes are evident in his comments on the *Marginalia.*

Poe's first essay describes the practice of writing his thoughts in the margins of the text he is reading, pointing out that this is no idle chitchat but rather a dialogue with himself, allowing boldness, originality, and a lack of conceit or pretentiousness. The limited space, says Poe, is more of an advantage than an inconvenience because it requires the reader to focus his thought and note only the most important points. Alongside Poe's commentary Valéry points out two major differences in his own habit of taking notes. First, he does not write in the margin of his books, preferring instead his notebooks, where thoughts can be developed more fully, and second, his notes almost never concern what he has read.[25] Restating a familiar theme, Valéry emphasizes that his notes record observations about the mind itself, how it functions. For many people, says Valéry, notebooks become a confidential friend in whom they confide confessions and impressions they would never reveal in conversation: "There are men who dare to write what they almost dare not think" (CW 8: 178). For Valéry, writing notes represents a dialogue of the brain with an inner voice, the recording of the mind's reactions to its own thoughts.

Poe mentions that reading another person's work can occasionally inspire original, spontaneous thoughts in the reader's mind.

To this possibility of a gratuitous discovery, Valéry reacts with strong distrust of inspiration:

He who in unguarded moments and in his impromptu talk is favored with happy discoveries, and invents forms and models of an original nature—is generally the *same* as he whose pains and prolonged attention will finally produce *at least* the *same* effects.
A powerful mind seeks to obtain from itself by conscious labor the results that are analogous to those it has sometimes been able to produce *by the very fact that it was not concerned to attain them.* (CW 8: 179)

Spontaneous thought perceived as original is merely an accident that must be subjected to the scrutiny of the conscious mind.

Poe reflects on the difficulty of transferring the marginal notes from their sources, pointing out that separating the comments from the context would render them incomprehensible. His solution to this problem is to provide the essential part of the author's concept where necessary in order to make the note comprehensible, leaving the rest to "the acumen and imagination of the reader." Valéry's comments on this discussion are less concerned with Poe's dilemma, being more preoccupied with his own thoughts on the effect of the works of others on his own mind:

The value of a work for a given reader is commensurate with the importance of these parallel reactions to his reading. The work may finally be judged a very bad one; if the notes in question have been numerous and explicit, the book has proved its value as a stimulant. (CW 8: 181)

The last line of this quote has important implications for Valéry's views on influence. He was convinced that the power of a work to generate other works is a sign of its greatness; making a value judgment on its quality is not necessarily relevant to its ability to engender future literary productions.

The final brief paragraph in Poe's essay on marginal notes inspires Valéry to make a long commentary on another aspect of his concept of influence, the power of the mind to alter itself. Poe remarks that the habit of making notes in reaction to his reading might have in some instances altered his mind or might not have altered it often. In any case, he concludes, "these are points upon which I say nothing, because upon these there can be nothing cleverly said" (CW 8: 181). This remark triggers a response from Valéry for whom the effects of the mind upon itself is a subject of great importance: "Poe stops at the very moment when he was about to develop the most interesting reflections of his preamble" (CW 8: 181–82). Valéry then takes up the subject where Poe leaves off. The *action* of the mind coming to grips with a text is more important to Valéry than the thought produced in the marginal note. The dynamic functioning of the intellect as it reacts to disordered thoughts, abolishing some, going deeper into others, reorganizing patterns, "no subject," says Valéry, "is more stimulating for the mind" (CW 8: 182). Valéry adds a third dimension to Poe's description of marginal notes. The original author records his thought in the text to which the reader reacts by scribbling notes. Valéry observes at the same time his own mind in the process of reacting to the text, formulating thought that is transformed into language. This very activity has an effect upon the brain, a mechanism constantly refined and changed by its own action. Valéry sums up his addendum to Poe's essay with this comment: "The essential object of the mind is the mind" (CW 8: 182).

The second text from the *Marginalia* that Valéry translated deals with the transfer of thought into expression. Poe introduces this piece with a quote from Montaigne: "People talk about thinking, but for my part I never think except when I sit down to write" (CW 8: 183). Poe finds that in his own experience, when the brain offers a confused conception, he takes pen in hand to transform the thought into a more precise form. To those who contend that there are thoughts which cannot be put into words, Poe responds by pointing out an apparent lack of deliberateness or method as the source of the problem. The thought is made logical through the effort of written expression. Valéry questions whether the same thought exists after it has been verbally treated. He sees the mind operating on the thought in such a way as to transform it in the process of giving it written expression. Again, his preoccupation with the dynamic forces of the intellect is evident. Another element affecting the expression of thought, remarks Valéry, is the action of one word upon another. The transfer of our primitive mental production into language is the most complex process the brain accomplishes. The mind must be turned upon itself in order to understand the process. As Valéry explains so eloquently, language distinguishes us as human: "We ourselves change into *inter-human* currency what our 'inner lives,' that is to say, our *inhuman, extrahuman, subhuman,* lives have brought forth for us" (CW 8: 186).

There is one category of thoughts that Poe finds especially difficult to adapt to language. For want of a better word he calls them "fancies," the "shadows of shadows" that seem to arise from the soul rather than the intellect and come to him upon the brink of sleep. These "fancies," accompanied by a pleasurable ecstasy not found in wakefulness or in the world of dreams, appear to be, in Poe's words, "a glimpse of the spirit's outer world" (CW 8: 187). Rather than coming through the intellect, these impressions seem to come through the five senses, which are "supplanted to five myriad others alien to mortality" (CW 8: 187). This discussion interests Valéry at the moment when Poe states that his faith in the "power of words" is so great that he believes it possible to "embody the evanescence of fancies." The intellectual effort required to transform vagueness, intuition, and inspiration into a literary work dominates Valéry's thinking as he reads this passage by Poe. Valéry's marginal note expresses his basic approach to literary criticism:

> Critical judgments about literary works never take into account the difficulties that are inherent in the object which the author has striven to evoke for the readers or those with which he has contended by the very form he has chosen. The result is that the notion of technical value in literature is generally ignored.
>
> Edgar Allan Poe, who let nothing stand in his mind without disturbing it with his precise questions, could not fail to touch on the essential problem of the passage from thought to language—and from formlessness to form. The rule is to resolve this problem without stating it—to resolve it by the work itself. (CW 8: 187–88)

The only way to judge a written work, in Valéry's mind, is to examine the connection between what the author intended to do and how well he accomplished it through the use of language. In other words, the critic must focus on the author's ability to transform formlessness into form. He believed that Poe was the first to recognize this essential link.

Valéry's last fragment translated from the *Marginalia* bears a title he added himself: "Fatal Superiority." His own parallel reactions to the text are longer than the three paragraphs translated from Poe. Valéry's commentary deals with one of his favorite subjects, the idea of a superior intellect, the "mute and inglorious" hero that caught his attention in "The Domain of Arnheim." Poe's opening remark in this fragment from the *Marginalia* proposes a concept that Valéry brought to life in his character Monsieur Teste:

> I have sometimes amused myself by endeavoring to fancy what would be the fate of an individual gifted, or rather accursed, with an intellect *very* far superior to that of his race. Of course, he would be conscious of his superiority; nor could he (if otherwise constituted as man is) help manifesting his consciousness. Thus he would make himself enemies at all points. (CW 8: 190)

The first sentence cited above could very well serve as an introduction to *The Evening with Monsieur Teste*. The rest of the quotation provokes a refusal in Valéry's thinking:

> I find a dubious point in these profound observations. It does not appear to me certain that a man of supreme intelligence must necessarily manifest the consciousness of his own superiority, or at least in such a way that it irritates the temperate intelligence of those who are his near equals. The hypothesis of a mind's general superiority implies the ability to foresee the fatal consequences of its manifestations. This very great mind would be able to hide within itself. (CW 8: 190–91)

Teste embodies the superior intellect that Poe imagines, but Valéry is careful to purge from his character the fatal flaw of manifesting his superiority. The purity of Teste's mental power is spared any sort of outside contamination by the fact that it is known only to him.

In his description of the individual endowed with superior intellect Poe sees the possibility of such a person being taken for a madman because of the extreme power he possesses. He is convinced that such individuals have existed, but their biographies will not be found among "the good and great." We must search, says Poe, "the slight records of wretches who died in prison, in Bedlam, or upon the gallows" (CW 8: 192). Valéry does not buy this argument, calling it "essentially romantic." "No one is more popular," remarks Valéry, "than a great criminal" (CW 8: 192). He points out that anonymous madmen have played a great role in history, such as those who built the Pyramids. Valéry offers a definition of his own: "A madman is not defined by the contents of his thoughts but by the judgment he makes about the value of these contents, by the illegitimate powers a thought usurps" (CW 8: 192). He transformed Poe's concept of an intellectual madman into a mental mechanism capable of identifying its own potential defects, the first of which is the desire to become known to others.

Valéry's translations of fragments from the *Marginalia* stimulated responses in three areas central to his own thinking: the mind's observation of its own processes, the link between formlessness and form as a basis for judging a literary work, and the idea of an individual endowed with pure intellectual power. The transformation of these basic concepts into his own work brought out Valéry's originality as a writer.

After returning from England, Valéry had to make a decision about a career, a thought that tormented him a great deal because of his need to earn money and reserve time for his intellectual endeavors. Taking Huysmans' advice to seek employment in the civil service, Valéry took the examination for entry into the War Office, where he was appointed to a position in 1897. He had hoped that this type of work would allow him the time and energy for intellectual pursuits, but the job was so mind-numbing that he resigned after three years. In 1900 he married Jeannie Gobillard, niece of painter Berthe Morisot, and left the War Office to become administrative assistant to Edouard Lebey, director of the French press association Agence Havas. This position, which Valéry kept until Lebey's death twenty-two years later, allowed him time to read and continue writing, although he rarely published before 1917.[26]

In 1945, a few months before his death, Valéry wrote several paragraphs in his *Notebooks* examining the effect Mallarmé and Poe had on his mental development during the period 1892–96. He recalls that only he and Mallarmé isolated and adored in secret the "abstract Idol of the perfect self (*du moi parfait*)," the meaning of which he explains by using the English term "*self-conscious-ness*, the legacy of Poe" (C 29: 536–37). For Valéry, the concept of the mind observing its own mechanism had its origins in Poe's work and therefore required a special term for which there was no French equivalent.   Thus, the expression "self-consciousness" became part of Valéry's inner vocabulary while he was a young man and continued to have special significance in his maturity.

In the same *Notebook* reference Valéry goes on to examine the connection between the influence of Mallarmé and Poe on him. While observing Mallarmé's mind struggling with the complex problems of poetic language and the art of literature, Valéry glimpsed the possibility of discovering a "universal attitude" within his own mind. "This sort of enlightenment (*lumière*)," explains Valéry, "came to me especially from four lines of Poe—here and there. I quickly fortified myself with faith in my own absolute power—pure and unrelenting, to the point of soon feeling even more brutal than Mallarmé" (C 29: 537).   Poe's influence on Valéry is unique and goes far beyond the effect of the American writer on his predecessors.   It had the effect of turning Valéry against literature and orienting him toward the quest of pure intellectual power.

Before he abandoned writing for publication, Valéry embodied his concept of "conscious consciousness" in the character Monsieur Teste.   Transforming the idea of pure intellectual power into a prose piece proved to be a difficult task.   In the process of creating his first work of fiction, Valéry relied on Poe as a model, as we shall see in the next chapter.

CHAPTER THREE

Dupin-Teste: The Poe Connection

Is it not indeed, possible that, while a high order of genius is necessarily ambitious, the highest is above that which is termed ambition?

—Poe, "The Domain of Arnheim"

After his crisis of 1892 Valéry reduced everything, as he put it, "to the single brute notion of mental power" (C 8: 419). Out of the determination to "guillotine all literature" came two of Valéry's most famous prose pieces, *The Evening with Monsieur Teste* and *Introduction to the Method of Leonardo da Vinci*, both of which develop the idea of a superior intellect. While Teste embodies pure intellectual potential, Valéry's Leonardo represents a synthesis of artistic genius and power of analysis as they apply to a number of creative activities. Valéry began working on the two commissioned pieces in 1894, completing the essay on Leonardo in 1895 and *Monsieur Teste* the following year. The creation of the fictitious character Edmond Teste reveals direct links to Valéry's immersion in Poe's works during the early 1890s.

Although he had given up any ambition of becoming a well-known poet and writer, Valéry did not completely turn his back on literary interests. After moving to Paris in 1894 he joined several friends, including André Gide and Pierre Louÿs, as editor of the literary review *Le Centaure*, which published two issues before folding in late 1896. The first issue features two poems by Valéry, "Summer" ("Eté") and "View" ("Vue"), the author being identified only by the letter V. The second and last edition contains *The*

Evening with Monsieur Teste along with an announcement of future articles, including one on Poe by P.V., which apparently was never written.

The origin of *Monsieur Teste* dates back to early 1894, when Valéry was invited to write an article of about twenty pages on a subject of his own choosing to be published in *Le Centaure*. He spent August of that year in Montpellier trying to create the piece, which caused him a great deal of anguish. "Teste was conceived," recalls Valéry, "—in a room where Auguste Comte spent his early years—at a period when I was drunk on my own will and subject to strange excesses of consciousness of my *self*" (CW 6: 3; O 2: 11).[1] Thirty years later he recounted in detail the mental state that led to the creation of Teste. He recalls suffering from "the acute ailment called precision" (CW 6: 3; O 2: 11), which rendered everything that came easy to him worthless. Literature, even demanding works of poetry, represented a "sacrifice of the intellect" because the purity and perfection required to make common language precise would find few readers, most of whom prefer instead to exercise only passive attention and expect amusement. At the age of twenty-three, Valéry made a decision that had a profound effect on his writing career: "it seemed to me unworthy to divide my ambition between the desire to produce an effect on others and the passion to know and acknowledge myself as I was, without omission, pretense, or complacency" (CW 6: 4; O 2: 12). He rejected not only literature but also philosophy, theology, and all other forms of accepted beliefs. His goal was to reduce himself to his *"real* properties," to discover his own potential and limitations, and to proceed from that point. His brain became an inner island where he retreated to develop and fortify his resources. It was out of this state of mind that Teste was born.

Obsessed by the fantasy of an ideal brain, Valéry decided to create a character to embody this intellectual monster, the "demon of possibility,"[2] as he liked to call Teste (CW 6: 6; O 2: 14). Many readers saw in Teste a close resemblance to Valéry's idol Mallarmé and assumed that he was the dominant inspiration and model for the character. In a letter to Albert Thibaudet written in 1912, Valéry denies this assumption and, in fact, says he created a character that Poe could have brought to life:

"M. Teste" has for me no willed connection with Mallarmé. It is, like everything else of mine, a commissioned work. With the help of notes quickly thrown together, I made up that pseudo portrait of nobody, a caricature if you like of someone who might have been invented by—Poe, once more.[3]

As Valéry mentions above, he wrote the text under a certain amount of pressure, relying on various notes he had taken with him to Montpellier. He mentions this fact again in a letter to Gide, adding that his main concern was to fill twenty pages with writing.[4] Creating the text was a discouraging and disappointing experience as he describes it in another letter to Gide: "disgust or lack of time or lack of talent, *the effects* that I wanted ended up being suppressed or nonexistent. Therefore my *mechanical* attempts let me down, failed."[5] Although Valéry was always his own severest critic and very much a perfectionist, his comments show that he did have difficulty preparing the text and relied heavily on notes—some personal, others undoubtedly suggested by his study of Poe. We know that during this same period and before, he was reading Poe almost exclusively, so some degree of influence on Valéry's early attempt at prose writing would not be surprising. What we find is an extensive dependence on Poe's character Dupin as a model.

C. Auguste Dupin is the shrewd detective in three tales, "The Murders in the Rue Morgue," "The Purloined Letter," and "The Mystery of Marie Roget." His remarkable analytical powers and brilliant reasoning are brought to bear on crimes the local police and public believe to be unsolvable. In the first tale, Dupin is intrigued by the gristly murders of a certain Madame L'Espanaye and her daughter, a crime that has horrified all of Paris for several weeks. When an innocent clerk, appropriately named Le Bon, who had once done a favor for Dupin, is accused of the murders, Dupin takes a special interest in the progress of the investigation. He discovers a police chief who is a "good guesser" but has "erred continually by the very intensity of his investigation." Dupin sees the case as a riddle to be solved when he remarks, "An inquiry will afford us amusement." By applying creative imagination and feats of logic, Dupin identifies a most unlikely culprit, an orangutan of the Bornese species brought to Paris as a pet by a sailor from a Maltese vessel. Why did such a bizarre tale interest Valéry? He was fascinated by the intellect of C. Auguste Dupin, who possesses the analytical powers of both a scientist and a poet.[6] Poe's hero seems to understand the operations of the mind that can solve any problem. It is a rarefied version of these analytical powers that Valéry portrays in his character Monsieur Teste.

The task of bringing Teste to life did indeed present quite a dilemma to his creator. Valéry's mind was captivated by the idea of an extraordinary genius who talks very little, considers writing a waste of time, and, so that his genius might be uncontaminated, prefers to remain anonymous. How then could this lofty intellectual, unknown to the rest of the world, be portrayed even in a slightly believable way to the reader? Valéry accomplishes this feat in exactly the same way that Poe did, by creating a narrator endowed with a superior intelligence capable of recognizing a true genius and appreciating his more subtle qualities, which go unnoticed by the rest of society. Both Poe and Valéry create an alter ego for the main character. It is this unnamed character who transmits to the reader fragmented glimpses of the physical and intellectual characteristics of Dupin and Teste.

The structures of "The Murders in the Rue Morgue" and *The Evening with Monsieur Teste* are strikingly similar, each text being composed of three parts: (1) a short introduction by the narrator, who not only impresses the reader with his own comments on the functioning of the mind but also prepares the way for an encounter with a far superior intellect; (2) the presentation of the main character introduced into the stories in exactly the same manner; and (3) the description of an evening promenade during which we see how Dupin and Teste observe the outside world.

The very first sentence of each text reveals the intellectual focus of the narrative. Poe's narrator declares: "The mental features discoursed of as the analytical are, in themselves, but little susceptible of analysis" (M 2: 527; OP: 7).[7] Poe describes here that aspect of the mind which intrigued him and became an obsession for Valéry. They both wanted to know how the intellectual mechanism works; however, it is this same mechanism that must be turned upon itself in order to understand how the mind operates. Valéry sometimes uses the English words *self* and *self-consciousness* to refer to the intellect attempting to comprehend its own functioning. Although Poe mentions in his opening sentence that the mind's analytical features do not lend themselves to analysis, Valéry was convinced of the opposite. Teste represents a mind which has come closest to achieving this self-consciousness in Valéry's sense, that is, the ability of the intellect to understand its own operation, its limits, and its potential. His text begins with the narrator's modest statement of intellectual superiority: "Stupidity is not my strong point" (CW 6: 8; O 2: 15).

In each story the narrator continues with a commentary on the virtues of possessing a keen intellect. We see that the development of such a mind provides its own gratification. The narrator in *Monsieur Teste* recounts that the victorious moments of his mind compose "a *happy* life," while Poe's narrator remarks that the analytical faculties are "a source of the liveliest enjoyment." One of the obvious differences between the two narrations can be seen immediately in the introduction: Poe takes pleasure in showing the practical application of the well-developed analytical powers of his hero while Valéry's character disdains any manifestation of his potential. For Poe, observing the intellectual faculties in action, as in the game of whist he describes, is a means of understanding how these analytical features of the mind work. We can see in the description of the whist player certain intellectual characteristics of an Edmond Teste: "mind struggles with mind. . . . He makes, in silence, a host of observations and inferences. . . . The necessary knowledge is that of *what* to observe" (M 2: 529–30; OP: 9). Teste too is a keen observer capable of separating the nonessential from the essential to be retained. He tries to create in his mind a mechanical sieve that will help him recall the important things he has observed. Teste's intellect is constantly struggling with itself, training its faculties, refining perceptions, and maturing.

For Valéry, these qualities are worthy of being developed solely for themselves. Applying the analytical powers of the mind to a practical situation in order to show proof of existence represents a sort of debasement. Much of the first two pages of *The Evening with Monsieur Teste* deals with defining a true genius who, according to the narrator, distinguishes himself from other superior minds by

.virtue of not committing their first error, that of becoming known:

What they call a superior man is a man who has deceived himself. To be astonished at him, one must see him—and to be seen, he must show himself. And he shows me that he is possessed by an inane infatuation with his own name. So every great man is flawed with an error. Every mind said to be powerful begins with the mistake that makes it known. In exchange for the public's dime, he gives the time required to make himself noticeable, the energy spent in conveying himself, preparing to satisfy someone else. He goes even so far as to compare the crude sport of fame with the joy of feeling unique—the great private pleasure. (CW 6: 9; O 2: 15–16)

Valéry creates in Teste the ideal head, the unknown genius aware of his own potential, as can be seen in the narrator's remark: "I dreamed that the most vigorous minds, the canniest inventors, the most precise connoisseurs of thought, must be unknown men, misers, or those who die without confessing" (CW 6: 9; O 2: 16). Poe had already imagined this same type of person, whom he describes in "The Domain of Arnheim," as the "mute and inglorious" genius far greater than Milton. Both writers imagine the existence of an intellect superior to the few minds we call geniuses. The detective Dupin demonstrates the superior analytical faculties that fascinated Poe, but Valéry goes a step farther in creating his character: Teste is the silent, uncelebrated genius whom Poe had only imagined.

After a two-page introduction in which each narrator comments upon the fine qualities of a well-developed intellect, we find a rather abrupt transition from this commentary of a general nature to the specific details of an encounter with a person who possesses the qualities just described. It is upon reading this part of *The Evening with Monsieur Teste* that one has the impression of recognizing a similar transition in "The Murders in the Rue Morgue:"

Poe:
    The narrative which follows will appear to the reader somewhat in the light of a commentary upon the propositions just advanced.
    Residing in Paris during the spring and part of the summer of 18—, I there became acquainted with a Monsieur C. Auguste Dupin. (M 2: 531; OP: 10)

Valéry:
    These ideas came to me during October of '93, at those moments of re-
pose when thought takes pleasure simply in existing.
    I was beginning to think no more about them, when I made the acquain-
tance of Monsieur Teste. (CW 6: 10; O 2: 16)

In each case there is (1) a reference made to the ideas just presented in the introduction, (2) an allusion to chronological time,
and (3) the first mention of the main character. It is curious that
Valéry makes a precise reference to the date of the encounter because chronological time has no importance at all in the various
Teste episodes.

We also find a close similarity in the description of how the
encounter between the narrator and the main character takes
place. Neither Dupin nor Teste possesses remarkable physical
traits that might attract attention. On the contrary, in public they
are both so self-effacing that only the sharpest observer perceives an
unusual inner concentration beyond their exterior blandness.
Valéry's narrator follows Teste to a café where he studies his eyes
and listens to the few words exchanged with a waiter. Poe's narrator makes Dupin's acquaintance by chance in a reading room in
the Rue Montmartre. Both narrators soon begin a close relationship with the main characters. In neither case are there any details given as to what sort of dialogue might have taken place between the narrator and the main character when the ice was finally broken and a friendship established. One has the impression that great minds recognize each other without need of verbal
communication.

Although only a scant description of this friendship is revealed,
the details are interesting because of their similarities. For example, the narrators make the same remarks about the unusual habits
of Dupin and Teste. Dupin is "enamored of the Night for her own
sake" (M 2: 532; OP: 11) and Teste's narrator remarks: "I never
saw him except at night" (CW 6: 10; O 2: 17). Both characters are
exempt from the everyday routine of earning a living; Teste has a
small income from stocks and Dupin manages to get by on a mea-
ger inheritance. This release from the workaday world affords
them not only the time, but the concentration necessary to develop

their intellectual faculties to full potential. Toward this same end they also free themselves from the demands of a social life. Dupin is a bachelor, as is Teste, at least when we meet him in *The Evening with Monsieur Teste*. Both authors minimize the social aspects of their characters. Poe's narrator mentions that "it had been many years since Dupin had ceased to know or be known in Paris" (M 2: 532; OP: 11). Valéry's narrator notes that Teste "never smiled, nor said good morning or goodnight; he seemed not to hear a 'How are you?'" (CW 6: 10; O 2: 17).

Thus the two characters are liberated from the banal activities of holding down a job and dealing with other people, time-consuming tasks that occupy most of our waking hours. Valéry's narrator remarks that Teste "had *killed the puppet*" (CW 6: 10; O 2: 17). Teste dominates even his conditioned reflexes to the point of being truly master of himself. This control over certain external aspects of his person reflects an inner dominance attained by conscious discipline. In the following brief sketches of Dupin and Teste, we can see in their physiognomies a concentration on inner powers.

Dupin:
His manner at these moments was frigid and abstract; his eyes were vacant in expression; while his voice, usually a rich tenor, rose into a treble which would have sounded petulantly but for the deliberateness and entire distinctness of the enunciation. (M 2: 533; OP: 12)

Teste:
His speech was extraordinarily rapid, and his voice low. Everything about him was unobtrusive, his eyes, his hands. Yet his shoulders were military and his step had an astonishing regularity. (CW 6: 10; O 2: 17)

The two adjectives, "frigid" in Dupin's case, and "military" used in describing Teste, while portraying a preciseness in the external movements of the two characters, also show an extreme self-control and concentration. It is as if this economy of physical gestures might allow body energy to be turned inward. The eyes, mentioned in both cases, do not focus on things around them but seem instead to be totally distracted by thought. The quality of the voice strikes each narrator, who notices that his subject is more absorbed by reflection than by expression. Emphasizing that Teste's exterior portrait is unimportant, Valéry says that "he may be thought of as invisible" and that he has "no face, and no more-or-less picturesque representation of his person" (CW 6: 158).[8] It is then all the more significant that the very minimal traits he ascribes to Teste are similar to Dupin's.

The same observation can be made concerning the setting of Valéry's narrative, which is short on detail but reminiscent of Poe. In order to focus on the inner aspect of his character Valéry says that he "only lightly indicated" the surroundings, a room and a theater. In *Monsieur Teste* we find a very brief sketch of the room where Teste and the narrator frequently seclude themselves. The only unusual aspect of this room is its distinctive Poesque atmosphere:

Poe:
At the first dawn of the morning we closed all the massy shutters of our old building, lighting a couple of tapers which, strongly perfumed, threw out only the ghastliest and feeblest of rays. By the aid of these we then busied our souls in dreams—reading, writing, or conversing, until warned by the clock of the advent of the true Darkness. (M 2: 532–33; OP: 12)

Valéry:
In the greenish room smelling of mint, there around the candle was nothing but the dull abstract furniture—a bed, a clock, a wardrobe with a mirror, two armchairs—like a creation of the mind. (CW 6: 18; O 2: 23)

Both rooms are distinguished by certain sensory qualities—the pervading smell, the sound of the clock, the warmth of the candles surrounded by semi-darkness. Other ordinary objects in the room seem to fade into the dimness outside the candle glow. Again, the very banality of the external description serves to emphasize the mental concentration of each character.

Exactly how Dupin and Teste's intellectual mechanisms operate will remain a secret. Each narrator relates certain characteristics of the extraordinary mind he observes, confessing that he himself does not understand its functioning. We do know, however, that intelligence in their case does not mean pure acquisition of knowledge, book learning, or feats of memory. It is a question here of the mind as a mechanism capable of taking diverse observations, facts, and even flashes of intuition and making them coherent. Dupin and Teste are able to render chaotic thought into logical patterns *and* understand how this process works. These fictional brains even go beyond the computer, since they are capable of programming themselves. They are superhuman, since we do not know of any minds capable of such intense self-concentration and comprehension.

A good memory certainly helps in the intellectual process just described; however, it is more a question of selective memory than total recall. Teste tries to transform his memory into a mechanical sieve in order to get rid of trivia and retain essential things. He has also disposed of all his books, since they are of no use to him. In Poe's story we again find interesting similarities in his description of the whist player, whose real skill, says the narrator, begins where the rule book leaves off and whose intense powers of observation help him recall what he needs to know later on.

Returning now to the texts of the two narratives, we will see how Poe and Valéry represent in the concrete the idea of unusual mental power. Both authors point out that such a mind goes so far beyond our normal concept of the human intellect that the term *aberration* might appropriately describe it. Valéry refers to Teste as a monster, adding that "monsters of flesh quickly perish" (CW 6: 6; O 2: 14). The word *aberration*, he says, could describe Teste in the sense that the word means "some excess of vitality, an overflow of internal energy, resulting in an abnormal development of certain organs or of physical or psychic activity" (CW 6: 66; O 2: 63). Poe too represents in Dupin a sort of aberration; his mind, says the narrator, is difficult to classify in a normal context: "What I have described in the Frenchman was merely the result of an excited, or perhaps of a diseased intelligence" (M 2: 533; OP: 12). Symptoms such as an "excess of vitality" and an "excited intelligence" seem to be those of one suffering from some psychic disorder. Both Poe and Valéry mention that Dupin and Teste might be judged insane, if their minds ever came to the attention of the public:

Poe:
Had the routine of our life at this place been known to the world, we

should have been regarded as madmen—although, perhaps, as madmen of a harmless nature. (M 2: 532; OP: 11)

Valéry:
The mind seems to me so made that it cannot be incoherent to itself. That is why I was careful not to classify Teste among the mad. (CW 6: 16–17; O 2: 22)

Thus, a man who becomes the witness of his own consciousness deviates to such a great degree from the intellectual norm that both narrators are at a loss for words to describe him and must resort to using unsuitable terms such as *diseased* and *mad.*

The idea of a mirror-like intellect observing itself thinking fascinated Poe long before Valéry took up the subject. This double aspect of the mind is central to both authors' fictional characters. Poe's narrator amuses himself "with the fancy of a double Dupin— the creative and the resolvent" (M 2: 533; OP: 12).[9] The creative function of the mind is observed by its analytical other half, thus arriving at total self-comprehension. Valéry's narrator makes a similar observation about Teste: "After a good deal of thought, I came to believe that Monsieur Teste had managed to discover laws of the mind we know nothing of" (CW 6: 11; O 2: 17).[10] Teste does not create anything, but through the narrator we are led to believe that the creative potential is there and that Teste understands exactly how it functions.

Each narrator is awed by the fantastic potential of the superintellect he observes but again is not able to discover the secret method by which it operates. He can only relate to the reader certain outward manifestations of its activity, which on occasion reminds him of the physical exercises of an athlete eager to maintain his skills and flexibility. Both narrators compare the mental activities of Dupin and Teste to gymnastics that produce remarkable mental powers. The narrators are also fascinated by what might be the consequences if this intellect, which is complete master of itself, were turned outward toward the world. Dupin very smugly gives a demonstration of his intellectual capabilities from time to time to the astonishment of the narrator:

He boasted to me, with a low chuckling laugh, that most men, in respect to himself, wore windows in their bosoms, and was wont to follow up such assertions by direct and very startling proofs of his intimate knowledge of my own. (M 2: 533; OP: 12)

Since Teste avoids any sort of exhibitionism, his power remains latent, although the narrator is fully aware of its possibilities: "If this man had changed the object of his inner meditations, if he had turned upon the world the controlled power of his mind, nothing could have resisted him" (CW 6: 13; O 2: 19). This superiority is demonstrated in Poe's story when Dupin surprises his interlocutor by recounting exactly the subject of the latter's thoughts. The narrator exclaims: "Tell me, for Heaven's sake, the method— if method there is—by which you have been enabled to fathom my soul in this matter" (M 2: 534; OP: 13). But the method is, of course, never revealed. Valéry takes up this idea of the mental powers of Teste turned toward other human beings in his second text, "A Letter from Madame Emilie Teste." While trying to describe her husband, Madame Teste points out an extraordinary characteristic: "The object his eyes fix upon may be the very object that his mind means to reduce to nothing" (CW 6: 22; O 2: 26). Teste, however, has no intention of becoming famous through the practical application of this power. His ambition is purely self-contained; he constantly asks himself one question—"*Que peut un homme?*"—what is the *potential* of the human brain.

We come now to the third part of the overall structure of the two narratives. There is clearly a transition between the descriptive second part containing very little dialogue (the actual words of Teste are quoted only three times) and the third part in which the two characters leave the solitude of their rooms, observe the outside world, and engage in dialogue quoted by the narrator. Again, there is a similarity in the transitional sentences, both of which indicate the time of day and the place. Poe: "We were strolling one night down a long dirty street, in the vicinity of the Palais Royal" (M 2: 533; OP: 12–13). Valéry: "Exactly two years and three months ago this evening I was with him at the theater . . ." (CW 6: 14; O 2: 20). A dialogue follows in each case, allowing the reader to get to know Dupin and Teste in a more direct way. The

events in this part have nothing in common. Teste goes to the theater, walks home, and goes to bed. Dupin talks about a bizarre
murder case that confuses the Paris police, then reveals the guilty
party (an orangutan) to a stupefied public. But if we look beyond
the events, we recognize a common intellectual attitude in the two
characters.

Dupin and Teste both detach themselves from the collective
mentality. At the theater Teste does not focus his attention completely on what is happening on the stage; he observes as well the
audience absorbed in the spectacle. Teste remarks: "Let them enjoy and obey!" (CW 6: 15; O 2: 21). The narrator notices this too
and replies: "The stupor that held all the others told us that something or other sublime was going on" (CW 6: 16; O 2: 21). Teste
watches the play from an unusual perspective: he sees the reflection
of the performance in the spectators. Teste remarks: "The supreme
simplifies *them*. I wager they are all thinking, more and more,
toward the same thing" (CW 6: 16; O 2: 21). The play has a leveling effect on the crowd, which is attentive to the details on the
stage, but does not see the spectacle in its totality as does Teste.

A similar situation exists in Poe's story when Dupin observes
with the same Teste-like detachment the horror of the crowd upon
learning the details of an unusual double murder. He notes the
collective reaction of the public and a certain leveling of thought
which the narrator mentions: "I could merely agree with all
Paris in considering them an insoluble mystery" (M 2: 544; OP:
23). The chief of police, like a spectator at the theater, can only see,
says Dupin, "one or two points with unusual clearness, but in so doing he, necessarily, lost sight of the matter as a whole" (M 2: 545;
OP: 24). Dupin shows his great esteem for discipline and method
when he criticizes the police: "There is no method in their proceedings, beyond the method of the moment" (M 2: 545; OP: 23).

Dupin and Teste are capable of seeing an event in its totality and
detaching themselves from the emotion that leads the public
astray. Teste remarks that "the supreme simplifies *them*. . . . They
will be equal at the climax or common limit" (CW 6: 16; O 2: 21).
In Poe's tale we see proof of this observation when the crisis of the
grotesque murders bewilders both the public and the police. Dupin
and Teste are exceptional beings, since no collective law seems to

apply to them. Teste assures us of this when he says: "Yet the law
is not so simple . . . since it does not include me; and—here I am"
(CW 6: 16; O 2: 21). If the spectacle simplifies the minds of the
crowd, Teste places himself above this effect and, like Dupin, takes
shelter in the domain of objectivity.

The intellectual portrait of the two main characters is in no way
complete, but neither writer intended it to be so. Valéry, like his
American predecessor, presents a few enticing glimpses of his
hero, then leaves the reader's imagination to fill in the rest.
Their technique is basically the same: both narrators inspire in
the reader a sense of awe by the use of questions, praises, and constantly expressed astonishment. The reader is left with the impression of seeing only the tip of the iceberg, which in this case is
the infinite potential of the human brain. Poe invents ingenious
detective plots to show off Dupin's analytical powers, but Valéry
avoids any such intellectual exhibitionism, since he is more interested in self-comprehension for its own sake.

In 1894, when Valéry was immersed in reading Poe, he realized that his own ambition was leading him in two contradictory
directions: (1) toward the desire to produce an effect on others
through literary works, poetry in particular; and (2) toward an understanding of how his own mind functioned, which meant many
tedious hours spent observing his brain as it came to grips with
mathematics and science. Both of these desires were reinforced by
his reading of Poe. But it was Poe's description of how his mind
operated during the creation of "The Raven" that fascinated Valéry
to the point of becoming an obsession. If one could analyze the intellectual process during the creation of a poem, perhaps, thought
Valéry, one could also observe the mind as it assimilates concrete
and abstract notions and eventually discover the secret of how the
mind functions. This lofty ideal of total comprehension of the intellect, embodied in Teste with the help of Poe, remained with
Valéry during the rest of his life. Some forty-five years later,
Valéry remarked in a letter to his friend Henri Mondor that during this period when Poe "possessed" him, the latter's influence
worked against poetry rather than for it.[11] Valéry emphasizes
here, once again, that through Poe he became more interested in
how the mind operates than in what it produces. Teste's refusal to

exhibit his intellectual powers through practical application reflected Valéry's belief at the time that the desire to produce an effect on others would detract from his goal of pure self-comprehension.

The case of Dupin-Teste provides an excellent example of Valéry's own theory of literary influence. The study of a literary contact between two writers, says Valéry, must bring out the originality of the one undergoing the influence, otherwise we are talking about simple imitation: "Nothing is more 'original,' nothing more 'oneself' than to feed on others. But one has to digest them. A lion is made of assimilated sheep" (CW 14: 10; O 2: 478). Valéry was convinced that all writers are subject to influence, either positive or negative:

> *What a man does* either repeats or refutes *what someone else has done*—repeats it in other tones, refines or amplifies or simplifies it, loads or overloads it with meaning; or else rebuts, overturns, destroys and denies it, but thereby assumes it and has invisibly used it. (CW 8: 241; O 1: 634)

Poe had a very positive influence because of the originality he inspired in Valéry's first attempt at writing prose fiction. Teste is far from being another Dupin. If we apply Valéry's own description of literary influence, we see that he "purifies" Teste by rejecting any necessity to prove his analytical powers, which are developed for their own sake; he "amplifies" him in the sense that he expands upon the idea of the pure intellect by placing Teste in various situations in which the reader observes his mind from different points of view (in later texts, those of his wife, a friend, and Teste's own private journal); the author "simplifies" Teste by concentrating solely on the subject of his intellectual potential, avoiding any sort of complicated intrigue which might detract from his central theme; and, finally, Valéry "loads and overloads him with meaning" by creating in Teste the absolute goal of total self-comprehension and complete intellectual consciousness. Teste is indeed an original character, although we can still recognize in him a few traces of "assimilated Dupin."

After the publication of *The Evening with Monsieur Teste* in 1896 Valéry continued to develop the main character of his "drama of consciousness." Descriptions of Teste and his thoughts are found throughout the twenty-nine volumes of the *Notebooks*.[12] In the 1920s Valéry published three new pieces, "A Letter from Madame Emilie Teste," "Extracts from Monsieur Teste's Logbook," and "Letter from a Friend," all of which mirror the intellectual hero from different angles.[13] When Gide tried to convince Valéry to publish some of his work in 1912, Valéry replied with the idea of putting together a collection of prose and verse that would include the original Teste piece and an unpublished fragment, "the ex-beginning of 'Agatha' which would be the *interior* of Teste's night."[14] This text had been entitled "Manuscript Found in a Brain" before Pierre Louÿs urged Valéry to change it so that the connection with Poe's "MS. Found in a Bottle" would not be so apparent.[15] Referring to the piece by various titles, "Agatha or the Saint of Sleep" ("Agathe ou la sainte du sommeil"), "Agatha or Sleep" ("Agathe ou le sommeil"), or simply "Agatha" ("Agathe"), Valéry continued to work on it for many years, especially in 1912 and in the 1920s, but never achieved the perfection he envisioned. The manuscript was found among his papers and published posthumously by his daughter in 1956.[16] The fragment is of particular interest to our study because of the direct influence Poe's tale had on Valéry's second attempt at writing what he called a "conte."

As in the case of *Monsieur Teste,* Valéry described in a letter to Gide, dated January 15, 1898, the impossible task he had set for himself:

> One morning recently, in my study *sub lumine,* I began writing the following story which I shall never finish because it's too difficult. Given one of those women who sleep two or three or ten years without waking, I assume (quite arbitrarily) that she has dreamed the whole time, and that when she wakes she can recount her dream. . . . This is a problem in transcendent (or imaginary) psychology, difficult to conceive. The successive zones of alteration of the images, etc., the variations in thought, as little by little it turns vacant—this would be interesting.[17]

Valéry struggled with the text during the next three years (1898–1901), mentioning his discouragement to Gide in two more letters[18] and describing the project to his friend Gustave Fourment in a letter that begins "I am writing . . . something crazy."[19] Valéry feared that recreating the life of a mind would appear to be obscure to readers while, in his view, it was simply unfamiliar. He continues in his letter to Fourment: "But just you try introducing *thought* and something *new* into literature; sustained *continuity* in a period of mindless confusion. It's a project so absurd that, in the end, I rather like this deadly stiff bit of writing."[20] Representing the progressive changes of mental states was so challenging that Valéry seems to have pursued his task out of pure stubbornness, reminding us of Monsieur Teste's remark: "What one *can do* with *words*. That is everything" (CW 6: 139; C 27: 365). Never satisfied with his attempt, Valéry gave up the idea of including "Agatha" as part of a *Monsieur Teste* collection; his "Manuscript Found in a Brain" washed ashore years later, unbeknownst to him.

Valéry scholars have taken an interest in "Agatha" for two main reasons.[21] First, the text is a fine example of Valéry's early prose poems, a genre that was initiated by Baudelaire and Rimbaud and perfected by Mallarmé and Valéry. Second, "Agatha" represents Valéry's attempt to recreate in literary form his concept of pure consciousness as it observes its own functioning. Ursula Franklin gives an accurate and succinct description of the text: "*Agathe* is the poetic mono/dialogue of a mind beholding itself think, and therefore speak, during the fragment of a night— *Agathe* is a fragment of a poem in prose."[22] Franklin's term "mind-persona" aptly identifies the female narrator who is also the universal mind that thinks and writes down the experience of self-awareness. The "mind-persona" describes in poetic language its own progression through internal phases from consciousness, to reverie, to deep sleep and back to full lucidity. This drama of the intellect is represented by cyclical movements expressed in poetic images and modulation of tone.

Valéry's prose poem of intellectual drama and Poe's tale of adventure, "MS. Found in a Bottle," do not appear, at first reading, to have much in common. Poe's nameless main character embarks on a sea voyage, survives a horrendous storm, is hurled by collision onto a phantom ship and finally plunges into the grasp of a whirlpool. As in the case of Dupin-Teste, however, underneath the apparent differences lie points in common that reveal Valéry's affinity for Poe's literary techniques. The two manuscripts, one found in a bottle, the other in a brain, are both recounted in first-person narration, describe a solitary and mysterious nautical journey representing a sequence of mental states, make use of similar images, and attempt to circumscribe and preserve the life of the mind through the self-conscious act of writing.

The opening paragraph of "MS. Found in a Bottle" no doubt captured Valéry's attention immediately. The narrator begins: "Of my country and my family I have little to say. Ill usage and length of years have driven me from the one, and estranged me from the other." Thus, the banalities of biography and cultural background, details that held little interest for Valéry, are dispensed with from the start. The narrator, a man of hereditary wealth with an education "of no common order," admits to being a genius who possesses "habits of rigid thought," another trait that Valéry admired. A skeptic who reads the German moralists with a critical mind, amusing himself by detecting their falsities, Poe's main character takes pride in the lucidity of his scientific mind, which is not led astray by superstition or wild flights of the imagination. These were all qualities that greatly impressed the young Valéry when he first read the tale. By describing the intelligence, lucidity, and objective approach of the narrator, Poe is preparing the reader for a journey into the incredible, which he wants us to believe.

"MS. Found in a Bottle" can be enjoyed purely as an adventure story, while on another level it can be seen as an intriguing allegory. Richard Wilbur, in his essay "The House of Poe," argues convincingly that most of the American author's prose fiction has "undercurrents of meaning" deliberately embedded in the tales by their creator. As a case in point, Wilbur sees in "MS. Found in a Bottle"

an allegory of the mind's voyage from the waking world into the world of dreams, with each main step of the narrative symbolizing the passage of the mind from one state to another—from wakefulness to reverie, from reverie to the hypnagogic state, from the hypnagogic state to the deep dream.[23]

Rereading the tale with this interpretation in mind, we discover a number of striking similarities with Valéry's "Agatha," especially the descriptions of the sequence of the mental states described by each narrator.

Since both the tale and Valéry's prose poem are recounted in the first person, the reader follows the mind observing its own transformations as it goes from lucidity to deep sleep. The first stage described by each narrator is wakefulness, which gradually slips into reverie, a state where elements of reality take on dream-like qualities. As we have seen, Poe's narrator describes himself as a person who maintains rigid control over his mental faculties. His embarkation on a ship at the port of Batavia[24] on the island of Java represents his departure from the waking world. The sailing is peaceful and calm as the narrator observes his surroundings, describing the ship in detail. Soon disquieting changes signal his passage into a state of reverie. The crystal-clear atmosphere is replaced by "the dusky-red appearance of the moon," and he notices "the peculiar character of the sea." The transition from the perfect clarity of the horizon and from the translucent water represents the passing from a state of wakefulness to the early stages of sleep, the "dusky-red appearance of the moon" suggesting light as seen through closed eyelids and the changing water symbolizing the clouding over of the mind as it slips from reality.

We turn now to "Agatha" whose opening line, "The more I think, the more I think," announces the intellectual theme of the piece. The state of wakefulness is expressed by the description of the narrator in bed: "My body is scarcely aware that the indistinct and easy volumes of the bed support it; upon it, my sovereign flesh regards and stirs the darkness" (CW 2: 205; O 2: 1388). As in Poe's tale, the transition into sleep is described as a shift from clarity into the "velvet midnight." Poe's "dusky-red appearance of the moon" is suggested in Valéry's poetic line: "This paltry glimmer resolves into a dull and fleeting cheek, a pointless face soon smiling against me, responsive, itself consumed by luster-swallowing dusk" (CW 2: 205; O 2: 1389). Reminiscent of Poe's narrator, who is reassured by the fact that he can still see the bottom of the sea through the water, Valéry's "mind-persona" remarks, "It is my depth I touch," indicating that she is still anchored to the real world, although aware that she will soon drift loose. This state is soon to change as Valéry's narrator too casts off on a sea voyage into obscurity:

The darkness fathers forth a few scraps still, of a flimsy seascape, ruffles them, and the icy crupper of a horse. . . . My continuancy softly pursues the methodical destruction of a whole series of foci of this sort, necessary in the annihilated domain. (CW 2: 206; O 2: 1389)

The image of the destruction of real-world perceptions is much more dramatic in Poe's tale. The break with reality is described by the narrator: "I was startled by a loud, humming noise, like that occasioned by the rapid revolution of a mill-wheel, and before I could ascertain its meaning, I found the ship quivering to its center" (M 2: 137; OP: 171). When the storm passes, the narrator discovers that he and an old Swede are the sole survivors, and thus begins a state of aimless, solitary wandering over which the narrator has no control.

In both texts the loss of control is expressed in whirlpool images. Poe's narrator describes the sensation of being raised by the "black stupendous seas" to an "elevation beyond the albatross," then becoming "dizzy with the velocity of our descent into some watery hell." Agatha is "swimming in the fullness of high water," when she is overcome by the swirling sea:

Human, almost upright in the coiled spring of the sea, swathed in enormous cold, upon whom the whole hugeness weighs, even to his shoulders, even to his ears despoiled of variable noise, I still touch the strange absence of soil, as if a ground of notions altogether new; and with the last scraps of my strength I tremble. (CW 2: 206; O 2: 1389)

Both narrators have been swept into reverie, which they describe as an eerie silence at the bottom of the vortex. Agatha seems to anticipate another rise and plunge when she observes: "Yet icier deeps, concealed below, forgo me but will mount again to drink me in some dream" (CW 2: 207; O 2: 1389). This thought could have been uttered by Poe's narrator, who from the bottom of an even greater abyss looks upward and beholds: "At a terrific height directly above us, and upon the very verge of the precipitous descent, hovered a gigantic ship" (M 2: 140; OP: 174). A remarkably similar image is found in Valéry's text at the moment when the "mind-persona" is on the brink of passing into a dream-like trance: "Hearing expands; to the very horizon, and overhangs a gulf that grows immense. A continually more subtle creature leans over the void to catch the slightest sound" (CW 2: 208; O 2: 1390). From the abyss, Poe's narrator is hurled through space onto the rigging of a phantom ship; Agatha, escaping from the void of her own abyss, exclaims: "I plumb a space where the possible breathes and I fly!" (CW 2: 208; O 2: 1390). The abrupt transition into a dream state is followed in both cases by an unusual calm during which both narrators describe their efforts to grasp their situations as the mind struggles to maintain its lucidity and self-awareness. Agatha remarks: "The quality of this calm is so limpid that if I am edged for a few moments around the same thought, I infer, from their mere diversity, this very thought" (CW 2: 209; O 2: 1391). Poe's narrator discovers that the crew of the second ship are unconscious of his presence. Like phantoms, they wander about as if he did not exist, abandoning him to total solitude.[25] His former lucid mental faculties seem to have no effect as he tries to comprehend the situation. He describes a new dimension that goes beyond worldly intelligence:

A feeling, for which I have no name, has taken possession of my soul—a sensation which will admit of no analysis, to which the lessons of by-gone times are inadequate, and for which I fear futurity itself will offer me no key. To a mind constituted like my own, the latter consideration is an evil. I shall never—I know that I shall never—be satisfied with regard to the nature of my conceptions. Yet it is not wonderful that these conceptions are indefinite, since they have their origin in sources so utterly novel. A new sense—a new entity is added to my soul. (M 2: 141; OP: 175)

And thus, the mind, cut off from its earlier self, observes its own transformations, its own mystery, which defy the former operations of comprehension. A similar sensation of the mind isolated from the body, a fundamental change of consciousness, occurs in "Agatha":

At this hour that is not an hour, who cares for my history? I despise it like a book. For this is the ideal chance: to strip all mortal order of memory, annul my experience, illumine what is inapposite and, by mere night dream, to escape so free that I no longer recognize even my own body. (CW 2: 207; O 2: 1390)

Each narrator notes the change with expressions of excitement in anticipation of making a new discovery.

This dream state in both texts is represented as being timeless and drifting. Valéry, like Poe, mentions a sibyl, whose powers to predict the future are useless. Agatha remarks: "no longer do I hear the endless murmur of the profound inexhaustible sibyl who calculates each particle of approaching futurity" (CW 2: 207; O 2: 1390). The captain of Poe's phantom ship appears to be suspended in time: "His forehead, although little wrinkled, seems to bear upon it the stamp of a myriad of years. His gray hairs are records of the past, and his grayer eyes are sybils of the future" (M 2: 144; OP: 178). All sense of time and direction is lost. On the floor of the captain's cabin are "mouldering instruments of science, and obsolete, long-forgotten charts" (M 2: 144; OP: 179). The mind, adrift in time and space, attempts to circumscribe its own thoughts. Both narrators turn to writing as a means of recording the solitary dialogues of the mind with itself, thus preserving fragments of consciousness, which is all that will be left after the annihilation of the body.

Valéry's "mind-persona" engages in a dialogue with itself and speaks of preserving in writing observations on its own awareness: "Who is asking? The same who replies. The same who writes, effacing the same line. They are but writings on water" (CW 2: 207; O 2: 1389). We have the impression that these "writings on water" might never be read, but Agatha feels compelled to objectify her thoughts as a defense against chaos. Her observation reminds us of Valéry's own struggle to write the text, which seemed impossible to create and, in fact, was not intended to be read by others.

Poe's narrator experiences the same need in his state of isolation and impending death. He slips into the captain's private cabin and takes "the materials with which I write, and have written" (M 2: 142; OP: 176). The use of the present tense indicates his continuing efforts to record his thoughts until the end; the present perfect reveals his backward glance that describes the sequence of mental states up until the present one. The mind can understand itself only by observing its past operations, through the manifestations of what it *has been,* a point Agatha makes:

You can only know yourself in reverse. You carry *backward* a power, a kind of discernment; and, being able to see only the opposite way to the one you travel, you analyze what is finished, you act out only what is done already. (CW 2: 209; O 2: 1391)

The possible futility of the act of writing is expressed when Poe's narrator remarks: "It is true that I may not find an opportunity of transmitting it to the world, but I will not fail to make the endeavor" (M 2: 142; OP: 176). By writing a journal which he plans to cast into the sea at the last moment, the narrator becomes both participant and spectator of his own mental drama, which will live after him in the form of manuscript fragments. Thus, death of consciousness will be overcome through the written word. J. Gerald Kennedy, in *Poe, Death, and the Life of Writing,* sees "MS. Found in a Bottle" as a tale that is "intrinsically a fable of composition, imaging the perils of inscription."[26] Another observation he makes concerning Poe's story also applies to Valéry's prose poem: "The narrator is compelled to record his impressions by the human need to achieve coherency of experience through language, yet the very object of language, the never-to-be-imparted secret, lies beyond the reach of words."[27] The suspense in "Agatha" and "MS. Found in a Bottle" lies in the anticipation of discovering this "never-to-be-imparted secret," which is different in the two texts.

The theme of discovery is presented in a rather contrived manner in Poe's tale. The narrator recounts that he "unwittingly daubed with a tar-brush the edges of a neatly-folded studding-sail," his strokes spelling by chance the word "discovery" when the sail is hoisted. As the phantom ship moves relentlessly through magnificent and horrifying seascapes, the narrator speaks of "a curiosity to penetrate the mysteries of these awful regions" that is stronger than feelings of despair at the thought of impending death. The exhilaration of the mind on the brink of making a new discovery is revealed in the narrator's remark: "It is evident that we are hurrying onwards to some exciting knowledge—some never-to-be-imparted secret, whose attainment is destruction. Perhaps this current leads us to the southern pole itself" (M 2: 145; OP: 180). Much to his horror, the ice opens on both sides and the ship descends in concentric circles, plunging madly into a whirlpool, with all going down. The sole survivor is the manuscript, which does not contain the final fragment revealing the "never-to-be-imparted secret."

Valéry's narrator is also carried along from one mental state to another by the expectation of discovering exciting knowledge. In spite of the silence and darkness of the night she exclaims:

How pure the will to tomorrow, the road I take to tomorrow! I feel uncertainty speed from the forehead of time, the event arrive, its vigor, its languor, the dissolution of experience, and the rebirth of the voyage, as pure and hard as itself, adorned in unending mind. The new sheds itself in advance, by way of a shift more imperceptible than the angle of the sky. (CW 2: 208–9; O 2: 1390–91)

On the brink of discovering consciousness in its purest state, Agatha is poised on the edge of a circle: "I have seemed to linger about the rim of an impenetrable circle with which I feel sure that there is something that would provide me long enjoyment . . ." (CW 2: 210; O 2: 1391). In a dream state the mind is no longer linked to the finite self and can thus rise to the outer edge of the vortex to gaze inward. What does Valéry's "mind-persona" seek? Contemplating the circle, symbolizing the *"cervelle"* or brain, she hopes to discover

something brief, universal: an abstract, imminent pearl would roll into a deep fold of common thought: an astonishing law, cosubstantial with its seeker, would inhabit there: work of a moment to get this pearl free: a few words would fix it forever. (CW 2: 210; O 2: 1391)

The pearl, symbolizing a gradual maturation that results in perfection, thus also representing the slow quest for pure consciousness, at a yet undetermined point would appear within the folds of the mind. The "astonishing law" is the object of Valéry's own lifelong quest: an understanding of how the universal mind functions. But not only does the "mind-persona" aspire to "get this pearl free," she also wants to give it permanent form through writing, "a few words would fix it forever."

Valéry's narrator remains in a state of anticipation, conscious of the presence of the absolute thought but unable to grasp it. Like the cyclone which is strongly felt but cannot be seized, pure consciousness remains out of reach: "Whether it be a great brightness, always at the tail of the eye, or a being as inviolate as the center of an orbit, its dwelling yields neither image nor doubt" (CW 2: 210; O 2: 1391). The desired discovery is both formless and definite; it exists but cannot be made manifest. Poe's narrator makes an observation that sums up the essence of Agatha's search. Attempting to describe the structure of the phantom vessel, he remarks: "What she *is not*, I can easily perceive; what she *is*, I fear it is impossible to say" (M 2: 142; OP: 176). Agatha arrives at the same negative definition of her desired discovery. Unable to possess "its form nor its powers," she continues, "—but of these I discover endlessly everything they are not, and of this lack I make a working symbol" (CW 2: 210; O 2: 1391). Valéry's "mind-persona" is convinced that pure consciousness exists, but can only recognize it as an absence. Near the culmination of the prose poem, Agatha senses that she is close to uniting with supreme lucidity when she observes "Now I am near perhaps on the verge of laws," but again they elude her grasp. The search for perfect order having come to naught, the mind must accept its imperfect state: "I maintain a disorder within me the better to attract my own powers or whatever awaits them" (CW 2: 211; O 2: 1392).

The dénouements of Valéry's prose poem and Poe's tale, both dramas of consciousness played out through evolving mental states, can be contrasted in terms of zenith and nadir. In the tale, the mind, released from its earthly shackles, makes a final spiraling plunge into unconsciousness; in the prose poem the mind rises to its zenith of pure concentration where system replaces individual thoughts. Instead of oblivion and death, Valéry's "mind-persona" experiences a rebirth at the moment when supreme lucidity overcomes chaos. Observing this privileged moment, Agatha remarks: "The assemblage of diverse modes of knowing . . . now forms a system quite null and indifferent to what it might produce or fathom, when the fancied shadow softly yields utter birth, and it is mind

. . ." (CW 2: 211; O 2: 1392). This system exists in a pure state without necessity to apply or explain itself; it is the absolute intellectual potentiality that Monsieur Teste seeks.

In the final brief paragraphs Agatha makes another discovery when she remarks: "At this point, above the calm, shines the fact that *relevance* is master of the world, the binding of the idea to the point of its apparition" (CW 2: 212; O 2: 1392). Valéry seems to be inserting here a concept he discovered in Poe, the idea of "consistency," a term Valéry uses in English and defines, according to his understanding of Poe, as "the quality of a thing or a system conceived or existing in such a way that its parts are in symmetrical relation with one another."[28] In terms that suggest a familiarity with Poe's *Eureka,* the final lines of Valéry's prose poem speak of the rise of ideas in a "meaningless order" to a point where they become *one,* the supreme thought, which is bound to the "point of its apparition," that is to the human brain. "Agatha" is a precursor of Valéry's major poem *The Young Fate* (*La Jeune Parque*), which will be examined in our chapter on *Eureka.*

"MS. Found in a Bottle" and "Manuscript Found in a Brain" reveal striking similarities in spite of their very different literary forms. Both present a mono/dialogue of the mind as it progresses cyclically toward the infinite freedom from time and space achieved through reverie and dream. In his poem, Valéry assimilates images and descriptions that appear in Poe's tale: circles, whirlpools, icy seascapes and cyclones, contrasts between luminosity (represented by the words phosphorus and phosphoric in both texts) and darkness, and a useless sibyl to symbolize timelessness. Through the act of writing, the narrators attempt to plumb the abyss and transmit to posterity their fragmentary glimpses of the mind's quest to understand its own functioning.

As Valéry had originally intended, "Agatha" adds another chapter to his *roman du cerveau,* his novel of the mind. In Teste we discovered consciousness existing in its purest form while inhabiting a body that continues to function in the everyday world. Agatha is pure mind, separated from body, pursuing its quest of supreme comprehension. The prose poem represents Teste's dream, an idea that is suggested in the last paragraph of *Monsieur Teste.* A connection with Poe's "MS. Found in a Bottle" is even hinted at when Teste mumbles just before nodding off: "I am thinking, and that hinders nobody. I am alone. How comfortable solitude is! Nothing soft is weighing on me. . . . The same reverie here as in the ship's cabin . . ." (CW 6: 21; O 2: 25). And the mind embarks on a solitary sea voyage in search of that extreme point of consciousness where an "astonishing law" will be revealed. Creating the drama of pure intellect expressed in poetic form resulted in an original work that was inspired, in part, by Poe's tale.

Valéry's often-proclaimed dislike for prose fiction misled some critics to believe that he did not bother to read Poe's tales, preferring instead the literary essays and *Eureka*. Noulet's conclusion that Valéry would have found only "a logic of the unreal and a rigor of the absurd,"[29] had he read Poe's tales, is no longer valid in light of the evidence we have seen in the case of "The Murders in the Rue Morgue" and "MS. Found in a Bottle," traces of which have been assimilated into Valéry's early literary endeavors. Poe's tales also had an influence on two of Valéry's poems, which will be examined in Chapters 5 and 6.

CHAPTER FOUR

Poe, Valéry, and Modern Criticism

Criticism consists of posing new problems. Poe was the first to consider mental mechanism as the producer of works. No one followed him.
—Valéry (CW 8: 354; C 6: 717)

Exemplifying his own concept of influence, Valéry discovered in Poe's essay *The Philosophy of Composition* a few sentences that were to have a profound effect on him and lead to extreme originality in his literary production. In Poe he recognized the germ of a new approach to understanding artistic creation, to analyzing it, and eventually to establishing a basis on which to evaluate literature and art. Specific passages in Poe's essay had a direct influence on Valéry's *Introduction to the Method of Leonardo da Vinci* and inspired much of what he had to say concerning literary criticism.

Baudelaire's translation of *The Philosophy of Composition* is called *La Genèse d'un poème*, although a literal rendition of the title, *La Philosophie de la composition*, would have been correct in French and faithful to the original. Baudelaire's title is more accurate in the sense that the essay reveals in detail how Poe claims he wrote his most famous poem "The Raven." Since Valéry's main preoccupation was observing the operation of the mind during artistic creation, the description of the genesis of a poem or, more precisely, the possibility of describing such a mechanism fascinated him. A few sentences in Poe's essay signaled a new direction in Valéry's approach to literature.

The Philosophy of Composition, first published in the April 1846 edition of *Graham's Magazine,* begins with a discussion of the process of writing a novel. Charles Dickens had written a note to Poe commenting on the American writer's exposé of the mechanism of Dickens' *Barnaby Rudge.* In his note Dickens asked Poe whether he was aware that William Godwin had written his *Caleb Williams* backwards. Although Poe did not agree that this was the precise way in which Godwin created his work, he used the observation as a point of departure for presenting his own ideas on the process of writing a novel, indicating that he begins with the effect to be produced on the reader. The combination of incidents and tone must all lead to the construction of the effect. Following this example, Poe makes a comment that struck a chord in Valéry:

> I have often thought how interesting a magazine paper might be written by an author who would—that is to say, who could—detail, step by step, the processes by which any one of his compositions attained its ultimate point of completion. (T: 14; OP: 985)

The suggestion that the mind could observe itself during the process of artistic creation fascinated Valéry to the point of obsession as he became a keen observer of his own intellect.

Poe then speculates on the principal reason such an article had never been written, suggesting that the author's vanity is the most likely cause. "Most writers—poets in especial—," remarks Poe, "prefer having it understood that they compose by a species of fine frenzy—an ecstatic intuition—and would positively shudder at letting the public take a peep behind the scenes" (T: 14; OP: 985). Were the spectators allowed to witness the process of creation, they would discover an intellectual drama taking place, one that is characterized by tension, "vacillating crudities of thought," and "true purposes seized only at the last moment." Using theatrical terms such as "tackle for scene-shifting," "demon-traps," and "the red paint and the black patches," Poe completes his analogy of the mental acts that make up the "properties of the literary *histrio*" (T: 14; OP: 985). He goes on to say that he has no qualms at all about describing the details of his own compositions, which he recalls without difficulty. At this point, Poe makes a comment that had a profound effect on Valéry and determined the direction of his intellectual endeavors:

Since the interest of an analysis, or reconstruction, such as I have considered a *desideratum*, is quite independent of any real or fancied interest in the thing analysed, it will not be regarded as a breach of decorum on my part to show the *modus operandi* by which some of my own works was put together. (T: 14; OP: 986)

There are two key points in this passage that oriented Valéry's thinking. First, the idea that *the analysis is independent of the thing analysed* (my italics) became the core of his intellectual outlook and inspired a new critical approach that he applied to his study of Leonardo da Vinci. Second, Valéry was intrigued by Poe's revealing his *modus operandi* and, on several occasions, described the genesis of his own poems in similar terms.

In the character Monsieur Teste Valéry embodied his concept of the rigorous intellect as pure potential; we have seen the ways in which Poe helped the author transform his abstract idea into literary form. At about the same time that Valéry was working on the Teste piece (1894–95), he committed himself to another commissioned work, this time on a specific subject, Leonardo da Vinci. Juliette Adam, a Parisian literary personage at the time, asked Valéry to write the article for her journal *La Nouvelle Revue*, where it appeared on August 15, 1895. The essay, *Introduction to the Method of Leonardo da Vinci*, caused Valéry a great deal of difficulty, mainly because he was determined to experiment with a new critical approach that had nothing to do with the artist's biography nor specifically with his work. In a letter to Gide dated January 3, 1895, Valéry expressed his discouragement with the project: "What an error! To have to shape to this format the great Flying Man."[1] After discovering copies of Leonardo's manuscripts in the library at Montpellier, Valéry spent hours studying the artist's notes and drawings in search of the mind that had created them.

Inspired by his reading of Poe, Valéry set out to analyze the *modus operandi* of the great Leonardo and to reveal the synthesis of artistic creation and intellectual rigor. Valéry's goal was not to analyze *what* Leonardo had accomplished but rather *how* he had produced such extraordinary works in various fields. He wanted to discover the properties of the universal mind, characterized by its ability to be creative in both art and science. Valéry found in Poe the point of departure for an innovative treatment of an artist who had already been studied from numerous angles. Because of the originality and eloquent analysis Valéry brought to the subject, his essay on Leonardo is considered to be one of his best prose pieces.

The decision to deal with Leonardo da Vinci by imagining the mind behind the work deviated so drastically from the more familiar historical or biographical approach that Valéry realized a preliminary explanation would be necessary in order to engage the reader in his attempt to recreate Leonardo's mind. The arguments he uses to prepare the reader for a new approach appear to come directly from *The Philosophy of Composition*. Valéry makes clear to the reader that his purpose is not to describe the Leonardo whose name is already illustrious. He states that he is "trying to give one view of the details of an intellectual life," (CW 8: 7; O 1: 1156), which, although a "crude model," is preferable in Valéry's view to a sequence of anecdotes, a list of dates or observations on a museum catalogue. Having stated his new approach, Valéry then defends it in terms that paraphrase Poe's comments in *The Philosophy of Composition:*

Many an error that distorts our judgment of human achievements is due to a strange disregard of their genesis. We seldom remember that they did not always exist. This has led to a sort of reciprocal coquetry which leads authors to suppress, to conceal all too well, the origins of a work. We fear the latter may be humble; we even suspect them of being natural. And although there are very few authors with the courage to say how their work took shape, I believe there are not many more who venture even to understand the process. (CW 8: 8; O 1: 1156–57)

Like Poe, Valéry proposes a new approach by suggesting that an attempt be made to consider the mental process at the source of the work. After remarking that one rarely reflects upon how works are created, he reiterates Poe's comment that the lack of such analyses is due to the author's "coquetry." (Poe uses the term *autorial vanity*.) Restating Poe's idea that writers would "positively shudder at letting the public peep behind the scenes," Valéry uses the verbs *suppress* and *conceal* to describe the writer's desire to avoid revealing the genesis of a work. What do writers fear? Perhaps they are afraid the public will be disappointed by the humble origins and thus think less of an artistic creation. Poe and Valéry agree that most authors would prefer to have the public believe that a literary or artistic creation springs forth on its own, having as its source the author's genius which produces a work of perfection. For Poe and Valéry such an idea is simply a myth. An "ecstatic intuition," using Poe's expression, does not create a poem. Valéry expresses a similar idea when he states that we often suspect the origins of works as being "natural," in the sense of coming to fruition on their own. In truth, observes Valéry, the process is "humble"; the facility of a flash of intuition plays only a minor role in a creative endeavor. The rest consists of transforming through conscious labor what Poe calls "vacillating crudities of thought." Valéry echoes Poe's sentiments when he says that few authors have the courage to examine how their work took shape, and, he believes, there are even fewer who are capable of understanding the process.

In an effort to clarify even further his approach to the study of Leonardo, Valéry uses a theatrical analogy similar to Poe's in *The Philosophy of Composition*. Valéry introduces this idea in a very straightforward manner: "Within the mind a drama takes place" (CW 8: 10; 0 1: 1158). He goes on to explain that "drama, adventure, agitation, any words of the sort can be used provided that several of them are used together" (CW 8: 10; 0 1: 1158). Through Leonardo's manuscripts Valéry searched for elements that reveal the conflict, the action, the opposing thoughts and finally the dénouement of this extraordinary mind during the process of creation. Referring to Leonardo's notes, Valéry remarks:

They help us to realize by what starts and snatches of thought, by what strange suggestions from human events or the flow of sensations, and after what immense moments of lassitude, men are able to see the shadows of their future works, the ghosts that come before. (CW 8: 10; O 1: 1158)

Poe describes the writer's mental drama in similar terms of doubt and conflict. He warns that the public would shudder "at the true purposes seized only at the last moment—at the innumerable glimpses of idea that arrived not at the maturity of full view—at the cautious selection and rejection—" (T: 14; OP: 985). Common to both descriptions are the dramatic tension of the mind in conflict with itself, the gratuitous thought rejected, the despair and lassitude, and the struggle to transform "sensations" or "fancies" into concrete structures. To convince the reader that the mental drama he describes is not limited to the extraordinary intellect, Valéry suggests that we observe someone who believes he is alone. Valéry uses theatrical terms to portray such a person deep in thought: "he *recoils* from an idea, *grasps* it, denies or smiles or stiffens, and mimes the strange predicament of his own diversity" (CW 8: 10; O 1: 1158). It is this drama of the intellect that Valéry sought to recreate in the case of Leonardo. He was well aware of the enormity of the challenge and the uniqueness of the experiment. "A consciousness of the operations of thought . . . ," remarks Valéry, "exists but rarely, even in the keenest of minds" (CW 8: 13–14; O 1: 1161).

In the apparent disordered thought of Leonardo's notebooks Valéry looked for a method, a unifying theory that would unlock the secrets of the universal mind. He observes that Leonardo "has an extraordinary sense of symmetry that makes him regard everything as a problem" (CW 8: 32; O 1: 1175). He imagines Leonardo's mind as functioning through a combination of will and intuition. The artist's projects might be conceived in flashes of the imagination but they are realized through rigorous scientific method that brings together "a particular vision and the materials that one has chosen" (CW 8: 41; O 1: 1182). Whether he is dealing with stones, colors, or words, the artist discovers secret affinities that manifest themselves through form. Valéry imagines a progression in the structures of thought, "first through a sort of primitive psychic onomatopoeia, then through elementary symmetries and contrasts, till it reaches the ideas of substances, metaphors, a faltering sort of logic, formalism, entities" (CW 8: 44–45; O 1: 1184–85). Elements are given a new order that defy their ordinary use. Picking up on Poe's idea expressed in *The Philosophy of Composition,* Valéry remarks: "On this order depends the effect. The effect is the aim of ornament, and thus the work of art takes on the character of a machine to impress a public; to arouse emotions and their corresponding images" (CW 8: 45; O 1: 1185). It is the search for the mechanics revealed through scientific laws driving the "machine" that becomes Valéry's major preoccupation in his study of Leonardo. He sees art as a problem of *rendering* images, whether it be through words, color, or musical notes. For Valéry art is not a vehicle for transmitting a personal feeling to another individual. Through the means at his disposal the artist creates an effect:

> What is called in art *realization*, is in fact a problem of rendering—one in which the private meaning, the key attributed by every author to his materials, plays no part, and in which the principal factors are the nature of these materials and the mentality of the public. (CW 8: 61; O 1: 1197)

Valéry was convinced that Poe was the first to see these "mechanics of effect." In a concluding paragraph of his essay Valéry specifically mentions Poe and places him in the realm of universal minds along with Leonardo:

> Edgar Poe, who in this century of literary perturbation was the very lightning of the confusion, of the poetic storm, and whose analysis sometimes ends, like Leonardo's, in mysterious smiles, has clearly established his reader's approach on the basis of psychology and probable effects. From that point of view, every combination of elements made to be perceived and judged depends on a few general laws and on the particular adaptation, defined in advance for a foreseen category of minds to which the whole is specially addressed, and the work of art becomes a machine designed to arouse and assemble the individual formations of those minds. (CW 8: 61–62; O 1: 1197–98)[2]

Aware that this concept of calculated effect in art went against the "ordinary notion of sublime," Valéry realized that he was reorienting criticism in a new direction by placing artistic creation on an analytical basis, an approach directly inspired by Poe.

Valéry admired in Poe and Leonardo their passion for science and art and the interrelationship they saw between two disciplines that appear on the surface to be unrelated. A leap of the imagination is as essential to science as it is to art; conversely, a methodical approach is the key to producing a work of art as well as to making a scientific discovery. Epitomizing this basic truth, remarks Val-

éry, is Leonardo's research on aviation, an example of the flight of
the imagination backed up by drawings that attempt to produce the
technical solutions to the problem. Valéry took pleasure in seeing
Leonardo proven right as science caught up with the artist's postu-
lations. He remarked in an essay on Degas that "as far as the
flight of birds is concerned, I will say in passing that high-speed
photography has confirmed the impressions given by Leonardo da
Vinci in his sketches" (CW 12: 41; O 2: 1192). Eight years after
Valéry's Leonardo essay was published the Wright brothers
realized the artist's dream.

Valéry's reconstruction of the famous artist's intellect is a work
of fiction inspired by Descartes, Poe, and Leonardo's notebooks.
Valéry's reading of Descartes stimulated his interest in an objective approach to considering the operations of the mind.[3] This
concept was reinforced by his study of Poe, who Valéry believed was
the first to focus on the intellectual analysis of the creative process.
Leonardo's notebooks represented for Valéry a secret laboratory
where the artist's projects could be seen in the process of gestation.
Valéry reconstructed Leonardo's method by imagining how such a
mind should have operated. While in Teste the extraordinary intellect remains pure potential, Leonardo's genius is revealed
through his work, although in this case it is still not the product
that interests Valéry but the mental process.

The essay on Leonardo, written when Valéry was only twenty-
three, embodied an idea that fascinated him, that of the creative
mind in operation. Throughout his lifetime he returned to the
Leonardo he had created in 1895. In 1919 *Introduction to the Method
of Leonardo da Vinci* was reprinted along with a new piece on the
same subject, *Note and Digression,* in which he reexamines his earlier essay, commenting on his own thought processes as he created
the original work. Other essays by Valéry on the Italian artist include *Leonardo and the Philosophers* (1928), *The Written Work of Leonardo
da Vinci* (1939), and a preface to a French publication of Leonardo's
notebooks (1942). In *Note and Digression* he recalls the powerful impression that drew him to attempt a recreation of Leonardo: "I felt
that this ruler of his own resources, this master of draftsmanship,
of images, and of calculations, had found the central attitude from
which the enterprises of knowledge and the operations of art are

equally possible" (CW 8: 66; O 1: 1201). Discovering how his own mind functioned and how these functions applied to artistic creation became the central focus of Valéry's thought and work. Like Leonardo's, Valéry's notebooks are the secret laboratory of his projects, "the ghosts that came before."

Poe's *Philosophy of Composition* had a direct influence on Valéry's first, and very successful, critical essay. In a much broader sense Poe had an effect on Valéry's approach to what we call today "literary theory," although Valéry would reject this term in his own case because his conclusions are based on his practice of observing himself create, thus he would not consider them theory. "I 'know' literature," he insisted, "from having cross-questioned it in my own fashion—and not otherwise" (CW 14: 201; O 2: 629). Also, he made no attempt to present his views on criticism in a codified way, even though they are central to his approach to literature, both as a reader and a writer. His ideas on how to evaluate artistic creations, found throughout his *Notebooks* and his published work, repeat certain basic tenets that can be traced to Poe.

Keeping in mind Valéry's concept of "counter-imitation" as a factor in literary influence, it is significant to note his own negative reaction to the critical approach of his generation. His reading of Poe confirmed certain observations that went counter to the practice of French literary critics of his time. Valéry's response was to reject the ideas in vogue and investigate new directions. He states the problem very bluntly:

Whether it is a question of Taine or Brunetière or Sainte-Beuve or others, these men are useless, they say nothing. They are long-winded mutes. They don't know anything about criticism. The problem itself is foreign to them. They calculate infinitely the age of the captain. Biography, morality, influences are the means given to the critic to hide his ignorance of the object and the subject. (C 7: 881)

Among the three critics Valéry dismisses with such disdain, the French scholar Hippolyte Taine (1828–93) had the greatest influence on European and American criticism in the late nineteenth and early twentieth centuries. In the introduction to his *History of English Literature* (1863) Taine argued that a literary work must be examined as the expression of the psychology of an individual, which in turn is determined by the *milieu* and the historical period, thus the famous formula "la race, le milieu et le moment."[4] In Taine's view, literature is part of the general historic process seen as an organized unity; it both depends on society and represents it. His concepts of "race" and "moment" have largely been discounted, but the term *milieu* generally refers to all external conditions of literature, such as the physical environment, the private life of the individual, and the political and social realities. Taine's argument that the study of a literary work is directly related to these external factors rankled Valéry, for whom art and literature are not a social document. Valéry regarded Taine as a sort of pseudo-scientist who was totally ignorant of the special relationship between the artist and his work.

While rejecting Taine's criticism as irrelevant, Valéry vents his strongest hostility toward Charles Augustin Sainte-Beuve (1804–69), who wielded extraordinary power as a critic, especially during the period 1840–65. Sainte-Beuve committed two cardinal sins that Valéry was never willing to forgive. First, "Beuve" (Valéry removed the "Sainte" in one of his *Notebook* references) blatantly misjudged the literary merits of several contemporaries, including Baudelaire, Balzac, Flaubert, and Stendhal. Second, the critic was guilty of the "biographical fallacy" by committing the error of making no distinction between the writer as a social being and the writer as a creator. Valéry saw Sainte-Beuve as a failed poet and novelist who turned to criticism with a vengeance. The sheer quantity of his critical essays, now filling some fifty volumes, and the fact that they were published regularly in newspapers made him the leading critic of his day.[5] Valéry's disdain for what he considered the inanities of Sainte-Beuve, Brunetière, and Lemaître is expressed in a *Notebook* entry which is a parody entitled "Resumé of known criticism." As can be seen in his sarcasm, Valéry deemed these critics unworthy because they had no understanding of the creative process:

Everything rather than the essential! I will talk about his mistress, his ancestors, his publishers, his investments, his reading—I will not talk about some words he uses and about others he doesn't use,—about the structure of the effects that he seeks—about the reader he imagines. (C 6: 632–33)

In Valéry's view the critics he mentions are not interested in the literary works themselves nor do they distinguish the properties on which the work can be judged. He sees Sainte-Beuve as a gatherer of facts, even as a gossiper, who had no inkling of what went on in the writer's head.

Valéry's cavalier attitude toward Ferdinand Brunetière (1849–1906) does not seem to be wholly justified, although it is understandable in light of the fact that the critic was mystified by Mallarmé's poetry and expressed a clear distaste for Baudelaire as a person and as a decadent poet.[6] On the other hand, like Valéry, Brunetière argued that criticism must concentrate on the works of literature themselves and eliminate the major importance attributed to biography, psychology, sociology, and other disciplines. Brunetière describes the history of literature in terms of inner causality, the influence of works on works. He recognizes both a positive and negative influence; authors imitate or reject. The tendency to do "something other" than works accomplished by predecessors appears to be the driving force of change, an idea Valéry also expresses in his statement: "Whether in science or the arts, if we look for the source of an achievement we can observe that *what a man does* either repeats or refutes *what someone else has done*" (CW 8: 241; O 1: 634). Literature, they both agree, moves by action and reaction, continuation and revolt, with an original work marking a change in its development.[7] In spite of sharing certain aspects of Bunetière's thought, Valéry relegates him along with Taine and Sainte-Beuve to the category of biographical critics, rejects them wholesale, and sets off in a new direction inspired in part by his reading of Poe.

Condemning the dominant literary critics of his day was Valéry's first step in expressing his own originality. As a practicing poet he spent many hours observing his own mind during the process of creation and was convinced that there was a clear distinction between the social self and the creative self. His goal was to understand the relationship between the creative mind and the work and between the work and the reader. For Valéry, Poe was an innovator whose approach to literature was far ahead of his time:

Poe was the first to think of giving literary works a theoretical foundation. Mallarmé and myself: I think I was the first to try having no recourse at all to the old notions, but to make a fresh start on purely an analytical basis. (CW 8: 356–57; C 12: 703)

Valéry's belief that Poe was the first to consider literary works on an analytical basis comes from his reading of *The Philosophy of Composition*. Here we find another case of a specific sentence having a profound effect on him by confirming his own observations and giving him the courage to pursue an idea to its extreme limits. The sentence is found at the beginning of *The Philosophy of Composition* in Poe's introductory remarks, after he explains his intention to describe how he composed "The Raven:"

It is my design to render it manifest that at no one point in its composition is referrible either to accident or intuition—that the work proceeded, step by step, to its completion with the precision and rigid consequence of a mathematical problem. (T: 14–15; OP: 986)

Did Valéry really believe that Poe composed his poem in the manner described? New evidence in a recently published manuscript indicates that he did not. James Lawler discovered the typescript of a talk Valéry presented at la Maison des Amis des Livres on May 31, 1922, in which Valéry discusses at length his impressions of Poe's work.[8] The text of the speech offers a rare glimpse of what Valéry *did not* like in Poe; comments in his published work and the *Notebooks* are almost without exception laudatory.[9] First, he did not care for "The Raven," indicating that it is not the best of Poe's poetry. He even calls it "*un poème réclame*," a term that translates roughly as "a publicity poem," meaning it was created specifically to appeal to the elementary tastes of the public at large.[10] In his second negative comment, Valéry states that Poe's description of how he created "The Raven" is "unworthy of his faculties." After explaining to his audience that Poe claims to have composed the poem by starting with the last word, Valéry remarks: "That is a mistake. Poe did not do that; he composed it in quite a different way."[11] From these remarks it is very clear that Valéry did not accept Poe's explanation literally, but herein lies an essential point in understanding Poe's influence on Valéry: Poe suggested to him ideas that reoriented his thinking. Although Valéry did not really believe that Poe created his poem "with the precision and rigid consequences of a mathematical problem," the *possibility* of such an approach excited Valéry to the point of pursuing it to its ultimate extreme, to the point of making the analysis itself his main focus. This is an example of the true meaning of influence for Valéry: an idea found in one author's work can be transformed beyond recognition in another's. Poe's step-by-step analysis of how he wrote "The Raven," pure fiction in Valéry's view, nonetheless triggered in him the determination to reject former notions of literary analysis and proceed in a new direction. Analyzing the creative process in and of itself became for Valéry the primary consideration, an activity that goes beyond Poe's intention in *The Philosophy of Composition.*

Through his analysis of the creative process Valéry arrived at a distinction between the author, the work, and the reader. Poe's careful calculation of the effect of various aspects of his poem upon the reader confirmed Valéry's belief that "a work of art is an object, a human product, made with a view of affecting certain individuals in a certain way" (CW 13: 142).[12] He goes even further by making an analogy with economics, indicating that there are two independent transformations, "the one which goes from the author to the *manufactured object* and the one which expresses the fact that the object or the work modifies the consumer" (CW 13: 142). Although this might appear to be calculated effect carried to the extreme, Valéry consistently points out in his work that art is not direct communication between the creator and the receiver. In his essay "The Creation of Art" he makes this clear: "In questions of art there are three main factors to distinguish: a creator or author; a concrete object which is the work; and a recipient—a reader, spectator, or listener" (CW 13: 124).[13] His description of the relationship between the author and his work is again reminiscent of Poe. The author, remarks Valéry, sees in the creation of his work "a whole *context* of incidents, hesitations, parts that have been deleted or never executed, makeshifts and surprises" (CW 13: 125). Drawing from his own experience he points out that an idea that comes to him suddenly and gratuitously might fit into a work so perfectly that it would strike the reader as being "natural," as nec-

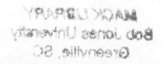

essarily following what precedes it in the text. Creation is a mental struggle between the author and the object, thus, observes Valéry, it is difficult for an author to perceive "the effect of a whole work as a finished, isolated construction" (CW 13: 125–26). The role of the writer or artist is "to combine determinate elements with a view to acting upon an indeterminate person" (CW 13: 129), the very process Poe describes in *The Philosophy of Composition.*

The "determinate elements" for the writer are certain properties of language such as words, rhythms, and sounds. Going from his general remarks to a specific example in the same way that Poe did in *The Philosophy of Composition,* Valéry recalls how he created one of his poems:

> Here is a recollection; here is what I find as the origin of a poem I wrote some years ago. One day I was obsessed by a rhythm which suddenly became quite palpable in my mind after a period during which I had been only half-conscious of it as a *lateral* activity. The rhythm asserted itself with a certain authority. I had the feeling that it wanted to be embodied, to attain the perfection of being. But the only way in which it could become clearer in my consciousness was to borrow or assimilate elements of *speech,* syllables, words; and at this stage in their formation, the syllables and words were determined no doubt by their musical value and affinities. (CW 13: 129–30)[14]

Valéry continues his step-by-step description, recalling that the syllables and words began to fill the rhythm, and a definite line "made its appearance," one that seemed impossible to modify. "The machine had been set going," remarks Valéry, but the conscious effort of the poet had to take over to complete the work set in motion by one gratuitous line. In this particular description of how he composed a poem Valéry does not mention length, but a brief observation in his *Notebooks* indicates that he agrees with Poe's arguments in *The Philosophy of Composition* that a poem should not be too long, no more than one hundred lines, in order to preserve the unity of effect. Valéry notes: "Proof: in practice the reader always breaks up long poems. Think of Poe" (CW 1: 417; C 6: 124). He was recalling Poe's statement in *The Philosophy of Composition*: "What we term a long poem is, in fact, merely a succession of brief ones—that is to say, of brief poetical effects" (T: 15; OP: 986). Valéry expresses a similar idea in "Rhumbs": "Long epic poems, when they are things of beauty, are beautiful in spite of their length, and then only in parts" (CW 14: 213; O 2: 638). A long poem that tells a story can be summarized and thus, in Valéry's mind, it is not really poetry. "A true poem," he observes, "is something that cannot be summarized. You can't abridge a melody" (CW 14: 213; O 2: 638). The unity of effect lies in the music of the words and the rhythm, which the reader must experience; the poem defies mere description.

Valéry analyzes the different stages of the creative process, emphasizing that inspiration and enthusiasm play only a minor role. He prefers to concentrate on the conscious use of the elements of language, which are the building stones of the construction to which the reader will react. Once the object is complete and out of the hands of its creator, the effect on the reader will take place independently of the author's specific intentions, although they often coincide.

Valéry described the experience of hearing his poem "The Graveyard by the Sea" ("Le Cimetière marin") analyzed in detail by Professor Gustave Cohen at the Sorbonne.[15] As the poet listened to the professor's exegesis, he reflected upon a striking dichotomy: the poem considered as *fact* and the particular circumstances that accompanied the creation of the poem. He comments: "I wrote a 'score'—but I can hear it performed only by the soul and the mind of others" (CW 7: 151; O 1: 1506). In spite of what he intended to do, the poem stands on its own. Cohen's analysis of his poem exemplified Valéry's perception of the relationship of the author to his work:

> There is no true meaning to a text—no author's authority. Whatever he may have wanted to say, he has written what he has written. Once published, a text is like an apparatus that anyone may use as he will and according to his ability: it is not certain that the one who constructed it can use it better than another. (CW 7: 152; O 1: 1507)

While listening to Cohen's analysis Valéry was struck by the clarity of the professor's explanations in contrast to the "chaos of the mind" that the poet had to overcome to create the poem.

On another occasion Valéry reacted in quite a different way to

written comments on his collection of poems *Charmes*. This time
he was impressed by the creative power his poems engendered in
the reader. Alain, pseudonym of Emile-Auguste Chartier (1868–
1951), professor at the Lycée Henri IV in Paris, wrote detailed
marginal notes in a new edition of Valéry's poems and then returned the copy to the poet. Valéry discovered in Alain's comments "the murmur of the discursive monologue responding to the
reading" (CW 7: 154; O 1: 1508). Valéry was fascinated by the
reader's reactions, on which he in turn comments at length.[16] His
poems awakened creative instincts in the receiver, whose reactions
are just as valid as his own. Anticipating the question "Is Alain's
commentary really close to your thought?" Valéry replies: "My
verses have the meaning attributed to them. The one I give them
suits only myself and does not contradict anyone else" (CW 7: 155;
O 1: 1509). He emphasizes that the object of poetry is not to
communicate a specific idea, a purpose that prose can serve. Once
prose has achieved its objective of communicating an idea, it per-
ishes. Valéry sees the function of poetry as being quite different.
Since its goal is not to communicate ideas, it survives through its
form, the sounds, the rhythms, and the effect of words upon each
other. Valéry expresses this conviction with a poetic image: "*A
beautiful line is constantly reborn from its own ashes*, it becomes again—
as the effect of its effect—its own harmonic cause" (CW 7: 157; O 1:
1510). Then using a scientific analogy, he compares the poem to
mysterious bodies studied in chemistry:

The simple presence of these bodies in a particular mixture of other substances determines the latter to unite, the former remaining unaltered, identical with themselves, neither transformed in their nature, nor increased or
diminished in their quantity. They are then, present and absent, acting and
not acted upon. Such is the text of a work. The action of its presence modifies minds, each according to its nature and state, provoking combinations latent within a certain head, but whatever reaction is thus produced, the text is
found to be unaltered and capable of indefinitely generating other phenomena in other circumstances or in another person. (CW 7: 158; O 1: 1511–12)

While recognizing in Poe the first author to approach poetry with
an analytical mind, Valéry carried the idea of analysis even further by inventing in his own mind the science of poetry. The only

way to judge a poem or a work of art, he believed, was to observe
the reciprocal action of its elements upon themselves and upon the
receiver. The intrinsic aspects of the work are all that count; ex-
trinsic factors might be interesting but are irrelevant to the work
itself.

In *The Philosophy of Composition* Valéry found an approach to literature that confirmed his own views and inspired his rejection of
positivist literary criticism as practiced by Taine, Sainte-Beuve,
Brunetière, and other majors figures who dominated the literary
landscape of his generation. His introspection on the creative process led to observations that coincide with certain aspects of modern
critical theory, which is generally traced back to 1914 with the publication of Viktor Shklovsky's essay on Futurist poetry, "The
Resurrection of the Word."[17] The Russian Formalists were determined to establish the independent existence of literary studies
and turn away from the Positivists' preoccupation with biography
and history. The goal of Formalism, as expressed by Boris
Eichenbaum, was "characterized only by the attempt to create an
independent science of literature which studies specifically literary
material."[18] Recognizing the "biographical fallacy" and concentrating on the literary work itself were basic to Valéry's approach,
as we have seen. The Formalists rejected all mimetic and expres-
sive definitions of literature, which considered the work as an extension of the author's personality or of a given society. They advo-
cated concentrating on literature's distinctive qualities, on the
"literariness" of the text,[19] a position Valéry had adopted from the
very beginning of his self-observation.

One of the most striking similarities between Valéry's approach
and that of the Formalists is defining literature as a set of differences. Basic to this concept is *defamiliarization* or making strange.
To illustrate his point that art defamiliarizes things that are habit-
ual or automatic, Shklovsky uses a specific example that is also found
in Valéry: the contrast between walking and dancing. "A dance
is a walk which is felt," remarks Shklovsky, "even more accurately,
it is a walk which is constructed to be felt."[20] In "Poetry and
Abstract Thought" Valéry observes that "walking, like prose, has a
definite aim" (CW 7: 70; O 1: 1330). Dance, on the other hand,
having no utilitarian purpose, "is only an ideal object, a state, an

enchantment" (CW 7: 70; O 1: 1330). Walking and dancing, continues Valéry, "use the same organs, the same bones, the same muscles, only differently co-ordinated and aroused." The same contrast applies to prose and poetry, which use the same words, the same sounds or tones, but are combined in a different way to produce a specific effect.[21] "Prose and poetry," remarks Valéry, "are therefore distinguished by the difference between certain links and associations which form and dissolve in our psychic and nervous organism, whereas the components of these modes of functioning are identical" (CW 7: 71; O 1: 1331). The poet brings together sounds, rhythms, and repetitions in unfamiliar ways that strike us like a chord of music. These rare occasions when sound and sense are brought together in an "intimate and indissoluble fusion" in poetry are opposed to what Valéry calls "the crude simplifying and specializing of verbal notations," which is characteristic of prose. The contrasts between walking/dancing and prose/poetry express the view of both Valéry and the Formalists that literature is a special category of language based on fundamental oppositions. The primary purpose of ordinary language is to communicate clearly and efficiently a message relating to the outside world. By contrast, the function of poetic language is not to make connections with reality as such but rather to focus on the poem's own intrinsic features and their interrelationships. Poetry produces a fresh experience in the reader through artistic devices applied to language, such as contrast in speech sounds, rhythm, rhyme, and repetition of words or images. For Valéry and the Formalists, literary analysis must concentrate on these intrinsic devices and not on the content or social significance of poetry. The term *Formalism* was first used derogatorily by opponents of Eichenbaum, Shklovsky, and Jakobson because they emphasized the formal patterns of sounds and words instead of the subject matter of literature. Although Valéry particularly disliked all terms ending in "ism" because they tended to be too vague, his approach to literary analysis had a great deal in common with Russian Formalism. But at times Valéry even goes beyond the Formalists when he suggests that for the artist, "*the idea of a form* means as much to him as *the idea that asks to be given a form*" (CW 8: 124; O 1: 1245).

Valéry's thoughts on literature also have affinities with American New Criticism, which developed independently of European Formalism. Like their Russian predecessors, the New Critics view the literary work as a self-sufficient object and consider poetry as a distinctive use of language that is opposed to ordinary language. The term New Criticism came into use after the publication of John Crowe Ransom's book *The New Criticism* (1941), but its critical tenets were formulated by a number of authors, including I. A. Richards, Cleanth Brooks, Robert Penn Warren, and T. S. Eliot. Eliot's views are of particular interest to our study because of his importance as a poet and his long friendship with Valéry.

While Eliot eschewed the prevailing concern with literary history and the lives of authors, he considered Valéry's preoccupation with the creative process an extreme in the opposite direction. Valéry's ideal of the poet as literary scientist, a concept inspired by Poe, went too far in Eliot's thinking: "Looked at in this way, the 'cool scientist' is an alternative, rather than the antithesis to the 'disheveled madman': a different task for the same actor. Poe, to be sure, combined both roles, but it is only as the 'cool scientist' that Valéry sees him" (CW 7: xix). Referring to *The Philosophy of Composition*, Eliot goes on to remark that "what for Poe was an ingenious exercise, was deadly earnest for Valéry, and from very early years" (CW 7: xx). Valéry developed an obsession that led to a dead end, in Eliot's opinion. The French poet's one object of curiosity was himself, his own mind in the process of creation. Eliot complains that Valéry's poetics "provides us with no criterion of *seriousness*" (CW 7: xxiii). Because Valéry is so deeply preoccupied with the problem of process, the poem itself is not important. Eliot hastens to add that Valéry's poems are serious works, but he is bothered by the fact that the French poet seems to regard them as insignificant by-products of an intangible reality, the mind in action. The poem interests Valéry to the extent that it reveals the intellectual mechanism that produced it.

René Wellek sees a link between Valéry and the New Critics in their recognition of the "intentional fallacy," which is the error of interpreting a work by taking into account the conscious aim of the author, either stated or inferred.[22] The New Critics and Valéry believe that the writer's intention should be irrelevant to the critic's evaluation because the value of the text resides in the work itself and must be judged independently of what the creator wanted to achieve. As we have seen, Valéry separates the work from the author once the literary product has been published and becomes public domain. What the author intended no longer counts, as Valéry points out: "Bad poems are made of good intentions" (CW 14: 236; O 2: 678). And again, he emphasizes that the work must stand on its own: "My intention was merely *my* intention and the work is—what it is" (CW 14: 109; O 2: 557).

Valéry would have agreed with the views in Cleanth Brooks' essay "The Heresy of Paraphrase," in which he argues that poetry by its very nature eludes any attempt to reduce it to conventional modes of expression.[23] Both Valéry and Brooks object to the tendency of many critics and scholars to present the paraphrasable elements in literature as its primary substance. In their view the value of a literary work is to be found in imaginative relationships produced by the special properties of language. Valéry was fond of illustrating this point by recounting on more than one occasion a brief conversation between Degas and Mallarmé. Degas wrote verses but found this creative pursuit much more difficult than painting. He once remarked to Mallarmé: "Yours is a hellish craft. I can't manage to say what I want, and yet I'm full of ideas," to which Mallarmé replied in his customary gentle manner: "My dear Degas, one does not make poetry with ideas, but with *words*" (CW 7: 63; O 1: 1324; CW 8: 324; O 1: 784). In Valéry's mind, literature, especially poetry, *"is and can be nothing else than a kind of extension and application of certain properties of language"* (CW 13: 85; O 1: 1440). It is the critic's role to discover how the poet creates an organic unity through a structure of opposing elements. The concept of organic unity is expressed in W. K. Wimsatt's description of poetry as "that type of verbal structure where truth of reference or correspondence reaches a maximum degree of fusion with truth of coherence—or whose external and internal relation are intimately mutual reflections."[24] Valéry recognized the central element of "truth of coherence" in Poe's use of the word *consistency,* which Valéry understood to mean coherence among intrinsic properties, whether in a poem or in Poe's conception of the universe (CW 8: 165; O 1: 858).[25] The beauty that results from the fusion of certain properties of language and the images produced cannot be captured in paraphrase. The critic must examine the "chemistry" that produces the fusion, in Valéry's view. Thus, Valéry arrives at a position similar to that of the New Critics: the object of criticism must be the literary text itself, which is an autonomous verbal object endowed with various meanings accessible to sensitive readers. A literary text has special properties that act and react upon each other while at the same time producing a "truth of coherence" among the various elements.

Valéry's importance as a precursor of Structuralism has been pointed out by a number of critics, most notably by Christine Crow and Jean Bucher, who sees Valéry as a specialist in the knowledge of linguistic effects.[26] For Valéry, a poem is made up of various components that react according to literary and linguistic codes, producing effects that have no truth-value outside the poem itself. The poem can produce a plurality of meaningful effects rather than a single correct meaning. Valéry's interest in the reader's creative reaction, as we have seen in his comments on Alain's reading of *Charmes*, predates the reader-response criticism which has developed since the 1960s. Reader-response critics agree that the meanings of a text are the "creation" of the individual reader, thus there is no "correct" interpretation of the text, an idea that Valéry insisted upon in the 1920s. Labeling Valéry an early literary Structuralist must be done with caution, as Tzvetan Todorov points out in "Valéry's Poetics."[27] The major difference between Valéry and the Structuralists is that, as Todorov notes, for Valéry "the object of poetics is not a description of different forms of literary discourse, but that of the creative action, considered in an abstract and non-individualized way."[28] Valéry's primary interest is understanding "the *action that accomplishes*" rather than the "*accomplished act*."[29] Comprehending the *modus operandi* of the creative mind, an exercise suggested to him by Poe, became more important for Valéry than the work itself.

Most of Valéry's observations on literary analysis deal with poetry because it was the only genre that offered any real challenge to his intellect. Creating within a structure that imposes specific restrictions places greater demands on the poet's skills and brings greater rewards when perfection is achieved. Valéry recalls a personal experience that revealed to him the meaning and feeling of perfection in literature. While gazing through a shop window at a page of Racine's *Phedre*, he attempted to change the alexandrines, but the fragment resisted his efforts to make word conversions or to alter it in any way. "*Phedre* resisted me," remarked Valéry. "I thus learned, through direct experience and immediate sensation, what is meant by perfection in a work. It was a rude awakening" (CW 11: 195; O 1: 508).

It is precisely a lack of intellectual resistance that Valéry objects to in the novel: "As a reader of novels and histories I could not help observing all the freedom which these writings left me to modify [them] at my pleasure" (O 1: 1813). The unrestricted form and the goal of recreating truth are the conditions that make the novel inferior to poetry in Valéry's mind. In spite of his depreciation of the novel as a genre, Valéry wrote a homage to Marcel Proust, whose multi-volume novel *In Search of Lost Time* is considered to be one of the masterpieces of the twentieth century. With unusual candor for a critic, Valéry begins his tribute by saying that he has scarcely read a single volume of Proust's work and that he finds the very art of the novelist almost inconceivable. Nevertheless, he continues, literature has experienced a great loss with the death of this talented author. Valéry's essay is of interest not because of what he says about Proust, which is very little, but because he uses the occasion to set forth his views on the distinction between the novel and poetry. The novel, observes Valéry, "takes advantage of the immediate signifying power of language" (CW 9: 296; O 1: 770). Poetry, by contrast, "brings our physical organism directly into play" through a "continuous liaison between sense of hearing, the form of the voice, and articulate expression" (CW 9: 296; O 1: 770). Although Valéry considers the novel a "naive genre," he himself gives a rather naive description that most novelists would reject:

There must be no essential difference between the novel and the natural description of things that we have seen and heard. Neither rhythms, forms and figures of speech nor even any definite structure are obligatory. (CW 9: 297; O 1: 771)

After pointing out what the genre lacks, Valéry arrives at the essential quality that every novel must have, and here he falls back on Poe for his argument. In *The Philosophy of Composition* Poe emphasizes the importance of unity of *effect*, which for Valéry is also the primary requirement in the novel. "There is only one rule," writes Valéry, "but it must be kept on pain of death: it is essential—and sufficient—that the sequence of events should carry and even *pull* us toward an end" (CW 9: 297; O 1: 771). This statement, especially with the use of the dash, sounds as if it could have come straight from Poe. Valéry concludes his essay by making three more contrasts between the two genres. Evoking the "heresy of paraphrase" he remarks that "unlike poetry, it is possible to give a resumé of a novel" (CW 9: 297; O 1: 771). Along the same line of thinking, he remarks that the unique qualities of poetry cannot be translated, while a novel can be transferred to another language "without losing its essence." Again, Valéry objects to the novel's lack of form by noting that "it can be *elaborated* internally or *continued* indefinitely, just as it can be read at several sittings" (CW 9: 298; O 1: 772). In *The Philosophy of Composition* Poe recommends that all works of literature be limited so that they can be read in a single sitting in order to preserve the unity of effect. He then mentions the novel *Robinson Crusoe*, "demanding no unity," as an exception to the rule (T: 15; OP: 987). Thus, the two main points Valéry makes concerning the novel, the necessity of creating a strong effect and the lack of unity, repeat Poe's views on the same subject.

Valéry sees the novel as the antithesis of poetry, therefore his comments are implicitly negative. Opinions about novelists in his *Notebooks* reveal his lack of interest in appreciating the finer points of their craft: "Reading Flaubert is unbearable to anyone who can think" (CW 9: 334; C 6: 141). In contrast to his published remarks about Proust, in the privacy of his *Notebooks*, Valéry refers to him as a "deadly bore, not a whit of intellectual force" (CW 9: 341; C 13: 679). Although Valéry preferred Stendhal to Flaubert, he nevertheless complains in his *Notebooks* that he finds no intellectual resistance in the novelist's work: "After a hundred pages you can predict—every time—Stendhal's reaction to anything at all" (CW 9: 332; C 26: 882). Because of his negative attitude toward the genre, Valéry did not move beyond seeing its art as being identical with Realism and Naturalism. A novelist's efforts to describe anything and everything represented a lack of restrictions and refinement, in Valéry's mind, thus the genre was scarcely worthy of critical analysis. His emphasis on form over content, his rejection of the traditional novel, and his insistence on the reader's participation in the creative experience link Valéry with the New Novelists, who have attempted to reform the genre along these lines.[30]

The theater held greater interest for Valéry than the novel because dramatic works written to be performed must submit to restrictions on length and form, to a certain extent. Even so, he had an aversion to the spectacular, the violence, and the conflict laid bare that make up the very essence of drama: "This antipathy to violent or theatrical incidents explains me insofar as I am nonnovelist, nonhistorian, nondramatist" (CW 15: 315; O 2: 1524). For Valéry, everything that is dramatic is accidental and diminishes one's capacity to observe the mechanism that produces the action. He uses the heart as an analogy: "Whether or not the heart beats fast, the fact that it beats is what interests the mind. Fast is the modality" (CW 15: 314; O 2: 1524). He was puzzled by the pleasure one finds in tragedy; for him it is only a facile distraction, opposed to the contemplative state or to the state of charm produced by poetry. While not considering himself a dramatist, Valéry nevertheless wrote dramatic scenes, Socratic dialogues, librettos, and two unfinished plays under the title "My Faust." He recalled the origin of his desire to write the Faust pieces: "It was one day in 1940 that I found I was talking to myself in two voices, and began to write accordingly" (CW 3: 4; O 2: 276–77). It was this dialogue of the self with the self that inspired him to write for the theater rather than any desire to astonish or captivate the audience with a dramatic conflict. In his "Notes on Tragedy and a Tragedy," a critique of Lucien Fabre's *God Is Innocent,* Valéry expresses his admiration for the play's closely knit form and the poetic beauty of certain dialogues (CW 7: 235).[31] His interest in the theater and his critical point of view are linked to his belief that form and poetic elements are central to the aesthetic experience, which can occasionally be found in drama.

Although Valéry did not consider himself a professional critic and would, in fact, have found the term offensive, he nonetheless earned a living from 1922 to his death in 1945 by writing essays, prefaces, official speeches, and various other types of commissioned pieces. The sheer volume of this work (seven tomes of his *Collected Works*) is as impressive as the diversity of the subject matter: politics, history, science, literature, art, dance, and philosophy, not to mention poetics, which we will examine in the next chapter. But common to all his essays is Valéry's conception of form and his fascination with the activity of the mind as it is applied to many disciplines.[32]

Poe's influence on Valéry as a critic was both specific and general. The inspiration to try a new critical approach in his *Introduction to the Method of Leonardo da Vinci* originated in a few lines from *The Philosophy of Composition* that suggested the idea of examining the *modus operandi* by which a work is produced. Some twenty years later Valéry's comment in his *Notebooks* indicates that he was still convinced of the American poet's originality: "Poe was the first to consider mental mechanism as the producer of works" (CW 8: 354; C 6: 717). Valéry's recreating Leonardo's mental mechanism produced a bold and innovative critical study that deviated dramatically from the positivist criticism that dominated the literary scene during the last half of the nineteenth century. Rejecting a biographical or historical approach, Valéry attempted to discover the elements of artistic creation and the laws that govern them in an effort to understand the work of art as a machine designed to have an effect on the individual mind. It was not Leonardo's personal thoughts or feelings that Valéry sought to grasp but rather the universal qualities that manifest themselves in the artist and the scientist. Valéry's method was to trace the work, fragments in Leonardo's notebooks, back to the mind in order to put together the intellectual puzzle and then examine it. Along the way he combined elements from Leonardo with figments of his own imagination to create a fictitious character who in turn became his ideal.

Poe's *Philosophy of Composition* had both a positive and negative effect on Valéry early in his career. On the one hand, he believed that Poe understood better than anyone how literary works are created and it is this very mechanism that the critic must grasp; on the other hand, he rejected the aim of producing works for the purpose of having an effect on others, preferring instead to devote himself to understanding the creative mechanism. In his *Notebook B 1910* Valéry makes this clear:

There's always a rather sordid side to literature: a lurking deference to one's public. Hence the mental reservations, the ulterior motives basic to every form of charlatanism. Thus every literary production is an "impure" product.

This principle is absolute and the critic who fails to bear it in mind is a bad chemist. Therefore we should never draw conclusions from a man's work to the man himself, but from the work to his "mask"—and from the mask to the machine. (CW 14: 138; O 2: 581)

In *The Philosophy of Composition* Valéry observed the "machine" in the process of creating the "mask" designed to have a specific effect on the public. Instead of encouraging him to become more adept at creating "masks," Poe's essay inspired an obsession with the mechanism of the "machine." It was this "Intellectual Comedy" (CW 8: 66; O 1: 1201) that became the subject of Valéry's prose pieces and his poetry.

When Valéry remarked that Leonardo, Poe, and Mallarmé each had a deep influence on him, he was referring to the images of these masters that he recreated in his essays. He explained how the influence worked: "I would imagine their minds, and from that it was an easy step to forming an image of the mind" (CW 8: vii; O 2: 1537). This image was shaped through the works of those he admired. Valéry continues: "In truth, the work that interests me deeply is the work that invites me to picture the living and thinking system that produced it—an illusion, no doubt, but one that develops energies not to be found in the attitude of a purely passive reader" (CW 8: vii; O 2: 1537). He imagines Poe as a writer endowed with an acute sense of "self-consciousness," which for Valéry meant an understanding of one's own mental processes during the act of creation. He believed that Poe oriented criticism in a new direction by considering the mental mechanism as the producer of works and the only basis on which to judge creative endeavors. Valéry's critical approach goes far beyond Poe's in the sense that he attempted to discover how the mechanism works in order to apply its secrets to understanding all disciplines.

CHAPTER FIVE

Poetics and Poetry

Poetry to me has never been an end in itself, always a means to some end.

—Valéry (C 3: 610)

During the two decades after the publication of *Introduction to the Method of Leonardo da Vinci* (1895) and *The Evening with Monsieur Teste* (1896), very little of Valéry's work appeared in print. Two poems came out in the literary journal *Le Centaure* in 1896, the poem "Valvins" in an album dedicated to Mallarmé in 1897, and "Anne" in *La Plume* in December 1900. While Valéry was in London in 1897 the editor of *The New Review* asked him to write an article about Germany. His essay, "A Conquest by Method" ("La Conquête allemande"), turned out to be prophetic; Valéry recognized the elements that would lead to the outbreak of World War I. When the piece was reprinted in the *Mercure de France* in 1915, readers were impressed by Valéry's insights published eighteen years earlier. This article, along with many others on history, politics, and contemporary ideas, has contributed to Valéry's reputation as a brilliant thinker able to discern the psychological elements in complex situations.[1]

Privately, Valéry was writing a great deal during his period of so-called silence. He carried on an extensive correspondence, some of which is now available in three volumes, and his meditations fill six volumes of *Notebooks* dated 1894–1918. His friendships included many artists, composers, writers, and men of science, whose conversations he particularly enjoyed. In 1912 he mentioned

Edgar Poe among the men he would most like to have met (O 1: 36). He saw the creative world divided into scientists and artists, and, in his mind, Poe was the first poet in modern times to bridge the gap. During this period of maturation, Valéry continued to read Poe and to reflect upon the intellect's creative mechanism, although he still had no desire to publish the "exercises" that resulted from his self-observation.

Valéry's return to writing poetry came about through the encouragement of André Gide, who in 1912 tried to convince him to put together an edition of prose and verse to be published by the newly founded *Nouvelle Revue Française*. Intrigued by the idea, Valéry reread with a mature eye poems he had written twenty years earlier, recognizing flaws that stimulated his mind to perfect the earlier pieces. As he began to revise, the idea came to him for a new poem of about twenty or thirty lines which would be a sort of "farewell to these adolescent games" (O 1: 1620). The result was a four-year creative surge that produced a masterpiece of over five hundred lines, some eight hundred pages of variant versions, many references in the *Notebooks,* and two essays describing the poem's genesis.[2] *The Young Fate* (*La Jeune Parque*),[3] published in 1917 when Valéry was forty-six years old, launched his fame as one of France's greatest poets. The creative force behind this poem did not wane; three years later "The Graveyard by the Sea" ("Le Cimetière marin"), Valéry's best-known poem, and the collection *Album of Earlier Verse* (*Album de vers anciens*) were published. In 1921 the review *Connaissance* ran an opinion poll to find out who their readers considered to be the greatest contemporary French poet. When Valéry won the contest, he had to overcome his embarrassment before writing a polite note to the editor: "This astonishing bit of news which you have so kindly communicated to me fills me with melancholy as for myself and with regrets for the other poets, innocent victims" (O 2: 1487). Even before this proof of success had been publicly acknowledged, Valéry was already at work on new poems, which came out in the collection *Charmes* in 1922.

While the publication of his poems brought fame, Valéry's greatest satisfaction was the exhilaration of observing his creative forces at work. These observations appear in many of his essays, speeches, and university lectures in which his poetics are presented as candid descriptions of his own experience. A recollection of his return to writing verse gives an indication of the very definition of poetry:

I perceived that I was again becoming sensitive to the ring of language. I lingered to catch the music of speech. The words I heard touched off in me some kind of relations and the hidden presence of imminent rhythms. Syllable took on color. Certain turns and forms of speech sometimes appeared of themselves on the frontier of the mind and voice, and seemed to demand life. (CW 7: 133; O 1: 1492)

Valéry was fond of reminding his audience that poetry is the development of certain properties of language. Works of prose begin with ideas; poetry begins with linguistic elements. In Valéry's mind, Poe was the first poet to expose the mental mechanism that consciously calculates the effect of language upon the listener. As early as 1889, when he praised Poe for his modern concept of the conscious poet, Valéry had observed from his own experience that conscious effort and control of technique were the major factors in artistic creation. Fifty years later, in a lecture on poetics in 1939, Valéry expressed again his belief that Poe reoriented poetry by steering it away from storytelling and divine inspiration.

Valéry declared himself Poe's disciple at the age of eighteen when he wrote his first article "On Literary Technique." As we have seen in Chapter 2, most of the ideas in the essay come from *The Philosophy of Composition.* Like Poe, Valéry declares that the primary concern of the poet is to create a calculated effect on the listener. Inspiration plays only a minor role, and what it produces must be incorporated into the poet's conscious effort to create the desired effect. In his first letter to Mallarmé (October 1890) Valéry mentions his preference for short poems "concentrated toward a final impact, in which the rhythms are like the marmoreal steps to the altar, crowning the final line" (CW 8: 406–7; O 1: 1581–82). The ideas expressed in his first article and the early letters to Mallarmé formed the basis of his poetics, which he continued to develop throughout his lifetime.

During the last eight years of his life (1937–45), Valéry presented his poetics in a systematic way at the Collège de France, where a chair had been created in his honor. From the voluminous notes he used to give the classes, only his introductory lecture and an essay titled "On the Teaching of *Poetics* at the Collège de France" have been published.[4] Other sources for the content of the poetics courses are found in notes published by Georges Le Breton in *Yggdrasill*[5] and in Lucienne Julien Cain's essays based on notes taken from Valéry's lectures.[6]

The essay "On the Teaching of *Poetics* at the Collège de France" seems to have been directly inspired by Poe's *Philosophy of Composition.* After remarking that the history of literature has made great strides over the years, judging by the number of university chairs created, Valéry makes a statement that reminds us of Poe's comment on the lack of attention given to the genesis of works. The second sentence of Valéry's lecture reads: "It seems strange by contrast that the form of intellectual activity which engenders the works themselves should be studied hardly at all, or taken up only incidentally and with insufficient precision" (CW 13: 83; O 1: 1438). Poe also wondered why the process by which a work is accomplished had not been the subject of critical examination. Valéry then goes on to expound on one of his favorite themes, the incompetence of critics who dwell on irrelevant details and fail to see the intrinsic qualities of a work of literature. Instead of a history of literature based on the events and "accidents" of the authors' lives, Valéry proposes in his course to examine the *"history of the mind in so far as it produces or consumes 'literature'"* (CW 13: 84; O 1: 1439). Clarifying one more point, he adds that *"literature is and can be nothing else than a kind of extension and application of certain properties of language"* (CW 13: 85; O 1: 1440). Thus, concludes Valéry, the purpose of his course on poetics will be to examine the literary effects of language and to distinguish these effects from other uses.

In the introductory remarks to his course at the Collège de France, published as "The Opening Lecture of the Course in *Poetics*" (CW 13: 89–111; O 1: 1340–58), Valéry explained his intention to revive the term *poetics* in a sense consonant with its etymology, stating that his desire was to "express the very simple notion of *making*" (CW 13: 92; O 1: 1342). Poetics, in his mind, is not a study of rules and precepts but rather observations on the operations of language used for a specific purpose. His aim in the lectures was to examine the mechanism used by the writer, in this case himself, as he comes to grips with the elements that make a poem a work of art. Many of the terms commonly used, such as *form, style, rhyme, influences,* and *inspiration,* are vague, complains Valéry. His goal was to make these expressions more precise by using them in the context of his own experience. Although subsequent lectures have not been published, much of what Valéry presented in his courses was taken from his *Notebooks.* The most important points of his poetics are covered in various essays, which we will examine in detail as they relate to Poe.

Among the notes for his poetics course there is a brief reference to a lecture on Edgar Poe given on January 14, 1939 (O 1: 64). Lucienne Julien Cain attended the lecture and later wrote an essay based on her recollection of Valéry's presentation. She notes that Valéry, "so disdainful of the events in the lives of authors, including his own,"[7] made an exception in Poe's case by recounting the details of the poet's sad life. Since Valéry strongly claimed a lack of interest in biography, it is all the more significant to learn which aspects of Poe's life he chose to recount to his audience. According to Cain, he described Poe walking in Virginia Clemm's funeral procession in the terrible cold, wrapped in his departed wife's plaid shaw. Following this moving image of love, death, and solitude, Valéry evoked the cerebral Poe, who exchanged letters with Dickens and figured out the ending to *Barnaby Rudge* before the novelist had revealed it to the public. This particular anecdote fascinated Valéry because it provided proof of Poe's analytical powers. Valéry also recounted that Poe was reduced to giving his last pennies to Baltimore street sweepers to come to his lecture on *Eureka* in order to have an audience for "this wonderful work on Newton and Laplace."[8]

Valéry's purpose in recounting these tragic events was to impress upon his audience the miracle of lucidity that Poe managed to maintain throughout his life. Cain reports that Valéry used the English word *self-consciousness* to describe this unique quality he recognized in Poe. He defines Poe's "*auto-conscience,*" the French translation he uses alternately with the English term, as "this faculty of the mind that applies to itself the laws of scientific observation."[9] Cain remarks that it mattered little to Valéry whether Poe actually composed "The Raven" with the "precision of a mathematical problem," the French poet was carried away by the idea of "this will power to create a work under conditions that are completely understood by the mind."[10]

Among the truly unforgettable lessons, reports Cain, was Valéry's lecture on *The Philosophy of Composition*. The poet-professor explained that Poe wanted to set forth three essential points concerning poetic composition: the length of the poem, which can only be considered as such if it is short, the "province" (the psychic region where the poem is situated), and the tone. The key to the whole composition, explained Valéry, is what Poe calls "the effect." After describing how Poe began his poem by selecting a refrain with a sonorous vowel, Valéry recounted similar experiences in the composition of his own poems, some of which began with a certain rhythm or a series of vowel sounds. Two other points that Valéry emphasized were unity and originality. Inspired by Poe's comment that *"for centuries, no man, in verse, has ever done, or even seemed to think of doing, an original thing"* (T: 20; OP: 992), Valéry explored the possibilities of creating new effects within the strict prosody of French verse. His own originality is evident in *Charmes*, where he uses a wide variety of metrical forms, including every line from five syllables to the alexandrine with the exception of the nine- and eleven-syllable lines.

Valéry's lecture on Poe was among the most memorable, recalls Cain, because of his enthusiasm for the subject and the relationships he described in connection with his own experience. Fifty years elapsed between Valéry's first essay on Poe (1889) and his lecture on the American poet at the Collège de France (1939). Even in his maturity, he continued to recognize in Poe's literary essays his own preoccupations: the attention to conscious creation that reduces inspiration to a minor level, the ideal of "pure poetry," the importance of music in poetry, the relationship between form and content, and the definition of poetry as "charm" or "enchantment." It is these elements found in germ in Poe's essays and developed to "extreme originality," to use Valéry's expression, that we will examine in detail.

In his essay "The Place of Baudelaire" Valéry defined the break with Romanticism as "the substitution of a spontaneous act by a deliberate one" and he credited Poe with having oriented Baudelaire in this direction. Poe's brief comments in *The Philosophy of Composition* in which he ridicules the idea of composing a poem in a "fine frenzy" reinforced Valéry's distrust of inspiration in poetic creation. In his essay "On Literary Technique" Valéry proposes a "totally new and modern conception of the poet," who is no longer the "disheveled madman who writes the whole poem in the course of one feverish night" (CW 7: 315; O 1: 1809). Early in his career Valéry viewed the role of inspiration as minimal and subordinated it to the concept of the poet as "a cool scientist" inspired by Poe. Throughout his life Valéry continued to observe and reflect upon various aspects of inspiration in his own creative process, a subject Walter Ince examines in his study of the development of Valéry's poetic theory. From his early extreme position that valued the dominance of conscious technique, Valéry developed an appreciation of the more subtle variations of inspiration, which Ince divides into six types: "total," "intermittent," "intuitive," "exalted," "attributed," and "personal."

Both Poe and Valéry reject the idea of "total inspiration," which suggests that the poet is the scribe of an external muse or some transcendental power that dictates the poetic creation. Since conscious intellectual control was very important for Valéry, the idea of a poet's creative powers coming from an unconscious or outside source was just the opposite of his conception, based on his own experience. "It is enough to be *inspired*," he remarked facetiously, "and things happen of themselves. I only wish it were like that. Life would be bearable" (CW 7: 212; O 1: 1375). Conscious effort that produces a work of art gives the *impression* of something divine; the "rough" labor that produced it is no longer visible. In "Poetry and Abstract Thought" Valéry discounts the role of "total inspiration":

Faced with a beautiful poem, one can indeed feel that it is most unlikely that any man, however gifted, could have improvised without a backward glance, with no other effort than that of writing or dictating, such a simultaneous and complete system of lucky finds. Since the traces of effort, the second thoughts, the changes, the amount of time, the bad days, and the distaste have now vanished, effaced by the supreme return of a mind over its work, some people, seeing only the perfection of the result, will look on it as due to a sort of magic that they call INSPIRATION. They make of the poet a kind of temporary *medium*. (CW 7: 76; O 1: 1335)

Valéry is describing here, again, the hidden drama of the intellect that we have seen in his essay on Leonardo da Vinci and in Poe's *Philosophy of Composition*. It is the conscious mind that must create the impression of magic. Extending the false doctrine of pure inspiration to its extreme, Valéry concludes that "the poet, since he merely transmits what he receives, merely delivers to unknown people what he has taken from the unknown, has no need to understand what he writes, which is dictated by a mysterious voice" (CW 7: 76; O 1: 1335). Pushing this idea to the absurd, he remarks that a poet could even write poems in a language he did not know. After ridiculing the concept of pure inspiration, Valéry turns to a more realistic description of what he calls the poet's "spiritual energy of a special nature" (CW 7: 76; O 1: 1335). The "poetic state" or "poetic emotion" is a type of inspiration that Ince categorizes as "intermittent."[11]

The distinction between a certain kind of poetic emotion that many individuals experience and the "poetic state" of the writer in the act of creation is made in Valéry's "Remarks on Poetry," where he points out that in contrast to ordinary emotion the "poetic state" is combined with a "sense of a universe." This sense, continues Valéry, consists of

a dawning perception, a tendency toward perceiving a *world,* or a complete system of relations, in which beings, things, events, and acts, although they may resemble, *each to each,* those which fill and form the tangible world—the immediate world from which they are borrowed—stand, however, in an indefinable, but wonderfully accurate, relationship to the modes and laws of our general sensibility. So, the value of these well-known objects and beings is in some way altered. They respond to each other and combine quite otherwise than in ordinary conditions. They become—if you will allow the expression—*musicalized,* somehow commensurable, echoing each other. (CW 7: 198; O 1: 1363)

Rather than a flash of intuition, Valéry describes a certain state in which the poet envisions relationships between reality and a world beyond that the poet translates into concrete language.

These periods of privileged vision are not static, thus the term *intermittent inspiration* that Ince ascribes to them.

The third type of inspiration, "intuitive," is a type of illumination that occurs when the poet is in a "poetic state." Valéry gives numerous descriptions of this form of inspiration, usually followed by comments on the conscious effort required to make use of the gratuitous fragment. In "Memoirs of a Poem" he mentions that the starting point for *The Young Fate* was an inspiration to attempt in poetry something analogous to modulation in music. Another poem began with a "hint of a rhythm, *which gradually acquired a meaning*" (CW 7: 111; O 1: 1474). A similar experience occurred in a more dramatic way, as Valéry describes it: "As I went along my street, which mounts steeply, I was *gripped* by a rhythm which took possession of me and soon gave me the impression of some force outside myself" (CW 7: 112; O 1: 1474). The unexpected illumination inspired Valéry's humorous comment that "this grace had descended on the wrong head, since I could make no use of a gift which, in a musician would doubtless have assumed a lasting shape" (CW 7: 112; O 1: 1474). These examples of "intuitive inspiration" are the closest akin to the traditional concept of inspiration as something that occurs beyond the conscious control of the poet. But for Valéry, these gratuitous moments play only a minor role in the creation of a poem and are always followed by an extreme will of the conscious mind to make use of the "divine" gift. As M. Teste observed, "Finding is nothing. The difficulty is in acquiring what has been found" (CW 6: 11; O 2: 17).

"Exalted inspiration," as Ince points out, does not mean a loss of self-control.[12] This stage arrives when the poet feels the poem coming together, and he works in a state of excited tension, feeling a supreme assurance in his creative powers. "Exalted inspiration" occurs when the "poetic state," "intuitive inspiration" and conscious effort converge, and the artist is in the final stages of realizing his composition. The best description of this type of inspiration is found in Valéry's essay "Degas Dance Drawing," where he first speaks in terms of the painter but then extends the idea to all artists including himself:

In a great painter, there is a particularly intimate and *reciprocal* relationship between his sensibility and his acquirements which, in a state of what is commonly called *inspiration,* can attain a sort of possession, an almost perfect interchange and balance between desire and its satisfaction, between will and ability, idea and act, up to a point where this composite unity is resolved and ceases by its own excess, and the exceptional state of being which had formed itself from our senses, our energies, our ideals, our acquired gifts, disperses and undoes itself, abandoning us to our usual barter of *worthless moments* against *evanescent perceptions,* but leaving in its wake a fragment of something which could only have been acquired at a *time,* in a *world,* under a certain *pressure,* or thanks to a certain *temperature* of the mind quite other than those which can only contain and produce the *Nondescript* . . . (CW 12: 45–46; O 2: 1195)

Valéry continues the idea by emphasizing that these privileged moments when both interior and exterior forces merge in creative harmony are only fragments, and because of their brevity, it is unlikely that a whole work could be accomplished. When this "exalted inspiration" passes, "a good head is needed," remarks Valéry, "to make full use of inspiration, to master the happy chance, and bring things to a *finish*" (CW 12: 46; O 2: 1195).

The concept of "attributed inspiration" is particularly interesting because it goes beyond the poet to involve the reader in the creative process of experiencing a poem. What Ince calls "attributed inspiration" derives from Valéry's definition in "Poetry and Abstract Thought":

A poet's function—do not be startled by this remark—is not to experience the poetic state: that is a private affair. His function is to create it in others. The poet is recognized—or at least everyone recognizes his own poet—by the simple fact that he causes his reader to become "inspired." Positively speaking, inspiration is a graceful attribute with which the reader endows his poet: the reader sees in us the transcendent merits of virtues and graces that develop in him. He seeks and finds in us the wondrous cause of his own wonder. (CW 7: 60; O 1: 1321)

The description is reminiscent of Valéry's definition of a poem as "a machine for producing the poetic state of mind by means of words" (CW 7: 79; O 1: 1337), which derives from Poe's detailed account of calculated effect in *The Philosophy of Composition.* Valéry restates the idea of the reader's role in "Remarks on Poetry," saying that "inspiration belongs to and is meant for the reader, just as it is the poet's task to make one think of it, believe in it, to make sure that one attributes only to the gods a work that is too perfect or too moving to be the product of a man's uncertain hands" (CW 7: 215; O 1: 1378). Thus, the poet's role is to make the reader think the poem was created in a state of divine inspiration, a difficult task that can only be accomplished by conscious effort, in Valéry's view.

The sixth type of inspiration that Ince identifies in Valéry's creative development is "personal inspiration," the themes, emotions, and images that inspire the original qualities in his poetry. Valéry recognized as essential to every artist's work a certain view of the world that distinguishes him from others and motivates his creative endeavors. In "The Creation of Art" he states that every artist has conceptions that "provide the specialized acts of the artist with a kind of *metaphysical field* which orients them in such a way that movement in certain directions is facilitated and furthered, while in others it is obstructed and hindered . . . ." (CW 13: 118). Referring to his own experience, he remarks that at certain moments in his life he felt the effects of intellectual sensibility "violently enough to conceive the ambition of putting some part of it into literature" (CW 13: 119). He then describes the dominant theme of his poetry and other literary works that distinguish him from others:

I have wondered whether the efforts of the isolated intellect, its peculiar events, its joys and sorrows, its splendors and miseries, its grandeurs and servitudes, might not be represented through the medium of art. Up to now, when art has taken intellectual life as a subject, it has considered and portrayed the intellectual, the thinker, more than the intellect itself. But it seemed to me that the intelligence, in the exercise of its boundless investigations, aroused emotions which, despite their special tonality, were quite similar to those associated with the impressions we receive from the spectacles of nature, the events of emotional life, and matters of love or faith. This intellectual emotion is obviously less frequent than the other kinds. The art which captures and reproduces it can have only a limited appeal . . . . (CW 13: 119)

No other poet before or since Valéry has chosen as a dominant poetic theme the drama of the intellect, combined it with sensual images, and created a state of "charm." His fascination with the intellectual mechanism inspired him to "put into literature," as he says, the excitement and beauty he perceives in the operations of the mind. Poe remarks in *The Philosophy of Composition* that the death of a beautiful woman is "unquestionably the most poetical topic in the world" (T: 19; OP: 990). Valéry's "personal inspiration" has a different source: the intellect exercising its creative powers is for him the most poetic of all themes.

Valéry's early intransigent rejection of inspiration and great admiration for technique, which was confirmed in his reading of Poe, softened over the years as he continued to observe himself in the process of writing poetry. Although he never accepted the idea of "total inspiration," his observations on the subtle ways in which other forms of inspiration contribute to the creative process show how an initial influence can lead to unexpected results, in the sense here of producing a refined commentary on how inspiration operated in his own case. No other poet has described in such detail the role of various types of inspiration in the creation of poetry.

Another concept in Valéry's poetics that is linked directly to Poe is his notion of "pure poetry." Valéry's first use of this term is traced to a preface he wrote for a collection of poems by Lucien Fabre.[13] In the first part of his essay Valéry reflects upon the true object of poetry, which, he believes, has never been made clear. Because there is no consensus on what poetry is, a great variety of works in verse fall into this category. Valéry describes works that belong to the didactic or historical order, such as the *Aeneid* and *The Divine Comedy*, adding the comment that these works could have been treated in prose. They can be translated without loss of meaning, he adds, and we can "break them into separate moments of our attention" (CW 7: 40; O 1: 1270). This discussion brings to mind Poe's description of *Paradise Lost* in his essay *The Poetic Principle*. "This great work," remarks Poe, "in fact, is to be regarded as poetical only when, losing sight of that vital requisite in all works of Art, Unity, we view it merely as a series of minor poems" (T: 71). In his view, "a poem deserves its title only inasmuch as it excites, by elevating the soul" (T: 71). This degree of excitement cannot be maintained throughout a long poem, and is found in alternation with what Poe calls "depression." Poe then makes a statement that inspired Valéry's notion of "pure poetry": "After a passage of what we feel to be true poetry, there follows, inevitably, a passage of platitude which no critical pre-judgment can force us to admire" (T: 71). These moments of "true poetry" became Valéry's ideal of "poetry in its purest state."

In his essay Valéry, again like Poe, describes poems that have a didactic or historical intention. He then credits Poe with being the first to move poetry away from utilitarian purposes:

> Finally, toward the middle of the nineteenth century, we see asserting itself in our literature a remarkable will to isolate Poetry once and for all from every other essence than itself. Such a preparation of poetry in its pure state had been accurately predicted and advocated by Edgar Poe. It is therefore not surprising to see in Baudelaire the beginnings of this struggle toward a perfection that is concerned only with itself. (CW 7: 40; O 1: 1270)

For Valéry, "poetry in its purest state" means not only that it is free from all didactic or moralizing elements but also that through the harmony of its form and meaning it produces a state of charm or enchantment that has no other reason to exist except its own beauty. As Poe mentions, poems vary in the amount of "true poetry" they contain, a point Valéry makes in his essay "Contemporary Poetry":

> This is the great problem in our art: in some measure to prolong the happiness of a moment. There are happy minutes for everyone; no work is without its beauties. But I know of nothing rarer than a composition of some length—say a hundred lines—in which there are no inconsistencies and irregularities. (CW 7: 193)[14]

His concept of "pure poetry" remained an ideal that was realized occasionally but never sustained throughout an entire poem.

In a rather strange set of circumstances, Valéry's ideal of "pure poetry" became the center of an intense debate between two of his ardent admirers, the critic Paul Souday and the priest-critic-writer Henri Bremond, both of whom quote Poe to support their opposing views. The controversy started on October 24, 1925, when Bremond presented a lecture at the Académie Française on the subject of "Pure Poetry," which began with the following statement: "The modern theoreticians of pure poetry, Edgar Poe, Baudelaire, Mallarmé and Mr. Paul Valéry are not the dangerous innovators that one seems to believe."[15] Retracing briefly the history of poetics, Bremond argues that poets have always sought to recreate in their work a mysterious charm. The predecessor of the modern theory of "pure poetry," he claims, was the eighteenth century Jesuit, Father Rapin, who first described the "secret grace" and "the imperceptible charms" that distinguish poetry from prose. These special qualities seem to have a divine origin and are not the creation of the conscious mind. "To reduce poetry to the methods of rational knowledge," remarks Bremond, "is to go against its very nature, it's like trying to square the circle."[16] As for the role of music, Bremond argues that the verbal music found in poetry is an incantation that results not in pure pleasure but in a sort of divine communication through the "mysterious fluid" ("le fluide mystérieux") that it transmits.[17] He defines the concept of "pure poetry" in a religious sense: "Every poem owes its poetic character to the dissemination of the transforming and unifying action of a mysterious reality that we call pure poetry."[18] All the arts, concludes Bremond, "aspire to join prayer."[19]

Connecting "pure poetry" and religion provoked the ire of Paul Souday, who ridiculed Bremond's lecture in the newspaper *Le Temps*.[20] Bremond responded with a series of articles titled "Clarifications" ("Eclaircissements") published in *Les Nouvelles Littéraires* between October 31, 1925 and January 16, 1926.[21] Three aspects of this literary debate interest us here: the references to Poe in the arguments of both critics to support their positions, the fact that the controversy started in the hallowed halls of the Académie Française and ended up in two New York newspapers, and Valéry's attempt to settle the matter by explaining in detail his concept of the term *pure poetry*, which derives from Poe's use of the term in *The Poetic Principle*.

Bremond was particularly annoyed that Souday published his most scathing attack on him in the American press. In *The New York Times Book Review* of November 29, 1925,[22] Souday called Bremond a "pure mystic" for whom reason is a *bête noire*. Souday goes on to clarify a major point: "it is true that the theory of pure poetry was developed first in modern times. But that was not by

Father Rapin, nor any other Jesuit: it was by Edgar Allan Poe." Addressing an American audience in his article, Souday remarks "as you know" the concept of "pure poetry" derives from *The Poetic Principle*, in which Poe "protests against the 'didactic heresy' and particularly against moralism, which is a heresy in itself." Souday accuses Bremond of treating reason like a personal enemy and relying solely upon divine inspiration. Ridiculing Bremond's conclusion that pure poetry consists of a "mysterious fluid," Souday offers a more down-to-earth definition: "What gives words their poetic value is not such electro-magnetic 'currents'; it is the immaterial, rational harmony of verbal music and of thought, as Poe so transcendently realized."

The great debate on "pure poetry" continued for several years with Souday's essays in *Le Temps*, Bremond's counterattacks in *Les Nouvelles Littéraires*, and other critics getting into the act by siding with one or the other or by making fun of both. At one point Bremond becomes melodramatic, if not comic, when he states: "As for Valéry, we will call him in, knife in hand the next time, and have him choose between Edgar Poe and Souday."[23] Taking pen in hand rather than a knife, Valéry clarified his own position in an essay titled "Pure Poetry," which was published first in English translation in the *New York Herald Tribune* on April 15, 1928. In his opening comment, Valéry makes reference to the debate among critics: "There is a great stir in the world (I mean in the world of the most precious and useless things), there is a great stir in the world about these two words: *pure poetry*. I have some responsibility for this stir" (CW 7: 184; O 1: 1456). In an attempt to settle the matter, Valéry wrote one of his best essays on poetics. The points he makes bear a close resemblance to Poe's arguments in *The Poetic Principle*. Valéry emphasizes that works of literature contain fragments that are poetic, elements that are distinct from the ordinary use of language and that have a singular effect on the reader. Like Poe, Valéry observes that "what we call a *poem* is in practice composed of fragments of pure poetry embedded in the substance of discourse" (CW 7: 185; O 1: 1457). Agreeing with what Poe called the "heresy of the Didactic," Valéry points out that "pure poetry" has nothing to do with moral purity; he uses the word "pure" with the same meaning as Poe, that is, "pure of all nonpoetic elements" (CW 7: 185; O 1: 1457). Valéry points out that "pure poetry" is an ideal that might best be expressed by the term a*bsolute poetry*, thus eliminating any moral connotation. He then defines this concept as

a search for the effect resulting from the relations between words, or rather the relations of the overtones of words among themselves, which suggests, in short, *an exploration of that whole domain of sensibility which is governed by language*. This exploration is made gropingly. . . . But it is not impossible that it may one day be carried out systematically. (CW 7: 186; O 1: 1458)

In Poe's literary essays, Valéry recognized both the goal of "absolute poetry" (what Poe calls "true poetry") and the systematic efforts of the poet to realize this ideal.

In the second part of "Pure Poetry" Valéry treats another theme found in *The Poetic Principle,* the role of music in poetry. Poe remarks that "it is in Music, perhaps, that the soul most nearly attains the great end for which, when inspired by the Poetic Sentiment, it struggles—the creation of supernal Beauty" (T: 78). Valéry describes the difficult task of the poet, who must fine-tune his "crude instrument," language, in order to create "his machine for producing the poetic emotion" (CW 7: 191; O 1: 1463). The musician, on the contrary, already has before him well-defined elements that do not have a multitude of meanings and connotations. The poet is faced with a paradoxical problem: he must endow ordinary language with musical qualities. Valéry defines "pure poetry" as an ideal creation in which non-poetical elements are eliminated and music is attained:

If the poet could manage to construct works in which nothing of prose ever appeared, poems in which the musical continuity was never broken, in which the relations between meanings were themselves perpetually similar to harmonic relations, *in which the transmutation of thoughts into each other appeared more important than any thought,* in which the play of figures contained the reality of the subject—then one could speak of *pure poetry* as of something that existed. (CW 7: 192; O 1: 1463)

This ideal cannot be consistently realized, concludes Valéry, because of the pragmatic nature of language, the irrationality found in its vocabulary, and the difficulty in according sound and meaning. Nonetheless, "pure poetry" represented for him, as it did for Poe, "an ideal boundary of the poet's desires, efforts, and powers . . . ." (CW 7: 192; O 1: 1463).

It is evident in the above passage that Valéry's concept of "pure poetry" is closely related to music, which he considered to be the purest art form. At the age of eighteen he had been impressed by Poe's remarks on poetry and music in *The Poetic Principle*, where he read that man's thirst to experience Beauty beyond the grave can only be quenched, according to Poe, "*through* the poem, or *through* the music," which reveals "brief and indeterminate glimpses" of that Beauty (T: 77). Continuing the association between poetry and music Poe writes:

> We are often made to feel, with a shivering delight, that from an earthly harp are stricken notes which *cannot* have been unfamiliar to the angels. And thus there can be little doubt that in the union of Poetry with Music in its popular sense, we shall find the widest field for the Poetic development. (T: 78)

His definition of poetry as "the Rythmical Creation of Beauty" was adopted by Valéry, who applied musical techniques to a much finer and subtler degree than Poe had ever imagined. Already in his first article "On Literary Technique," Valéry proposes a musical device that is much more complex than the one Poe describes in *The Philosophy of Composition:*

> Let us suppose that instead of a single, monotonic refrain, several are introduced, and that each character, each landscape, each state of mind has its own; that they are successively recognizable; that at the end of the piece of verse or prose all those known signs flow together to form what has been called the *melodic torrent*, and that the terminal effect is the fruit of the opposition and encounter of this meeting of refrains—then we arrive at the conception of the *Leitmotiv* or dominant theme, which is the basis of Wagnerian musical theory. (CW 7: 321; O 1: 1811)

Valéry makes the connection between Poe and Wagner ten years later in a *Notebook* entry, where he praises Wagner for perfecting a system of correspondences in music by linking subject, drama, and sensations. In the next paragraph Valéry remarks that "Poe, Rimbaud, and Mallarmé opened the way for finding new technical means to make the leitmotiv possible in literature" (C 1: 800). It was Wagner's search for a method based on calculating the effect upon the listener that linked him to Poe in Valéry's mind.

The musical device that Valéry developed to the most subtle degree is modulation. Lloyd J. Austin examines the application of this device in several of Valéry's poems, most notably in *The Young Fate*.[24] Modulation is the leitmotiv of the poem, as Valéry confirmed when he described *The Young Fate* as "an endless research into the possibility of attempting in poetry something analogous to what in music is called 'modulation'" (CW 7: 111; O 1: 1473). The central theme, as described by the poet, is "the depiction of a sequence of psychological substitutions, and . . . the changes in a consciousness during the course of a night" (O 1: 1621–22). The creation of the poem began as a decasyllabic rhythm in a given stanza form. Musical devices were applied at two levels, as Valéry explains in his *Notebooks*: "First the musical sequence of syllables and lines—and then in the shifting and substitutions of idea-images—themselves following the states of consciousness and sensibility of the *Speaker*" (C 29: 92). Transitions from one idea to another are carried out through modulation used as a poetic device.

Brian Stimpson's detailed study *Paul Valéry and Music* gives an extraordinarily thorough examination of how Valéry uses techniques derived from music in his poetry, including melody, harmonics, and rhythm. Stimpson's analysis of Valéry's poem "The Sleeper" ("La Dormeuse") reveals a number of musical devices concentrated in a short poem. "Music is the single most important factor in Valéry's poetry," remarks Stimpson; "it is both the goal by which the poetic ideal is defined and the means by which it is attained in composition."[25] Valéry's definitions and applications of musical techniques go far beyond Poe's general comments in his literary essays.

For Valéry, melody in poetry is associated with theme or image. "Melody is an organized expectation," he remarked in his *Notebooks* (C 12: 705). He uses the expression "melody of a poem" to describe the structure of a poem's themes. Like a composer to whom part of a melody comes easily and then the rest must be developed through conscious effort, the poet too often works from a fragment he hears that must be fleshed out to form the basic structure of the poem. "To find a line of poetry, a melody, is to listen, to wait. And then—one always receives" (C 6: 651), observes Valéry. By comparing different versions of Valéry's poem "The Footsteps" ("Les Pas"), Stimpson shows how the melody of the poem evolved as the theme emerged. He suggests that the beautiful opening lines of the poem "were felt to be a melodic development which needed a reason or justification."[26] As the melody or theme of the poem evolves, a countermelody appears, and throughout the poem the two oppose and then unite in the last stanza.

Harmony as an analogous device in poetry is much more complex, as Stimpson points out:

Musical harmony depends upon the possibility of combining notes simultaneously and forming a sequence from these combinations of sounds; but the words of a poem are not notes which are actually sounded at the same time as each other and this crucial distinction must be recognized from the outset.[27]

Valéry uses the concept of harmony in several different ways. For him, the term refers to the relationships among the different parts of the poem, to the different levels of meaning of individual words, and to the poetic images produced by the timbre of the sounds. The building up of associations was an essential device for the Symbolist poets, especially for Mallarmé and Valéry. The ideal of "pure poetry" would be realized for Valéry when all the elements of the poem achieve perfection in their harmonic relationships. Through a detailed analysis of "The Pythoness" ("La Pythie"), Stimpson shows how Valéry applied harmonics to the creation of the poem.

The importance of rhythm in Valéry's poetry is evident in his preference for regular verse forms. "The regularity of form," remarks Stimpson, "allows a sense of pulse against which the poet may establish the rhythmic variations."[28] There is a kind of tension between the two which gives Valéry's mature poetry its sense of rhythmic vitality. Stimpson goes on to show that rhythm in Valéry's poetry is not simply a matter of counting syllables. Rhythm plays a major role in structuring the entire poem; it involves movement, ideas, and relationships between stanzas. Valéry understood the complexity of the concept that appears to be the most evident musical device. He remarked in "Problems of Poetry": "I have read or invented twenty definitions of *Rhythm* and have adopted none of them" (CW 7: 93; O 1: 1289). Although the term is difficult to define, rhythm is an essential part of the poetic process for Valéry. As mentioned earlier, "The Graveyard by the Sea" came to him first as a "rhythmic figure, empty, or filled with meaningless syllables" (CW 7: 148; O 1: 1503). Stimpson sees an evolution in Valéry's rhythmic style from his poems published in *Album of Earlier Verse* to those composed during the period 1917–22, especially the complex rhythm used to change moods in *The Young Fate.*

Titles of Valéry's poetic works reveal his preoccupation with music. *Charmes,* derived from the latin *carmen,* suggests "magical music," and the titles of poems in this and other collections are related to music, for example, "Aria for Semiramis," "Song of the Columns," "Colloquy (for two flutes)," and "Song Sotto Voce." Although Valéry did not play a musical instrument, his understanding and application of "the purest art form" are remarkable. As in the case of inspiration, the idea of music in poetry, described in Poe's literary essays, impressed Valéry early in his career and became the focus of his meditations for many years. Valéry's application of musical elements in his own poetry produced works of extraordinary originality.

In *The Philosophy of Composition* Poe describes the careful consideration given to the selection of the word that he used in the refrain in "The Raven," the famous "nevermore." The expression forming the close of each stanza, he calculated, "must be sonorous and susceptible of protracted emphasis." These considerations led him to choose "the long *o* as the most sonorous vowel in connection with *r* as the most producible consonant" (T: 18; OP: 989). Thus, the creation of "The Raven," as Poe recounts it in his essay, began with the considerations of form and then proceeded to content. First came the idea of a refrain, then the specific sounds, followed by the selection of a word containing the desired vowel and consonant. The word "nevermore" suggesting to him a melancholy tone, Poe was led to the theme of death, which, he states, is the most melancholy when allied with Beauty. He then arrived at the theme of his poem, the death of a beautiful woman, the "most poetic topic in the world," in his view.

Valéry was very impressed by the importance Poe gave to form, although he was not convinced that "The Raven" was written as described. What he discovered in Poe's essay was a poet who did not see poetry as an idea set in verse. The relationships between sound and meaning, form and content, and prose and poetry preoccupied Valéry from the very beginning of his writing career, and he often referred to these oppositions when talking about his own creative endeavors.

The most basic tenet of Valéry's poetics is the symbiosis of sound and sense. In his "Course on *Poetics*" he emphasizes the importance of these indissoluble elements: "The great problem is to control the sensuous art and the significative construction like two independent horses. The poet must drive both sound and sense, the phonetic variable and the semantic variable."[29] This inseparability originates in the poet's mind at the moment of the poem's conception. As Valéry remarks in his description of the genesis of "The Graveyard by the Sea," "There is not one time for the 'content,' another for the 'form'" (CW 7: 150; O 1: 1505). The poet does not start with an idea he wishes to develop and then find the poetic elements to express this concept. The two must come together simultaneously and complement each other, not an easy task to accomplish, as Valéry points out:

The value of a poem resides in the indissolubility of the sound and the sense. Now this is a condition which seems to demand the impossible. There is no relation between the sound and the meaning of a word. . . .
    Yet it is the poet's business to give us the feeling of an intimate union between the word and the mind. (CW 7: 74; O 1: 1333)

Valéry believed that Poe was a writer who made it his business to discover the links between the sonorous quality of words and the effects they produce on the mind.

In reaction to the emphasis too often placed on the *ideas* expressed in poems, Valéry goes to the opposite extreme by drawing attention to the importance of form. On the one hand, he detests grand eloquence because, as he says, "the form refutes the content" (CW 14: 184; O 2: 616). On the other, the lack of embellishment, which allows the idea to come through in its clearest form, is characteristic of prose, the essence of which is "to perish—that is, to be 'understood'—that is, to be dissolved, destroyed without return, entirely replaced by the image or the impulse that it conveys according to the convention of language" (CW 7: 146; O 1: 1501). In poetry, the form must suggest the content but not overpower it. Valéry expresses this idea with a beautiful analogy:

Thought must be hidden in verse like the nutritive essence in fruit. It is nourishing but seems merely delicious. One perceives pleasure only, but one receives substance. Enchantment, that is the nourishment it conveys. (CW 7: 179; O 1: 1452)

Drawing from his own experience, he recalls the delight of discovering a pleasing rhythm, which, through a great deal of patience and labor, led to the thought of his poem. Speaking of the genesis of *The Young Fate,* he remarks, "Another poem began merely with the hint of a rhythm, *which gradually acquired a meaning*" (CW 7: 111; O 1: 1474). The form gave birth to the content and was a stimulus to conscious work that led to the completion of the poem. From a negative point of view, Valéry observes: "The 'subject' of a work is what a bad one finally boils down to" (CW 14: 239; O 2: 679). While the content can be paraphrased, it is the form that gives the poem its unique quality and duration. Speaking of literary works, Valéry remarks: "Form is their skeleton; but some works have none. All works die, but those that had a skeleton last much longer, thanks to its survival, than ones that were soft all through" (CW 14: 238; O 2: 679). Valéry reverses the common order of priorities by declaring: "What is 'form' for anyone else is 'content' for me" (CW 7: 183; O 1: 1456). The "subject" of a poem is not only the thought it expresses but also all of the acoustical effects that make its expression possible.

Poe's definition of poetry as the "Rhythmical creation of Beauty," as realized through the musical effects of language, made a deep impression on Valéry at a time when poetry was making a transition from the intensely personal expression of the Romantics

to the disordered world of the Surrealists. For Valéry, poetry was
not a vehicle for conveying his deepest sentiments to an unknown
public. He strongly believed that order and strict adherence to traditional verse forms lead to perfection of the highest order, thus he
was not tempted by the many experiments in modes of verse
emerging around the turn of the century. He saw the poet's role as
one of imposing order to create a greater beauty, an idea he links
to Poe's conception:

The poet recreates the world (like a Domain of Arnheim) by way of unique
and various rhythms. He evokes the perfect Man dancing in a pure landscape and uttering magnificent words to a divine music.[30]

Poetry is above all enchantment achieved through the magical use
of ordinary language. "Poets have forgotten," says Valéry, "that
they practice the craft of a singer. Some of them have taken it to be
the craft of an orator—the rest, nothing" (CW 1: 406; C 19: 124).
As Poe points out in *The Poetic Principle*, the purpose of poetry is not
to instruct or to inculcate a moral, for which prose suffices.
Rejecting the idea that the ultimate objective of poetry is Truth, Poe
remarks in reference to the latter: "All *that* which is so indis-
pensable in Song is precisely all *that* with which *she* has nothing
whatever to do" (T: 76). Valéry takes up Poe's idea and elaborates:
"The poem is not related to *truth*; but the poet's act, his plan, his
work, the arrangement of his illogical fantasies, owe everything to
logic, which has judged and judged well *in secret*" (CW 1: 399; C 7:
154). By emphasizing the words "logic" and "in secret" Valéry is
thinking in terms of Poe's description in *The Philosophy of Composition* of the drama that takes place in the poet's mind, "the machine
behind the mask," the calculating mechanism that creates the
enchantment.

   This "myth of creation," as Valéry calls the poet's act of making
something from nothing, became the dominant theme of his own
poetry. The creative work progressing little by little, the struggle,
the pleasures, the anticipation, the patient waiting, all are part of
the mental drama that Valéry represents through his poetry.
Several of the shorter poems in *Charmes* show Valéry's preoccupation with the drama of sensation and conceptual awareness.[31] The

first poem in the collection, "Dawn" ("Aurore"), written in hepta-
syllables, is a hymn singing the praises of a new day commenc-
ing, while at the same time it can be enjoyed as the song of the
conscious mind awakening to its own capabilities, including expression through language.   The octosyllabic sonnet "Pomegran-
ates" ("Les Grenades") makes a striking analogy between the
ripening of the sumptuous fruit and the poet's mind bursting with
thoughts coming to fruition.   In "Palm" ("Palme"), the last poem
in the collection, we find the image of the growing tree enriched
through the loss of its fruit in the same way the poet's mind is
enriched by its own creations.   These brief examples, and there are
many others, give an idea of the originality of Valéry's poetry in
which the drama of consciousness is represented through sensuous
images.   After describing how he wrote "The Graveyard by the
Sea," Valéry remarked: "Yet the sole thought of constructions of
this kind remains for me the most *poetic* of ideas: the idea of
composition" (CW 7: 149; O 1: 1504).   Valéry goes a step farther
than Poe.   Not only did he observe himself while writing a poem,
the creative process itself became the theme of his poetry.

Contrary to his predecessors Baudelaire and Mallarmé, Valéry
expressed no enthusiasm for Poe's poems.   Evidence that the poems
made any impression on him at all is rare.   A passage in Valéry's
"Rhumbs" suggests that he was familiar with Poe's poem "The
Bells":

Bells, the bells of Genoa! "Ting-tee-rin," they say. "Ting-tong/ . . . /Tong/
. . . / /and I sit here, my eyes glued on the bell that's ringing just over there,
a hundred yards away, I have turned my head, my hand still holding the pen
ready—for what? Emptiness. Nothing is left but an intention, an impulse, a
wraith of writing. But writing *what?* The wall calls back my gaze to its
checkerboard. . . .

Ting/tee-rin/ting-tong. Those bells don't count the hours but sing them.
Liquidly, with an endlessly cloying sweetness, the notes trickle through the
air. Shrill notes and deep—on all the floors of space—as if the air, peopled
with presences, were scratching itself, itching with sounds that have lodged in
it, picking out its fleas.

An atmosphere golden with music; a chord stretched tight; myth of the
soul. (CW 14: 162; O 2: 599–600)

The onomatopoetic repetition, the different timbres, the changing moods, and the gradually overwhelming sound are all reminiscent of Poe's poem.

In a *Notebook* entry Valéry mentions Poe's poem "Ulalume" in the context of a dream he imagines. He looks out the window and tries to discover himself in the night sky. Recognizing familiar constellations, he does not see himself in them. Then he observes: "Other constellations—unknown to those who look, but well known in my heart—I knew which ones they were. I knew marvelously well this sky. There "Hérodiade" shone. There the pale "Ulalume" (C 8: 441). These poems by Mallarmé and Poe were shining examples of what he wanted to accomplish.

Valéry refers to "The Raven" in his early essay "On Literary Technique," praising the use of the refrain and the frequent alliterations, citing specifically the line "And the Raven, never flitting, still sitting, still is sitting" (CW 7: 319; O 1: 1810). But we find nothing like the encomiums that accompany Mallarmé's translations of Poe's poems or Baudelaire's imitations of certain images and lines of Poe's verse.

In order to discover a direct connection between Poe and Valéry's poetry we must look elsewhere, to the tales, one of which inspired a poem in the collection *Various Poems of All Periods.* Valéry's little-known poem "Disaster" ("Sinistre") draws part of its inspiration from Poe's long sea narrative *The Adventures of Arthur Gordon Pym.* On one of the early manuscripts of the poem Valéry wrote the notation "Gordon Pym." The conception, composition, and publication of the poem cover a span of fifty years. James Lawler, who studied the early manuscripts and revealed the direct connection with Poe's work, believes Valéry's poem was conceived in the early 1890s and possibly composed in 1909.[32] The date October 4–5, 1917, written on another manuscript, indicates that the poet worked again on the piece during his most intense period of poetic creation. The poem was published for the first time in 1939 and later included in a 1942 edition, *Various Poems of All Periods.*[33]

The opening stanza of "Disaster" brings to mind Poe's description of Pym as he lay in the hold of the whaling ship *Grampus* during a violent storm:[34]

What hour hurtles at the staves of the hull
That knock of darkness on which our fate cracks?
What force untouchable plays the castanets
In our tackle with a dead man's bones?

Quelle heure cogne aux membres de la coque
Ce grand coup d'ombre où craque notre sort?
Quelle puissance impalpable entre-choque
Dans nos agrès des ossements de mort?

The reference to the ship's hull in the first line is central to the theme of self seen as a victim of the elements. In Lawler's view, it introduces the allegorical contrast between dependence and self-reliant lucidity, one of Valéry's favorite underlying themes. The asymmetrical rhythm of the first line and the repetition of the plosive /k/ in the French version evoke the violence of the terrifying moment. After the second stanza describes the storm in more detail, the third and fourth focus inward toward the narrator, whose consciousness of imminent death inspires revolt:

Atrocious man, your heart within capsizing,
Drunkard, foreigner, astray on the sea
Whose nausea coupled to the ship
Wrenches from the soul a longing for hell,

Total man, I shudder and calculate,
Brain too lucid, capable of this moment
Where, within a phenomenal microcosm
Time is shattered like an instrument . . .

Homme hideux, en qui le coeur chavire,
Ivrogne étrange égaré sur la mer
Dont la nausée attachée au navire
Arrache à l'âme un désir de l'enfer.

Homme total, je tremble et je calcule,
Cerveau trop clair, capable du moment
Où, dans un phénomène minuscule,
Le temps se brise ainsi qu'un instrument . . .

Death and time once seized by the lucid mind seem less menacing. In the fifth stanza the speaker now condemns the structure he once held dear:

> A curse on that swine who rigged you out,
> Ark of rottenness with your moldering ballast,
> In your black holds, every created thing
> Rattles on your dead timbers drifting East . . .

> Maudit soit-il le porc qui t'a gréée,
> Arche pourrie en qui grouille le lest!
> Dans tes fonds noirs, toute chose créée
> Bat ton bois mort en dérive vers l'Est . . .

The image here, in Lawler's view, seems to be inspired by Poe's description of Pym: "The ballast now shifted in a mass to leeward (the storage had been knocking about perfectly at random for some time) and for a few moments we thought nothing could save us from capsizing."[35] The poem's narrator has to muster his inner qualities to resist the buffeting from the elements. Memories of the past fill the speaker's mind in the sixth stanza, but he does not give in to sentimentality. The realistic details of these lines contrast with the dramatic final stanza which is a mystical vision reminiscent of Pym's hallucinations. The figure of Christ bound to the mast is an unusual image in Valéry's poetry:

> I see Christ roped to the yardarm!
> Dancing to death, foundering with his herd;
> His bloodshot eye lights me to this exergue:
> A GREAT SHIP GONE DOWN WITH ALL ON BOARD! . . .

> Je vois le Christ amarré sur la verge! . . .
> Il danse à mort, sombrant avec les siens;
> Son oeil sanglant m'éclaire cet exergue:
> UN GRAND NAVIRE A PERI CORPS ET BIENS! . . .

The macabre scene suggests a loss of faith rather than an illumination, a point Lawler makes by comparing the image to the drowning of the poet's personal "idols." The critic sees in the poem an allegorical ballad treating one of Valéry's most original themes:

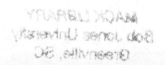

a tragic event of the intellectual sensibility. In the violence and drama of the poem we recognize the dramatic event of 1892, when Valéry came face to face with the death of his former self. "The ocean of the mind," remarks Lawler, "in its frightening depths, is precisely what we discover in Valéry's poem; and the one way of being its master, . . . was to adopt a stance brutally opposed to the 'silliness' that had taken him to the brink of suicide."[36] Although references in the *Notebooks* show that Valéry attempted many times to scrutinize the major turning point in his life, Lawler believes that Valéry's approach "is nowhere as charged with personal meaning as it is in 'Sinistre' ("Disaster")."[37]

There is one particular passage in the *Notebooks* in which Valéry describes his contempt for earlier idols that is suggested by the "rotten hulk" in the poem. The following passage also contains a reference to an enlightenment coming from Poe that emerged after the drowning of Valéry's former intellectual models:

There arose in me, about 1892, a certain scorn for poetry and poets, due to the intellectual weaknesses I found in most of them, even the most famous. I noted on the one hand that they lived on a capital of ideas that was miserably common and naive (so that a poet of the year 1000 B.C is still readable) and that they did not exercise all the powers of the mind; that they were ignorant of the *imaginative* developments we owe to the sciences, that is, to organized thought. Besides, their craft itself had made no advance in the way of perfection—that is, poetic continuity and composition—as music had done, with its technical progress from the sixteenth century to our time. A sentence from Poe's "Arnheim" had given me much to think about. (CW 1: 409; C 23: 273)

The shipwreck of his earlier beliefs was replaced by an optimism based on a scientific approach to creative endeavors and by the goal of perfection in artistic creation, both of which were inspired by his reading of Poe. Although "Disaster" climaxes in death, we know that it was followed by a resurrection of the poet's mind when he begins the quest for intellectual self-comprehension expressed in "Agatha," another of Valéry's creative endeavors influenced by one of Poe's sea narratives.

Valéry found Poe's literary theory much more interesting than his poetry. In his essay "From Poe to Valéry" T. S. Eliot states that "for Valéry the poetry of Poe is inseparable from Poe's poetic theories."[38]   There is no evidence in Valéry's published work or the *Notebooks* to support this statement, which Eliot does not elucidate. Valéry's numerous references to Poe's poetics are not linked in any way to examples in the poems, and certainly not in the manner that Valéry illustrates his poetic theory with references to his own poems.   In the same essay Eliot discusses the general influence of Poe's tales without any mention of a connection with Valéry's *Monsieur Teste*, "Agatha," or the poem "Disaster."   Eliot does allude to the importance of Poe's concept of "pure poetry" and the development of consciousness of language, both of which played a major role in Valéry's thinking.

Poe's description of the poet observing himself during the act of creating a poem became an obsession for Valéry and inspired the theme of much of his poetry.   Valéry even goes beyond Poe's idea that "the poem should have nothing in view but itself"; writing poems was for Valéry an exercise in observing his own consciousness.   Eliot sees a danger in Valéry's pursuit:

And, as for the future: it is a tenable hypothesis that this advance of self-consciousness, the extreme awareness of and concern for language which we find in Valéry, is something which must ultimately break down, owing to an increasing strain against which the human mind and nerves will rebel.[39]

In one sense Eliot was right.   As a poet, Valéry has many admirers but no imitators.   He carried Poe's idea of intellectual self-consciousness as far as it can go by making it a theme of both his poetry and prose fiction.   In Valéry's masterpiece of poetic self-awareness, *The Young Fate*, there is a possible connection with Poe's *Eureka*, which we will examine in the next chapter.

CHAPTER SIX

"On Poe's Eureka *"*

IN THE BEGINNING WAS FABLE.
It will be there always.
                    —Valéry, "On Poe's *Eureka*"

After reading and commenting on Poe's work for over thirty
years, Valéry wrote his only essay devoted entirely to his literary
mentor in 1921 at the age of fifty. He chose as subject one of Poe's
most difficult and lesser-known creations, the long "prose poem"
Eureka. Valéry's commentary, "On Poe's *Eureka*," was written as
the Introduction to a new edition of Baudelaire's translation of
Poe's cosmogony.[1] It was because of Baudelaire's determination to
make the work known in France that Valéry read *Eureka* as a
young man.

Although Baudelaire doubted that Poe's cosmological essay
would interest French readers, his initial hesitations were overcome by an unrelenting devotion, spurred on perhaps by Poe's preface, which offers the book "to the few who love me." A more practical reason for the effort was Baudelaire's dire need to earn translator's fees after the disappointing sales of his own collection of poems, *The Flowers of Evil*, in 1857. He managed to sell the translation of *Eureka* to a Geneva publication, the *Revue internationale*, which
ran it as a serial in 1859 before going out of business at the end of
the year, leaving the final installment unpublished. Discouraged
by the obscure fate to which *Eureka* seemed to be doomed,
Baudelaire convinced his editor Michel Lévy to publish it along
with a collection of the tales. The lack of interest in *Eureka* both-

ered Baudelaire a great deal, as can be seen in a letter to his mother, written December 31, 1863, in which he complains: "I've found a few people who have had the courage to read *Eureka.* The book will sell badly, but I should have expected that; it is too abstract for the French."[2] Baudelaire still persevered in his efforts to have the work reviewed by such notables as Taine, who refused to give it his critical attention. Finally, in 1864 an enthusiastic and perspicacious review came out in the *Moniteur,* written by Judith Gautier, daughter of the well-known writer Théophile Gautier, one of Baudelaire's old friends.[3] The project to translate *Eureka* and make it known in France had begun in 1856; Baudelaire devoted eight years to the work while his health declined more rapidly each year. Whether because of lack of time, strength, or inspiration we do not know, but Baudelaire mentioned apologetically that he could not devote an article to *Eureka* (OP: 1028). Valéry took up the task by writing the Introduction to the 1921 edition of the translation, thus paying homage to both Poe and Baudelaire.

Valéry was fascinated by the work, partly because it offered a challenge to his mind. He once remarked: "Nearly all the books I prize, and absolutely all that have been of any use to me, are books that don't make easy reading" (CW 14: 17; O 2: 483). He was reading *Eureka* in early 1892 before his intellectual crisis in the fall of that year, as he notes in a letter to Gide.[4] In an interview with Frédéric Lefèvre he remarked that his relationship with Mallarmé became closer after a discussion they had about *Eureka.*[5] Although Valéry does not mention a date, the conversation probably took place in 1894, when he met Mallarmé in Paris. Poe's cosmological poem continued to interest Valéry over the years. On June 24, 1901, Valéry mentions the work again to Gide:

I read *Eureka* to my boss.[6] I feel that perhaps I was wrong x years ago not to have written an article on Poe.[7] Now I have no desire to do it. Even so, Poe is unique. He is absolutely the only writer who had the intuition to link literature and the mind.[8]

Twenty more years passed before Valéry had the time and inspiration to write the *Eureka* essay, one of the earliest critical studies of the work in French or English.[9]

Valéry discovered an intellectual drama unparalleled in anything he had ever read. He was captivated by the idea that a certain truth of coherence could be discovered through poetic imagination coupled with scientific reasoning. Like Poe, Valéry too was
obsessed with logic, internal consistency, and universal laws. His
essay on *Eureka* reveals three modes of thinking, which we will
examine in detail. First, Valéry describes in a very personal style
how he discovered in Poe's "prose poem" the beauty of scientific
thought, which had never before been awakened in him because of
the drab way physics and mathematics had been presented to him
as a youth. Second, shifting to the ironic tone of a skeptic, Valéry
observes the "comedy of the intellect," imagining Poe's mind in
the process of creating his "supreme work." Third, Valéry responds to *Eureka* with his own creative thinking, speculating on
the limitations of human knowledge. He poses the same questions
that obsessed him in *Monsieur Teste* and in *Introduction to the Method
of Leonardo da Vinci*: "What is the potential of the human brain?"
"What are the limits of the mind?" "Can it discover universal
laws?"

Valéry was very impressed by Poe's scientific knowledge and
moved by the circumstances in which the poet tried to make his
work known to the public. In a lecture at the Collège de France
Valéry describes Poe reading *Eureka* to anyone willing to listen. It
was indeed difficult to find an attentive audience for his 143-page
explanation of the *"Physical, Metaphysical and Mathematical—of the
Material and Spiritual Universe:—of its Essence, its Origin, its Creation, its
Present Condition and its Destiny,"* which Poe announces as his theme.
First presented in a two-hour lecture entitled "The Cosmogony of
the Universe" at the New York Society Library on February 3, 1848,
Eureka was published later the same year in the Putnam edition.[10]
Poe considered it his "supreme work," as he explains in a letter to
Maria Clemm: "I have no desire to live since I have done 'Eur-
eka.' I could accomplish nothing more."[11] These words were
written just three months before his death on October 3, 1849.

Convinced that he had produced a masterpiece, Poe urged his
publisher to print fifty thousand copies. Out of the five hundred
copies of *Eureka* in the original printing only one-third had been
sold a year later. Reviewers expressed consternation, admiration,

and skepticism, as in the case of one writer who suggested that *Eureka* was perhaps a hoax perpetrated by the author of "A Descent into the Maelstrom."[12] One cause of consternation was the fact that the work defies the traditional divisions into literary genres. In the subtitles Poe refers to *Eureka* as "a Prose Poem" and "An Essay on the Material and Spiritual Universe," which he dedicated to the German scientist Alexander von Humboldt (1769–1859). As described in the Preface, the work is to be taken as a "Book of Truths," a "composition," an "Art-Product," a "Romance," or as a "Poem." The concluding sentence in the Preface states: "Nevertheless it is as a Poem that I wish this work to be judged after I am dead."[13] Many readers find the long scientific explanations more appropriate to an essay than to poetry.

As a warning to those who might be disconcerted by the ideas he intends to propose, Poe announces in his Introduction: "I shall be so rash, moreover, as to challenge the conclusions, and thus, in effect, to question the sagacity, of many of the greatest and most justly reverenced of men" (B: 7). He ridicules the methods of Aristotle and Bacon, saying that the sole use of inductive and deductive reasoning place strict and artificial limits on the intellect's powers. These restrictions have retarded the progress of science, which, Poe argues, makes its most important advances "by seemingly intuitive *leaps.*" Because of the "mental slavery" imposed by Aristotle and Bacon, their followers have failed to perceive "the broadest, the straightest and most available of all mere roads . . . the majestic highway of the *Consistent*" (B: 18). Scientific investigation was taken out of the hands of the "ground-moles" and given over to the "*only* true thinkers—to the generally-educated men of ardent imagination," such as Kepler and Laplace. Through the methods of these men of science, Poe arrives at his definition of "Consistency":

The Keplers, I repeat, speculate—theorize—and their theories are merely corrected—reduced—sifted—cleared, little by little, of their chaff or inconsistency—until at length there stands apparent an unencumbered *Consistency*—a consistency which the most stolid admit—because it *is* a consistency—to be an absolute and an unquestionable *Truth*.[14] (B: 19)

Poe compares the use of consistency to the operations of the cryptographers, who are able to solve the most complicated ciphers through guesses backed up by internal evidence. By this method, the great French Egyptologist Champollion deciphered the truths of the hieroglyphics that had remained a mystery for many centuries. Even the fact of gravitation, "the most momentous and sublime of *all* truths" was deduced from the laws of Kepler, and, Poe argues, "Kepler admitted that these laws he *guessed*" (B: 19). The point Poe wants to make so strongly is that the inductive and deductive routes cannot account for some of the greatest discoveries. He imagines Kepler explaining his discovery by saying "I grasped it with *my soul!*—I reached it through mere dint of *intuition*" (B: 20). Thus, intuition can go beyond logic but does not necessarily deny it. Instead of restricting the scientific intellect, reason must be used to support discoveries rather than limit them.

Having established his method and calling it "Consistency," Poe embarks on his explanation of the universe, its creation, the nature of its matter, and its destiny. As a starting point he proposes the *"Godhead,"* about which we know nothing. But with the aid of intuition, Poe makes what he calls "the sole absolute *assumption*" of his essay:

that what God originally created—that that Matter which, by dint of his Volition, he first made from his Spirit, or from Nihility, *could* have been nothing but Matter in its utmost conceivable state of — what?—of *Simplicity*? (B: 29)

The primordial particle, brought into existence by a divine act, is the basis on which Poe constructs his cosmogony: *"Oneness is a principle abundantly sufficient to account for the constitution, the existing phenomena and the plainly inevitable annihilation of at least the material Universe"* (B: 30). The makeup of the physical universe was effected "by *forcing* the originally and therefore normally *One* into the abnormal condition of *Many*" (B: 30). The diffusion of original unity produces divisibility, action, and reaction, with the forces of gravity causing attraction and electricity effecting repulsion. Poe then introduces consciousness and thought into his scheme:

Discarding now the two equivocal terms, "gravitation" and "electricity," let us adopt the more definite expressions "attraction" and "repulsion." The former is the body; the latter the soul; the one is the material; the other the spiritual, principle of the Universe. *No other principles exist.* (B: 37)

Once the Divine Act has completed the initial diffusion, there will be "a *satisfiable* tendency of the disunited atoms to return into *One.*" The unending process of expansion and contraction will continue "at every throb of the Heart Divine" (B: 139).

Before arriving at his conclusion, Poe gives a long explanation of Newtonian gravity, which, he asserts, enables us to account for nine-tenths of the Universal phenomena. This discussion is followed by a detailed account of Laplace's nebular theory, which Poe finds "beautifully true." It was Poe's descriptions of these discoveries that excited Valéry and sparked a desire to learn more about the sciences and mathematics.

In the opening paragraphs of his essay "On Poe's *Eureka*" Valéry recalls the strong impression Poe's work had made on him thirty years earlier. Valéry's readings in literature and philosophy bored him because of their lack of rigor while science held little attraction, at least as he had learned it in his high school days. "My studies under drab and dismal instructors," he remarks, "had led me to believe that science was not love. . . . I consigned mathematics to a species of tiresomely exact minds, incommensurable with my own" (CW 8: 162; O 1: 855). Discouraged by his weakness in mathematics, Valéry had already given up a youthful ambition to become a naval officer.[15] Poe's work acted upon him like a revelation that was to change his daily activities for the rest of his life. "In a few moments," recalls Valéry, "*Eureka* introduced me to Newton's law, the name of Laplace, the hypothesis he proposed, and the very existence of speculations and researches that were never mentioned to adolescents" (CW 8: 163; O 1: 856). A whole new intellectual world opened before him; he acquired an interest in the natural sciences that he pursued in his reading and mentions frequently in his *Notebooks.*

Revealing more than just factual information, *Eureka* communicated to Valéry a passion for the sciences that was to last a lifetime. Recalling this sudden conversion, Valéry remarks: "These sciences, so coldly taught, were founded and developed by men with a passionate interest in them. *Eureka* made me feel some of that passion" (CW 8: 163; O 1: 856). Poe's description of the intuitive leap followed up by verifiable facts fascinated him as an intellectual method. Thus, *Eureka* had an immediate effect on Valéry by awakening in him the desire to learn more about mathematics and the natural sciences on his own. His intellectual biography is marked by an obsessive attraction to mathematics that can be verified by perusing his *Notebooks,* starting in 1894 when there are numerous mathematical notations and formulas. During his law school days Valéry was tutored in mathematics by his close friend, the engineer Pierre Féline, but for the most part he was self-taught. After his intellectual crisis in 1892, he gave up reading literature and began to devour scientific works.

Valéry's extensive reading in the sciences after discovering *Eureka* is evident in *Introduction to the Method of Leonardo da Vinci.* This essay shows a particular fascination with the work of Michael Faraday (1791–1867), the British physicist and chemist who discovered the laws of electrolysis, the theory of electrostatics, and electromagnetic induction. Valéry sees a connection between the modern scientist and the Renaissance artist: "It was Faraday who discovered Leonardo's method as applied to the physical sciences" (CW 8: 57; O 1: 1194). Speaking again of Faraday, Valéry shows his familiarity with the works of the great French mathematicians:

After the glorious mathematical researches of Lagrange, d'Alembert, Laplace, Ampère and many others, he came forward with admirably bold concepts that were literally only the projection, in his imagination, of observed phenomena. (CW 8: 57; O 1: 1194)

Valéry admired Faraday's method of discovery, a leap of the imagination supported by verifiable facts, a concept similar to Poe's "Consistency" described in *Eureka.* Valéry was right in thinking that Faraday, like Leonardo, combined the powers of analogy of both scientist and artist. Faraday describes his approach to the study of the connections between magnetism, electricity, and light in a letter dated 1845:

You can hardly imagine how I am struggling to exert my poetical ideas just now for the discovery of analogies and remote figures respecting the earth, sun and all sorts of things—for I think that is the true way (corrected by judgment) to work out a discovery.[16]

Faraday's reference here to the "true way (corrected by judgment) to work out a discovery" is strikingly similar to Poe's definition of "Consistency," an affinity that certainly was not lost on Valéry.

Continuing his digression into modern science in the Leonardo essay, Valéry also reveals his knowledge of the works of James Clerk Maxwell (1831–79), known for his electromagnetic theory of light, and of Lord Kelvin (William Thomson, 1824–1907), honored for his work in solar energy, electricity, and electromagnetism. Not only was Valéry impressed by their discoveries, he was obsessed with finding out the intellectual method that led to them:

Such men seem to have had an intuitive grasp of the methods discussed in this essay. We might even permit ourselves to extend those methods beyond the physical sciences; and we believe that it would be neither absurd nor entirely impossible to create a model of the continuity of the intellectual operations of a Leonardo da Vinci, or of any other mind, determined by the analysis of the conditions to be fulfilled. (CW 8: 59–60; O 1: 1196)

Valéry's discussion of method then leads to a specific mention of Poe, who "established his reader's approach on the basis of psychology and probable effects" (CW 8: 61–62; O 1: 1197). "From that point of view," remarks Valéry, "every combination of elements made to be perceived and judged depends on a few general laws and on a particular adaptation" (CW 8: 62; O 1: 1197–98). He believed that Poe approached science with the mind of a poet, while at the same time bringing scientific method to the creation of literature.

The effect of *Eureka* on Valéry's intellectual pursuits was major. His love of science is evident in the innumerable analogies and references in his published works and in the *Notebooks*, which reveal his knowledge of mathematics, astronomy, physics, chemistry, biology, and medicine.[17] In his essays on poetics, Valéry drew many analogies from chemistry. He saw the properties of language as "pure elements" which react in different ways depending on their environment.

T. S. Eliot considered Valéry "a dilettante of science but a specialist in a science of his own invention—the science of poetry" (CW 7: xxiii). Poe's greatest influence, in Eliot's opinion, was bequeathing to Valéry the concept of the poet as scientist. But at the same time, Eliot finds Valéry's scientific analogies a bit annoying when he remarks: "Sometimes, I think, Valéry allowed himself to be carried away too far by his metaphors of the clinic and the laboratory" (CW 7: xxi). A passage from "Poetry and Abstract Thought" gives an example of the type of approach that Eliot finds exaggerated:

With every question, before making any deep examination of the content, I take a look at the language; I generally proceed like a surgeon who sterilizes his hands and prepares the area to be operated on. This is what I call *cleaning up the verbal situation.* You must excuse this expression equating the words and forms of speech with the hands and instruments of a surgeon. (CW 7: 53–54; O 1: 1316)

In Valéry's view, the precision, objectivity, and method designed to produce specific results that scientists use in their work can be applied to literary problems. Poe was the only poet he knew who had discovered these relationships.

The scientific knowledge set forth in *Eureka* made a very positive impression on Valéry. But at the same time, he expresses certain mental reservations in his essay on Poe's cosmology. Describing his reaction to *Eureka* the first time he read it, Valéry remembers being astonished and only half persuaded by the pretensions and the enormous task Poe set out to accomplish in his work. Although the solemn tone of the preamble and the extraordinary discussion of method provoked a skeptical response in him, Valéry recognized beneath the ambitious beginning something that had great appeal:

Those first pages, however, brought forward a ruling idea, while presenting it in a mysterious fashion that suggested partly a feeling of helpless awe and partly a deliberate reserve, the reluctance of an enthusiastic soul to reveal its most precious secret. All this was not calculated to leave me cold. (CW 8: 163; O 1: 857)

Valéry too had felt "helpless awe" and "deliberate reserve" when confronting his own ambition to understand how the mental mechanism works. He read *Eureka* as an adventure of the mind in which he was willing to participate.

Poe's idea of "consistency" captivated Valéry, who makes reference to the term several times in his *Notebooks*. He mentions that Poe does not give a clear definition of the concept in *Eureka*, but Valéry arrives at his own understanding:

> In Poe's system, *consistency* is both the means of discovery and the discovery itself. Here is an admirable conception: an example and application of reciprocal adaptation. Poe's universe is formed on a plan the profound symmetry of which is present, to some degree, in the inner structure of our minds. Hence the poetic instinct should lead us blindly to the truth. (CW 8: 164; O 1: 857)

Valéry sees an analogy with the work of mathematicians, who, he believes, do not consider their discoveries as creations but rather as preexistent forms revealed to them through disciplined effort, sensitivity, and desire. The internal symmetry of a mathematical formula has a beauty similar to that of a well-constructed poem.

The flaws that Valéry sees in *Eureka* are all part of the mind at grips with its own creation. He complains that Poe does not "explain with the degree of clarity that one might desire" and that "there are dark places and lacunae." Valéry objects to interventions inadequately explained and, he laments, "there is a God." But he takes pleasure in observing the mind in operation, describing it in terms similar to passages in his *Introduction to the Method of Leonardo da Vinci*. Of the weak points in *Eureka*, Valéry remarks:

> For a spectator of the drama and comedy of the intellect, nothing is more interesting than to observe the ingenuity, the insistency, the trickery and anxiety of an inventor at grips with his invention. He is admirably aware of all its defects. Necessarily he would like to display all its beauties, exploit its advantages, conceal its poverty, and at any cost make it the image of what he desires. (CW 8: 165; O 1: 858)

In Valéry's mind, *Eureka* is an "art-product," a term Poe used himself to describe the work in his preface. Its creator has arranged all the elements to create a "mask" designed to make a specific impression on the reader.

In spite of the chicanery Valéry sees in the work, he nonetheless finds that *Eureka* is based on a "profound and sovereign idea." He was struck particularly by the following proposition: "*Each law of nature depends at all points on all the other laws.*" Valéry then questions: "Is this not a formula for generalized relativity, at least the expression of a will toward it?" (CW 8: 166; O 1: 858). Answering his own query, he makes the connection with twentieth-century scientific discoveries while recognizing at the same time the aesthetics common to both science and art:

> That this tendency approaches recent conceptions becomes evident when, in the *poem* under discussion, we find an affirmation of the symmetrical and reciprocal relationship of matter, time, space, gravity, and light. I emphasize the word symmetrical, for the *essential characteristic of Einstein's universe is, in effect, its formal symmetry.* Therein lies its beauty. (CW 8: 166; O 1: 858)

Valéry read Einstein a great deal and translated his *Theory of Relativity* from English to French. While reading Poe's *Eureka* he was impressed by ideas that were later accepted as scientific "truths."

Placing *Eureka* in the domain of literature, Valéry refers to the work as an abstract poem constructed on mathematical foundations. He considers it a rare modern example of a cosmogony, one of the most ancient literary forms. Looking back on these books of genesis from many different literatures throughout history, Valéry judges them as "standards to measure the intellectual innocence of each historical era" (CW 8: 170; O 1: 862). Cosmogonies represent for him a record of man's intellectual development, touching on religion, philosophy, psychology, and science. Valéry has no illusions about the naive purpose of cosmogonies, but at the same time he greatly admires the intellectual attempts to grasp the origins and explanations of the universe. Viewing the art of cosmogony as a noble effort of the mind to extend itself to the infinite, Valéry remarks: "But it is the glory of man to waste his powers on the void, and it is something more than that. Often such crackbrained researches lead to unforeseen discoveries" (CW 8: 170; O 1:

862). In this great "drama of the intellect" that cosmogonies represent, he sees the history of thought, which could be summarized
in these words: *"It is absurd by what it seeks, great by what it finds"*
(CW 8: 170; O 1: 862). Thus Valéry admires in Poe's *Eureka* the intellectual faculties of the poet engaged in scientific speculations that
have been neither proved nor disproved by numerous important
discoveries made since 1847.

In the final part of his essay on *Eureka* Valéry examines the
mental processes by which the intellect attempts to construct the
concept of a universe. To begin with, he observes, we need the idea
of nothingness, which is already something. Valéry describes
this first step in theatrical terms: "It is a pretense of the mind,
which plays a comedy of silence and perfect shadows, in the midst
of which I know that I lie hidden and ready to create, simply by
relaxing my attention" (CW 8: 171; O 1: 863). The mind then
conceives an extreme disorder that can be rearranged at will, like
a card player who jumbles the deck for the joy of putting the cards
back in order later. A confusion that is truly infinite would represent an impasse for the mind, thus the possibility of order must be
created. "As for the idea of a beginning," remarks Valéry, "it is
necessarily a myth" (CW 8: 172; O 1: 863–64).

The next step is to imagine the Whole with its infinite diversity that in turn stimulates the mind to seek unity. All senses of
perception look for relationships, an act that leads back to one's
own power of perceiving. Valéry observes: "All the diversity of my
visual perceptions is harmonized in the unity of my directing consciousness" (CW 8: 173; O 1: 864). The term *Universe* is a mytho-
logical expression, argues Valéry, because as soon as we attempt to
explain it, "we exhaust ourselves in our liberty" (CW 8: 175; O 1:
866). Concluding his essay, he observes: "IN THE BEGINNING
WAS FABLE. It will be there always."

Valéry's fascination with Poe's *Eureka* lies in the example of the
mind's effort to discover the unity of consciousness. As we have
seen in *Monsieur Teste* and in the prose poem "Agatha," Valéry was
obsessed with the idea of finding universal laws that allow the
mind to grasp the most complex phenomena. In *Eureka* he sees the
mental mechanism seeking the supreme understanding, the origin of its own existence. Poe's cosmological poem represents the

extreme limits of intellectual self-consciousness, which is the focus of Valéry's essays and poetry. In Poe's description of the phases of human consciousness in *Eureka* there are affinities with Valéry's long poem *The Young Fate*.

The awakening of human consciousness described in *Eureka* and the theme of Valéry's poem show interesting parallels. On several occasions Valéry mentions that the subject of his poem is self-awareness, an idea he refers to in another context as "conscious consciousness, the legacy of Poe." *The Young Fate* is a mono/dialogue of self-observation, what Valéry calls "a sequence of psychological substitutions, the changes of consciousness during the period of a night" (O 1: 1622). Numerous similarities with "Agatha" suggest that the earlier prose poem probably inspired Valéry as he was creating *The Young Fate* between 1912 and 1917. The female narrator, observing her own consciousness during its different phases, wakes from sleep, returns to reverie and then reawakens. The first line of the poem, "Who is that weeping, . . ." ("Qui pleure là, . . ."), sets the scene for the internal monologue that progresses cyclically as the Fate attempts to comprehend the operation of her own psyche. Although it is difficult to analyze the poem in a linear fashion and one hesitates to commit the "heresy of paraphrase" in regards to Valéry's poetry, there are nonetheless identifiable similarities between the development of the phases in *The Young Fate* and levels of consciousness described in *Eureka*.

In the concluding pages of his cosmogony, Poe speaks of "the law of periodicity" guiding our imaginations, by which he envisions "a novel Universe swelling into existence, and then subsiding into nothingness, at every throb of the Heart Divine" (B: 139). He then makes the connection between the expanding and contracting universe and the individual consciousness: "And now— the Heart Divine—what is it? *It is our own*" (B: 139). The dynamic process at work in the universe is also present in each individual. The paragraph that follows must have made a strong impression on Valéry, who admired most in Poe the "cool scientist" capable of observing his own consciousness:

Let not the merely seeming irreverence of this idea frighten our souls from that cool exercise of consciousness—from that deep tranquillity of self-inspection—through which alone we can hope to attain the presence of this, the most sublime of truths, and look it leisurely in the face. (B: 140)

Poe then describes the phases of human consciousness that are analogous to the expansion, contraction, and return to unity of the universe. The sequence bears a remarkable similarity with the phases of consciousness in *The Young Fate*. The points of comparison are presented schematically below, then followed by a detailed discussion.[18]

Eureka	*The Young Fate*
Youth, period haunted by dreams; feeling *that we exist.*	Period of innocence, dreams. (Verses 107–40)
Maturity, "World-Reason," Doubt.	Consciousness of Surprise, immortality; sexual instinct. (Verses 141–84)
Crisis, consciousness of something greater than individual soul.	Crisis, an evening of turmoil. (Verses 185–210)
Conclusion, each soul is its own creator.	Realization of her dual fate; life and death united in each being

The beginning of *The Young Fate* evokes an atmosphere of memories, dreams, and awakening. The narrator questions the cause of her anguish, "I ask my heart what pain keeps it awake" ("J'interroge mon coeur quelle douleur l'éveille"). The theme of "conscious consciousness" becomes evident in the line "I saw me seeing myself" ("Je me voyais me voir"). The Fate then recalls the phases of her life: (1) the innocence of her youth; (2) the awareness of death and of her own instincts; and (3) the crisis that results from this consciousness. This same drama of consciousness is suggested in *Eureka:*

We walk about, amid the destinies of our world-existence, encompassed by dim but ever present *Memories* of a Destiny more vast—very distant in the by-gone time, and infinitely awful.

We live out a Youth peculiarly haunted by such dreams; yet never mistaking them for dreams. As Memories we *know* them. *During our Youth* the distinction is too clear to deceive us even for a moment. (B: 140)

In Valéry's poem the Fate recalls the innocent state of mind when she had lived without awareness of her own mortality.

Thing of harmony, ME, unlike a dream,
Firm, flexible, feminine, whose silences lead
To pure acts! . . . (CW 1: 75)

Harmonieuse MOI, différente d'un songe,
Femme flexible et ferme aux silences suivis
D'actes purs! . . . (O 1: 99)

Poe sees this period as a time when one does not even question the state of existence: "That there was a period at which we did *not* exist—or, that it might so have happened that we never had existed at all—are considerations, indeed, which *during this youth,* we find difficulty in understanding" (B: 140). This idea is expressed poetically when the Young Fate runs among the flowers, happy, giving herself to life: ". . . I was the equal and spouse of light" (. . . J'étais l'égale de l'épouse du jour"). In this state of innocent bliss, she offers her shoulder to the sun, seeming to exist outside time. Still ignorant of death, she feels an infinite joy in herself:

And in the burning calm of natural dreams
All those continual steps seemed to me eternal. (CW 1: 77)

Et dans l'ardente paix des songes naturels,
Tous ces pas infinis me semblaient éternels. (O 1: 100)

But one day, upon seeing her shadow, she becomes aware of time, being, and nothingness. The shock of this sudden awareness of her mortality transforms her into a stranger to life:

If only, oh Splendor, it were not for the enemy
My shadow at my feet, mobile, supple mummy
Effortlessly skimming, portrait of my absence,
The earth where I was fleeing that weightless death.
Between the rose and me I see it lurking;

Over the dancing dust it glides, never stirring
The leafage, passes and breaks on anything . . .
Glide, funereal bark! . . . (CW 1: 79)

Si ce n'est, ô Splendeur, qu'à mes pieds l'ennemie
Mon ombre! la mobile et la souple momie,
De mon absence peinte effleurait sans effort
La terre où je fuyais cette légère mort.
Entre la rose et moi, je la vois qui s'abrite;
Sur la poudre qui danse, elle glisse et n'irrite
Nul feuillage, mais passe, et se brise partout . . .
Glisse! Barque funèbre . . . (O 1: 100)

The Young Fate discovers an invisible consciousness outside herself, a moment Poe describes in *Eureka:*

But now comes the period at which a conventional World-Reason awakens us
from the truth of our dream. Doubt, Surprise and Incomprehensibility arrive
at the same moment, They say:—"You live and the time was when you lived
not. You have been created. An Intelligence exists greater than your own;
and it is only through this Intelligence you live at all." These things we
struggle to comprehend and cannot:—*cannot* because these things, being un-
true, are thus, of necessity, incomprehensible. (B: 140–41)

The Young Fate, shaken from her state of innocence, experiences a
double state of awareness: she is haunted by the invisible, a mysterious Absolute outside herself, and she recognizes within her body
a sensual "secret sister," the awakening of her sexual instincts.
The effect on her is just as Poe describes: doubt, surprise, and in-
comprehension. Torn between her desire for purity and the attraction of the real world, she finds herself being led toward death,
where this innocence and purity will be preserved, and toward
life, where the sensibilities of the body engage her. There are efforts to annihilate consciousness, but this exercise is only a comedy
of silence that the mind is playing on itself:

Sleep, my prudence, sleep. Shape this absence;
Turn back to the seed, into dark innocence. (CW 1: 101)

Dors, ma sagesse, dors. Forme-toi cette absence;
Retourne dans le germe et la sombre innocence. (O 1: 109)

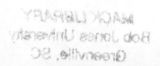

The Fate is haunted by the possibility of carrying out her own death, of accomplishing the absolute end of consciousness:

LET MY EYES, FIXED IN HEAVEN, TRACE MY TEMPLE,
AND LET REPOSE ON ME AN ALTAR UNEXAMPLED! (CW 1: 83)

QUE DANS LE CIEL PLACES, MES YEUX TRACENT MON TEMPLE!
ET QUE SUR MOI REPOSE UN AUTEL SANS EXAMPLE! (O 1: 102)

Poe describes in a similar manner the crisis that takes place at the moment of maturity:

No thinking being lives who, at some luminous point of his life of thought, has not felt himself lost amid the surges of futile efforts at understanding, or believing, that anything exists *greater than his own soul.* (B: 141)

The drama of *The Young Fate* evolves from this point of illumination in the intellectual self-awareness of the narrator. After passing through the phases of innocence, of consciousness of herself and the world around her, and of immortality, she reconciles herself to accepting her double nature and rededicates herself to life. Poe's text concludes with a description of the awareness of a double consciousness:

The utter impossibility of any one's soul feeling itself inferior to another; the intense, overwhelming dissatisfaction and rebellion at the thought;—these, with the omniprevalent aspirations at perfection, are but the spiritual, coincident with the material struggles towards the original Unity—are, to my mind at least, a species of proof far surpassing what Man terms demonstration, that no one soul *is* inferior to another—that nothing is, or can be, superior to any one soul—that each soul is, in part, its own God—its own Creator. (B: 141)

For Valéry, there is no Divine Creator, but the struggle toward total knowledge always returns to intellectual self-comprehension, understanding the unity of his own mind.

In *Eureka* Valéry discovered a passion for science and an appealing concept, Poe's "consistency," which Valéry recognized as an application of reciprocal adaptation that applies to both science and poetry. He was also attracted by Poe's idea that the profound symmetry of the universe is present in the inner structure of the mind. The drama of consciousness, represented poetically in *The Young Fate*, is the aspect of *Eureka* that had a great appeal to Valéry.

Conclusion: Unity of Effect

> It is when a book or an author's collected work acts on someone
> not with all its qualities, but with one or a few of them, that in-
> fluence assumes its most remarkable values.
>
> —Valéry (CW 8: 242; O 1: 635)

Valéry's concept of how true influence operates came from many years of observing his own mind's reaction to the works of others. Although he mentions that Leonardo, Poe, and Mallarmé had a deep influence on him, his obsession with specific qualities in Poe define the effect of the other two mentors.

Early in his intellectual development Valéry became aware that he had to overcome the tyranny of the past, otherwise he would produce inferior imitations of Mallarmé's poems. While admiring the elder poet's work, he had to seek his own originality, which meant doing "other than" Mallarmé. This negative reaction to another's work is part of the process of influence, in Valéry's view, and can result in "extreme originality," which is what happened in his case. While reading Poe he made a discovery that would have a major effect on his literary career. He recalls this moment of enlightenment many years later in a *Notebook* entry: "'There is a poetry of the very things of the mind.' That is what struck me as early as 1890 or so" (CW 1: 410; C 25: 460). And more succinctly, he remarks on another occasion: "Writing a poem is a poem" (C 8: 578). Poe inspired Valéry to examine the beauty and pathos of the intellectual drama, with its moments of joy, excitement, lassitude, and despair. This "poetry of the things of the mind" is the quality in Poe's work that assumes remarkable expression in Valéry's essays, prose fiction, and poetry.

A few sentences and ideas from Poe were nourished and embellished in Valéry's mind. He was challenged by Poe's comment in "The Domain of Arnheim" that no man has ever realized the highest degree of perfection in art. He coupled this goal with his desire to discover how the analytical faculties operate, another theme suggested to him in Poe's work. As a result, Valéry gave up writing poetry to concentrate on achieving an understanding of how the mind functions. This "drama of the intellect" that he spent so much time observing led to "extreme originality" in his prose creations and became his main focus when he returned to writing poetry. Intellectually, Poe gave Valéry the courage to break away from Mallarmé and discover his own unique talents. While discussions about Poe brought the two French poets together, it also separated them in the sense that Valéry realized he was fascinated by the faculties that produce a poem rather than by the poem itself. Valéry went beyond Mallarmé's desire to perfect poetic language; the younger poet wanted to understand how the human brain arrives at linguistic perfection.

In Leonardo Valéry saw the realization of Poe's bent for combining scientific analysis and artistic talent. The approach to his essay on the Italian master came straight from Poe. Valéry goes "behind the scenes," as suggested in *The Philosophy of Composition,* in his attempt to discover the mind that created the work. The fictionalized description of Leonardo's *modus operandi* represents Valéry's concept of the ideal mind in the act of producing artistic creations based on scientific principles. In his essay Valéry states that both Leonardo and Poe were seeking a "few general laws" that determine the effect of a work of art on individuals (CW 8: 62; O 1: 1197–98). The discovery of universal laws of the mind became an obsession for Valéry which he embodied in the fictional character Monsieur Teste.

Like the detective Dupin, Teste possesses the analytical and creative functions of a superior intellect. But the originality of Valéry's character lies in the fact that these qualities are refined to the point of turning upon themselves in order to discover how these functions operate. Dupin takes pleasure in applying his intellectual abilities to solve the most baffling crimes. Teste's greatest pleasure is simply observing the keen intellect in operation, a function that has a beauty all its own.   In his description of how influence works, Valéry remarks that what one person does often repeats what someone else has done, but "repeats it in other tones, refines or amplifies or simplifies it, loads or overloads it with meaning" (CW 8: 241; O 1: 634).   In the case of Dupin-Teste, influence seems to have operated exactly as Valéry describes.   Starting with the qualities in Dupin, Valéry refines and simplifies them in his character by eliminating all the complexities of exhibiting the mind's practical applications.   He overloads with meaning by portraying Teste as pure consciousness living the everyday life of a man, a monster of the intellect who has no predecessors.   The analytical and creative abilities of Dupin are exaggerated almost beyond recognition.   Valéry once remarked that Teste is "a caricature of someone who might have been invented by Poe."[1]

Valéry's disdain for prose fiction led some critics to believe that Poe's tales held little interest for him.   On the contrary, not only did Valéry enjoy reading the stories, he found in them a source of inspiration for his own creative endeavors.   "The Murders in the Rue Morgue" provided a model for *The Evening with Monsieur Teste.* Another of Valéry's attempts to write what he called "a novel of the mind" is the prose poem "Agatha," whose images bear numerous similarities to passages in "MS. Found in a Bottle."   And the poem "Disaster," symbolizing the shipwreck of the mind, is reminiscent of scenes in *The Adventures of Arthur Gordon Pym.*   Common to all Valéry's creative endeavors inspired by Poe's tales is the attempt to realize in writing the dramatic moments of cerebration.   These specific examples of direct influence contradict T. S. Eliot's impression that Poe's influence on Valéry came solely from ideas contained in his literary essays.[2]

Since Valéry wrote a great deal on the subject of poetics and described his own experience as a writer, the connection with Poe's literary essays is easier to see than in the tales.   Like Poe, Valéry was concerned with the process of poetic creation and the self-questioning approach to writing.   In *The Philosophy of Composition* Valéry discovered for the first time a poet who asked himself, "what goes on in the mind when I write a poem?"   Although he did not believe Poe wrote "The Raven" as described, the essay nonetheless suggested to Valéry the possibility of attempting to understand the creative process in action. In the same essay Valéry discovered the basic tenet of his approach to literary criticism, as he explains in an essay on Descartes: "A work expresses not what the author *is* but what he *wishes to appear,* by selecting, co-ordinating, harmonizing, concealing, and exaggerating" (CW 9: 44; O 1: 817). Poe gave Valéry the courage to reject the dominant critics of his day and approach literature from a new angle, that of the intrinsic properties of the work itself. In Valéry's view the role of the writer is "to combine determinate elements with a view of acting upon an indeterminate person" (CW 13: 129); the role of the critic is to evaluate how well the author succeeded. Valéry's analysis of the interrelationships between author and work and work and reader link him to modern concepts of literary criticism.

Valéry was fascinated by the complexities of thought and their relations to linguistic expression. As Poe points out in *The Philosophy of Composition,* conscious effort plays a greater role in writing a poem than gratuitous inspiration. Valéry also observed that in his own experience as a writer inspiration accounted for only part of the creative activities of the mind. Examining the spontaneous elements of creativity with the analytical approach of a scientist, Valéry identifies several types of inspiration that act upon the creative process in different ways. While recognizing that inspiration plays a role in writing poetry, Valéry's major preoccupation was to understand and control the techniques of poem making. He carried Poe's intellectual self-awareness to the ultimate extreme by making "conscious consciousness" the theme of his poetry.

The effect of *Eureka* on Valéry is also linked to his obsession with the drama of the mind. He saw in Poe's cosmology the heroic efforts of the intellect attempting to grasp its own beginning. Although Valéry sees this attempt as doomed to failure, other aspects of the work had a decisive influence on him. His interest in science, which became a passion after reading *Eureka,* affected the way he analyzed his own creative activities. Fascinated by Poe's attempts to discover universal laws, Valéry makes numerous references to the concept of "consistency" presented in *Eureka.* On the creative level, the awakening of human consciousness described in

Eureka inspired phases of awareness in Valéry's poem *The Young Fate.*

In one of the early *Notebooks* there is a sentence revealing the quality in Poe's work that became the driving force in Valéry's intellectual development and literary production: "Poe—or some demon—whispers: the very limit of analysis—where?" (C 1: 809). This is the question that became an obsession for Valéry. While observing the functioning of his own mind in an attempt to unveil its secrets, he discovered the most poetic of all themes: the beauty of the human brain in operation. Poe's works oriented Valéry toward the originality that was so precious to the French poet. No writer before or after Valéry has given poetic expression to the "drama of the intellect" as a dominant theme in poetry and prose.

Afterword: Poe in France since 1945

The inevitable question arises, "What happened to Poe in France after Valéry's death in 1945?" Although no other well-known French writers took up the banner for Poe, his work did not fall into oblivion. Judging from the many critical works and new editions turned out by French publishing houses, Poe continues to be a popular writer. I was struck by Poe's importance among French readers during a walk near the Champs-Elysées in July 1989 when the Bicentiennial celebration was in full swing. Paris bookstore windows were crammed with works on the Revolution. But, much to my surprise, in the center front of an elegant shop window was a new edition of Poe, displayed as the focal point with the historical tomes relegated to the background. An important publishing event indeed!

The new edition was prepared by French Poe scholar Claude Richard, who had died a year before his thousand-page volume of Poe's works came off the press. Although numerous twentieth-century critics in France have commented on various aspects of Poe's prose and poetry, Richard devoted a lifetime to studying the works of his favorite American writer. While teaching at the Université Paul Valéry at Montpellier, where he was professor of American literature, Richard organized a research team made up of students and teachers devoted to the task of presenting Poe to French readers in a new light. The goal of their research was to rectify the distorted image of Poe created by Baudelaire and handed down from one generation to another. The process of "demythification" was carried out by presenting texts to prove that the real Poe was not a poet of disorder but rather the "literary engineer" who fascinated Valéry. The researchers translated and edited many documents that had not been available to French readers, thus providing new sources on which to base a judgment of Poe.[1]

Richard also brought to the French reading public another aspect of Poe's writing career. In his monumental work *Edgar Allan Poe: journaliste et critique* Richard documents in great detail Poe's contributions to the field of journalism and literary criticism that had not been the object of critical study in France. Eager to try new approaches, Richard wrote several essays applying text-oriented theories of literary analysis to Poe's tales.[2] Through his critical studies, essays, new editions of prose and poetry, and bibliographies Claude Richard has made extraordinary contributions to Poe scholarship and has produced a constant flow of good-quality editions for French readers to enjoy.

A major literary debate that began in France in the 1960s and then spread beyond its borders has kept Poe in the limelight. The neo-Freudian critic Jacques Lacan illustrates his theories by applying them to Poe's tale "The Purloined Letter." Lacan is not interested in Poe the person or the writer but rather in his tale as a text for exemplifying the symbolic repetition of the unconscious effort to find an irretrievably lost object. His "Seminar on 'The Purloined Letter,'" published in 1966 provoked a reaction from his compatriot the deconstructionist Jacques Derrida, and the debate was on. Their opposing views inspired other critics to get involved in the controversy, which seems less concerned with Poe and more preoccupied with the "act of analysis" and the "act of analysis of the act of analysis," as Barbara Johnson describes the exchange of views.[3] Nonetheless, Poe's tale has inspired the application of modern literary theories and has renewed interest in a story written over a century ago.

Speaking of Baudelaire, Valéry once remarked that in exchange for what he had taken, he "gave Poe's thought an infinite expanse. He offered it to future generations" (CW 8: 204; O 1: 607). Valéry made an important contribution to this legacy both within France and beyond its borders. The torch of admiration for Poe has been passed to contemporary Hispanic writers, such as the Argentine Jorge Luis Borges, who admired both Valéry and Poe,[4] and the

Mexican Carlos Fuentes, who acknowledges his indebtedness to Poe and consciously incorporates elements from the tales into his own fiction. For Borges, Valéry passed on "the lucid pleasures of thought and the secret adventures of order,"[5] the legacy of Poe.

Notes

Unless otherwise indicated, emphasis in quotations appears in the original.

Introduction

1. Patrick F. Quinn states in his introduction to *The French Face of Edgar Poe* that he does not attempt to examine Poe's effect on Valéry (p. 7). Célestin Pierre Cambiaire's *The Influence of Edgar Allan Poe in France* mentions Valéry in two paragraphs (159–60). More recently, in *The Genius of Edgar Allan Poe*, Georges Zayed devotes five pages (51–55) to Valéry in Part I of his study, which discusses Poe's influence in France.
2. *Hudson Review* 2 (1949) 327–42. Repr. in Carlson, *Recognition* 205–19.
3. O 1: 854–67. An English translation of the essay is found in CW 8: 161–76. Eric W. Carlson's *Critical Essays on Edgar Allan Poe* reprints the same text (102–7). A different translation is given by Jean Alexander in her *Affidavits of Genius* 233–43.
4. "Situation de Baudelaire" in O 1: 598–613. English translation, "The Place of Baudelaire" in CW 8: 193–211.
5. "Quelques fragments des Marginalia," traduits et annotés par Paul Valéry, *Commerce* 14 (1927) 11–41. *Commerce* was a literary review published in Paris between 1924 and 1932. Valéry's translation of Poe's text is on the right-hand side of each page with comments by the translator printed on the left-hand side. The piece is presented in just the opposite format with Valéry's gloss translated by James R. Lawler in CW 8: 177–92. Valéry's translation has been republished in France: *Edgar Poe, Fragments des 'Marginalia', traduits et commentés par Paul Valéry* (Montpellier: Fata Morgana, 1980).
6. *Lettres à quelques-uns* 28–29. English translation in CW 8: 406–7.
7. Valéry's article entitled "Sur la technique littéraire" in its original version is found in O 1: 1809–11. An English translation by Denise Folliot is given with the French on the opposite pages in CW 7: 314–23. All quotes are from this translation. The phrases from Poe's *Philosophy of Composition* are found in *Edgar Allan Poe, Essays and Reviews*, comp. by G.

R. Thompson 23 and 16. Henceforth, all references to Poe's essays will be from this edition indicated by T followed by page number.

8. For example, one of the most respected Valéry critics, Emilie Noulet, believed that he had not bothered to read Poe's tales. See Noulet, *Paul Valéry* 85. T. S. Eliot discusses Poe's tales in the article mentioned in Note 2 above but makes no connection with Valéry's work.

9. O 2: 1381. Jean Hytier describes the manuscript, which was exhibited in 1956.

10. *Lettres à quelques-uns* 97–98; CW 8: 421. The italics are Valéry's.

11. Quoted in O 1: 70 by Valéry's daughter, who wrote the biographical introduction.

12. Valéry's lectures at the Collège de France were never published, but one of his students, Lucienne Julien Cain, recounted his lectures on Poe in her book *Trois essais sur Paul Valéry* 129–50. Georges Le Breton published notes from the lectures in the poetry review *Yggdrasill.* (See Chapter 5, Note 5.)

13. Valéry made this remark in his Introduction to René Fernandat's book *Autour de Paul Valéry.* The Introduction was translated into English by Malcolm Cowley and used as the Preface to CW 8, *Leonardo, Poe, Mallarmé.*

1. The Image of Poe Inherited from Baudelaire and Mallarmé

1. *The French Face of Edgar Poe* 68–69.

2. Poe's name first appeared in France in the November 1845 issue of the *Revue Britannique,* which published a translation of "The Gold Bug." Forgues served as editor of the periodical. See M. Gilman, *Baudelaire the Critic* 58–59. Gilman mistakenly refers to Forgues as Fargues. W. T. Bandy identifies the translator as Alphonse Borghers, pseudonym of Amédée Pichot. See W. T. Bandy, *Edgar Allan Poe: Sa vie et ses ouvrages* xiii.

3. Bandy, *Edgar Allan Poe: Sa vie et ses ouvrages* xiv–xv.

4. Baudelaire scholar Enid Starkie was apparently unaware of the Forgues article when she wrote: "Baudelaire's article on Poe, which appeared in 1852, was the first in any foreign language to be published on the American and it marks an important date in comparative literature studies." See E. Starkie, *Baudelaire* 215.

5. I quote from the English translation of Forgues' article published in E. Carlson's *Critical Essays on Edgar Allan Poe* 41–62. The preface and translation by Sidney P. Moss are reprinted from *Poe's Major Crisis* (Durham, N.C.: Duke University Press, 1970) 143–54. In this translation the first four paragraphs of the original article are not included, apparently because they do not relate directly to Poe. The complete article translated into English can be found in J. Alexander's *Affidavits of Genius: Edgar*

Allan Poe and the French Critics, 1847–1924 79–96. Alexander's introduction to the book is very helpful in understanding the French response to Poe.

6. Carlson, *Critical Essays* 45.
7. Carlson, *Critical Essays* 46.
8. According to Buranelli, *Edgar Allan Poe* 27, Mesmerism had an enormous impact in Europe and America. Buranelli explains the origins of Mesmerism:

> The problem presented by Franz Anton Mesmer, who died in 1815 within Poe's lifetime, was that he had the right facts (the trance and the curious phenomena resulting from it) but the wrong theory. Mesmer believed that he put his subjects into his celebrated trance by infusing their nervous systems with 'animal magnetism,' rays of a universal cosmic fluid. This original theory of the founder lingered after the true theory had been put forward by his followers, namely, that the trance resulted from suggestion in the subject's mind, its cause being psychological rather than physical.

Bandy in *Edgar Allan Poe: Sa vie et ses ouvrages* xx sheds some light on Baudelaire's interest in this story by citing a letter Baudelaire sent to his mother while still in secondary school in which he mentions a fascination with animal magnetism.

9. See Starkie, *Baudelaire* 28–29 for description of Baudelaire's mother's early days in England.
10. Baudelaire, *Correspondance*, ed. Claude Pichois 1: 676. Translation in Rosemary Lloyd's *Selected Letters of Charles Baudelaire, The Conquest of Solitude* 148.
11. These include *Histoires extraordinaires* (1856), *Nouvelles Histoires extraordinaires* (1857), *Aventures d'Arthur Gordon Pym* (1858), *Eureka* (1863), and *Histoires grotesques et sérieuses* (1865). For a list of the contents of the three volumes of short stories, see *Baudelaire on Poe*, ed. and trans. Lois Hyslop and Francis E. Hyslop, Jr., 167–68.
12. English translations are included in Hyslops' *Baudelaire on Poe* 37–86, and in Alexander's *Affidavits of Genius* 99–121.
13. Translations of the 1856 essay are included in Hyslop and Hyslop 89–118, and in Alexander 122–30. For an interesting comparison of Baudelaire's 1852 and 1856 articles, see Lloyd, *Baudelaire's Literary Criticism* 61.
14. In 1937 at the age of sixty-six Valéry was appointed Professor of Poetics at the Collège de France, a venerable institution founded in the sixteenth century by François I. The public was invited to the lectures, which Valéry gave every Friday and Saturday. Lucienne Julien Cain, a faithful auditor, recalled that Valéry, "so disdainful of the everyday events in other people's lives as well as in his own, in the case of Edgar Poe almost exclusively, took the time to evoke melancholy biographical details" (*Trois essais sur Paul Valéry* 137).

15. Lord Byron, English poet (1788–1824), died of fever shortly after arriving in Greece to participate in the revolution against the Turks.

16. Recounted in Baudelaire's 1852 article "Edgar Allan Poe: Sa vie et ses ouvrages" in *Oeuvres en prose d'Edgar Allan Poe* 1007. English translation in Hyslops' *Baudelaire on Poe* 47–48. Henceforth, references to Baudelaire's Poe translations will be from this volume, abbreviated OP, followed by page number. English translations of Baudelaire's essays on Poe will be taken from Hyslop and abbreviated H followed by the page number. Both references will be indicated in the text.

17. In "New Light on Baudelaire and Poe," *Yale French Studies* 10 (1952) 65–69, W. T. Bandy describes his discovery that much of Baudelaire's 1852 article had been taken from a review by John M. Daniel published in the *Southern Literary Messenger* in March 1850. According to Bandy, "twenty-five of the forty pages of Baudelaire's article are translated almost word-for-word from Daniel's review." Bandy gives a detailed comparison of Baudelaire's articles with those of Daniel and John R. Thompson in *Edgar Allan Poe: Sa vie et ses ouvrages,* which is devoted almost entirely to that subject. A discussion of Bandy's discovery is presented by Rosemary Lloyd in *Baudelaire's Literary Criticism* 51–52. Claude Richard in *Poe: journaliste et critique* juxtaposes Baudelaire's text and those of the American journalists. He compares the texts in detail, bringing to light similarities that add to Bandy's earlier analyses.

18. A detailed study of these comparisons can be found in Peter M. Wetherill, *Charles Baudelaire et la poésie d'Edgar Allan Poe.* The same author presents in English the main points of his book in "Edgar Allan Poe and Madame Sabatier," *Modern Language Quarterly* 20 (1959) 344–54. Patrick Quinn minimizes the importance of these similarities in *The French Face of Edgar Poe* 157–59.

19. *Correspondance* 2: 386. English translation in Rosemary Lloyd, *Selected Letters of Charles Baudelaire* 204.

20. *Correspondance* 2: 466–67; Lloyd, *Selected Letters of Charles Baudelaire* 221.

21. *Charles Baudelaire et la poésie d'Edgar Allan Poe* 136.

22. Both authors quoted by Léon Lemonnier, *Edgar Poe et la critique française* 18–26.

23. Paul Valéry, *Cahiers*, 29 volumes (Paris, Centre National de la Recherche Scientifique, 1957–61) 5: 882. Henceforth, all quotations from the *Cahiers* will be indicated C followed by volume and page numbers. Quotations from the *Cahiers* translated in CW will be indicated; otherwise the translations are my own.

24. The passage borrowed from Poe to which Valéry refers is found in Baudelaire, *Oeuvres complètes* 2: 111–15.

25. Baudelaire, *Oeuvres complètes* 2: 432. English translation is my own.

26. *The French Face of Edgar Poe* 4–5.

27. *Correspondance* 1: 344. English translation in Lloyd, *Selected Letters of Charles Baudelaire* 84.

28. *The French Face of Edgar Poe* 134.
29. *Correspondance* 1: 506. English translation in Lloyd, *Selected Letters of Charles Baudelaire* 116. Baudelaire had written to Saint-Beuve two years earlier (March 19, 1856) begging him to write a review of Poe's work: "Here, my dear protector, is a form of literature that may well not inspire as much enthusiasm in you as it does in me, but which will certainly interest you. Edgar Poe, who is not highly regarded in America, *must*, by which I mean I wish he could, become a great man in *France.* I know how good you are and how much you love new things, so I've boldly promised Michel Lévy your aid." *Correspondance* 1: 343; Lloyd, *Selected Letters of Charles Baudelaire* 83.
30. This quote and subsequent ones in this paragraph are from Barbey d'Aurevilly's article "The King of the Bohemians, or Edgar Poe" translated by Alexander in *Affidavits of Genius* 145–52. The article was first published in *Le Réveil,* May 15, 1858, 231–33.
31. Quoted by Chiari, *Symbolisme from Poe to Mallarmé* 68.
32. Stéphane Mallarmé, *Thèmes anglais* (Paris: Gallimard, 1937). This text plus another one, *English Words* (*Les Mots anglais*), are included in Mallarmé's *Oeuvres complètes* 886–1156. It is interesting to note that out of 1322 pages of Mallarmé's complete works, 270 pages are devoted to the study of English in addition to the 57 pages of translations and notes on Poe's poems.
33. Fowlie, *Mallarmé* 64.
34. Stéphane Mallarmé, *Correspondance* 1: 104. English version is my own translation.
35. Mallarmé, *Correspondance* 1: 243.
36. Mallarmé, *Correspondance* 1: 207. A reference to this same letter in Mallarmé's *Oeuvres complètes* 1442 gives the incorrect date as March 1866.
37. Mallarmé, *Oeuvres complètes* 234–44.
38. Mallarmé, *Oeuvres complètes* 1526.
39. T. S. Eliot, "From Poe to Valéry." Repr. in Carlson, *Recognition* 214.
40. *Symbolisme from Poe to Mallarmé* 103.
41. *Symbolisme from Poe to Mallarmé* 105.
42. *Symbolisme from Poe to Mallarmé* 104–5.
43. *Symbolisme from Poe to Mallarmé* 105. Huxley argues that Poe overuses rhymes and proper names to produce "musical-magical effects." Huxley begins his essay by stating that "Baudelaire, Mallarmé, and Valéry are wrong and that Poe is not one of our major poets." "Vulgarity in Literature," *Saturday Review of Literature,* Sept. 27, 1930, 158–59. Repr. in Carlson, *Recognition* 160–67.
44. The version presented here is from Mallarmé, *Oeuvres complètes* 189. W. T. Bandy discovered what he believes to be an earlier version of the poem among the John H. Ingram papers in the Alderman Library at the University of Virginia. See Bandy, "Mallarmé's Sonnet to Poe, The First Text?" in *Revue de Littérature Comparée* (jan.–mars 1963) 100–101.

45. *Stéphane Mallarmé, Selected Poetry and Prose* 51.
46. Fowlie, *Mallarmé* 71.
47. Fowlie gives an interesting reference to the repetition of this line in the second part of T. S. Eliot's "Little Gidding": "Since our concern was speech, and speech impelled us/ To purify the dialect of the tribe,/ And urge the mind to aftersight and foresight,/ Let me disclose the gifts reserved for age/ To set a crown upon lifetime's effort." Cf. Fowlie, *Mallarmé* 88.
48. English translation in Alexander's *Affidavits of Genius* 219–32. Two paragraphs of Alexander's translation (those dealing specifically with *The Philosophy of Composition*) are reprinted in Carlson, *Critical Essays* 85. De Gourmont's text is from *Promenades littéraires* (Paris: Mercure de France, 1904) 348–82. Rémy de Gourmont (1858–1915) was editor of the influential *Mercure de France* from 1885 until his death. T. S. Eliot called him "the critical conscience of his generation."

2. *Valéry's Views on Influence*

1. *Paul Valéry's Album de vers anciens: A Past Transfigured*, 22–23, Note 2. Among the examples of Valéry's preoccupation with originality found in the *Notebooks* Nash cites the following (my translations):
   > Having always lived in order to be other than others, having sacrificed everything for that.
   > Having had the disgust of recommencing what is written everywhere.
   > Having conceived something that has never been done. Having accorded it an infinite price (C 8: 500).
   > I don't like the ideas of others, and it is in order not to make my own the ideas of others that I have not published them. (C 10: 163)

   Valéry felt the need to be ever vigilant to the threat of influence. In "Remarks about Myself" ("Propos me concernant") he expresses this cautious attitude:
   > I recognize in myself a certain way of being influenced by others. It might be that another's act or thought so exactly conforms or is so directly opposed to some disposition or preoccupation of my inner self that it is stimulated to react strenuously, as if for the reasons of security, against the declared threat. An opinion that strikes me as being too much like my own causes me to doubt mine. (CW 15: 293; O 2: 1510)
2. This text is not included in *Oeuvres*, ed. Jean Hytier. Unpublished and undated, the typescript was given to editor Jackson Mathews by Julien P. Monod (CW 15: 393).
3. The original French text is "Souvenirs sur Paul Valéry," by Pierre Féline, *Mercure de France*, July 1954. Reference in CW 15: 407.

4. Original source is "Impressions et Souvenirs," *Maîtres et amis* (Paris: Camaieux de Jacques Beltrand, 1927). Reference in CW 15: 394.

5. Huysmans also mentions Poe as one of the few authors his main character des Esseintes can bear to read:

> To enjoy a literature uniting, as he desired, with an incisive style, a penetrating, feline power of analysis, he must resort to that master of Induction, that strange, profound thinker, Edgar Allan Poe, for whom, since the moment when he had begun to re-read him, his predilection had suffered no possible diminution.
>
> Better than any other writer perhaps, Poe possessed those close affinities of spirit that fulfilled the demands Des Esseintes had formulated in the course of his meditations. (*Against the Grain* 178)

   The importance of Huysmans' novel in bringing Poe's works to the attention of French writers has been the subject of debate. G. A. Cevasco in his article "*A Rebours* and Poe's Reputation in France," *Romance Notes* 13 (1971) 255–61 claims that *Against the Grain* played a major role in establishing Poe's fame in France. Bandy refutes this argument and cites numerous mistakes in Cevasco's article. See W. T. Bandy "Huysmans and Poe," *Romance Notes* 17 (1977) 270–71.

6. Valéry's original French version is printed on opposite pages in CW 7: 314–22.

7. This phrase recalls Baudelaire's: "A painting is a machine in which all the systems are evident to a practiced eye." Cf. Chapter 1, Note 25.

8. Thirty years later Valéry is convinced that Poe did not write "The Raven" as he describes in *The Philosophy of Composition.* See Chapter 4, pp. 115–16.

9. Mallarmé, *Oeuvres complètes* 229–30.

10. Pierre Louis changed the spelling of his name to Louÿs in the 1890s.

11. Quoted by Henry A. Grubbs, *Paul Valéry* 24.

12. *The Art of Paul Valéry: A Study in Dramatic Monologue* 11.

13. Emilie Noulet, *Paul Valéry* 10–11. Valéry's handwritten note, reproduced in photocopy, begins "Dear Sir," assuming that Noulet's perceptive analysis of his work had been written by a man. He praises her for recognizing that the central theme in his prose and poetry is consciousness, which, as he says, became his "mania."

14. Noulet, *Paul Valéry* 85.

15. Noulet, *Paul Valéry* 85.

16. *Correspondance d'André Gide et de Paul Valéry* 143. Letter dated December 1891.

17. *Correspondance Gide-Valéry* 162. Letter dated June 1892.

18. *Correspondance Paul Valéry-Gustave Fourment* 246. The letter from Louÿs to Valéry is quoted by Octave Nadal.

19. *Cahiers.* 29 vols. In 1908 Valéry made a first attempt to organize the voluminous notes by classifying them according to subject. After recopying about one thousand pages by hand, he abandoned the project until 1921, when a secretary took over the task of typing the notes while Valéry arranged them by categories. These typescripts and handwritten notes, discovered after his death, became the basis of a new two-volume edition of the *Cahiers* edited by Judith Robinson (Paris: Gallimard, 1973, 1974). More recently, Robinson and co-editor Nicole Celeyrette-Pietri have returned to the photocopied edition, which they are publishing in a printed version that corresponds to the handwritten volumes. The first volume, *Paul Valéry: Cahiers 1894–1914, Tome I,* has two prefaces and helpful notes to clarify references. Converting the remaining 28 volumes of the *Cahiers* into print will take many more years of tedious work.

20. In a letter to his friend Henri Mondor, who had sent Valéry his recently completed biography of Mallarmé, Valéry mentions this idea: "You cannot imagine, for instance, how the period when Mallarmé becomes the creation of Poe and arrives at a final judgment on Baudelaire put me back into my years of 1891–1892, when I too was obsessed with Poe. (Though it is remarkable that in my case this influence worked perhaps more against the purpose of poetry than for it)" (CW 8: 426; O 1: 1753).

21. Valéry describes his experience in "My Early Days in England." There is no known French version of the text, first published in *The Bookman's Journal,* London, December 1925, by an anonymous translator. See CW 15: 394.

22. "From Poe to Valéry," *The Hudson Review* 336.

23. Valéry translated Hardy's poem "Felling a Tree" and Einstein's "Theory of Gravitation." For a complete list of Valéry's translations, see *Bibliographie des oeuvres de Paul Valéry publiées de 1889 à 1965,* eds. Georges Karaiskakis and François Chapon, preface by Lucienne Julien Cain (Paris: Librairie Auguste Blaizot, 1976) 551.

24. First published in the Paris journal *Commerce* 14 (1927) 11–41, Valéry's text is presented with his marginal notes in CW 8: 177–92. When Valéry translated the selections from the *Marginalia* into French, he often changed the paragraph divisions and, in some cases, the syntax of Poe's text. The English version presented in CW reflects these changes.

    The selections in the *Marginalia* that Valéry translated are from *Democratic Review,* November 1844; *Graham's Magazine,* March 1846; and *Southern Literary Messenger,* June 1849.

25. Evidence in Valéry's personal copies of Poe's works contradict his claim that he does not make notes in books he reads. Judith Robinson-Valéry answered my query on this subject by responding in a letter that her husband Claude (Valéry's son) has kept in his personal collection his father's well-worn editions of Poe, which have many annotations written by Paul Valéry. The annotated books include *Histoires grotesques et*

sérieuses, Les Aventures d'Arthur Gordon Pym, Histoires extraordinaires, and *Eureka,* but not Poe's poems. Mme Robinson-Valéry believes that Valéry read Poe uniquely in French. She adds the following comment: "The number of these annotations is an indication of a deep interest in Poe on Valéry's part, and, despite their many different subject matters, they are reminiscent of his annotations of books by his favorite scientists." Letter from Judith Robinson-Valéry dated March 16, 1989.

26. A chronological list of Valéry's publications is given in Karaiskakis and Chapon, *Bibliographie des oeuvres de Paul Valéry* xxv–xxxix.

3. Dupin-Teste: The Poe Connection

1. Valéry described the creation of *Monsieur Teste* in a preface for the second English translation published in 1925 by Ronald Davis. The first translator of the piece was Natalie Clifford Barney in 1922. See CW 6: 163.

2. This expression suggests "Le Démon de la perversité" ("Demon of Perversity"), Baudelaire's translation of the title of Poe's tale "The Imp of the Perverse."

3. *Lettres à quelques-uns* 97–98.

4. *Correspondance Gide-Valéry* 281.

5. *Correspondance Gide-Valéry* 281.

6. The origin of the name Poe chose for his famous detective has been the subject of several hypotheses. Valéry was no doubt familiar with two historical French figures, André Marie Dupin (1783–1865), a well-known jurist and politician, and his brother the Baron Charles Dupin (1784–1873), economist and mathematician whose name is given to a geometry term, "the Dupin indicatrix." As Jones and Lyungquist point out in their article, "Monsieur Dupin: Further Details on the Reality behind the Legend," Poe came across the name of André Marie Dupin when he reviewed Robert Walsh's translation of Louis Léonard de Loménie's *Sketches of Conspicuous Living Characters of France.* The authors of the article go on to point out that Poe was probably familiar with the personage because of an earlier scandal of international proportions involving André Dupin. Michael Harrison supports the case for Baron Charles Dupin as being Poe's real-life model (*The Exploits of the Chevalier Dupin,* 3–14). W. T. Bandy's theory is the most original. He discovered a letter in which Poe mentions the name of a French teacher by the name of C. Auguste Dubouchet and suggests that Poe was amusing himself with a private joke that remained hidden for a long time. (See Bandy's "Who Was Monsieur Dupin?") In my opinion, the most convincing answer to this riddle is "all of the above."

7. Poe's opening sentence appears to be a rather abrupt introduction to the subject of the analytical mind. In his article "Poe as Phrenologist: The

Example of Monsieur Dupin" Donald B. Stauffer mentions that when Poe revised the tale for the Wiley and Putman edition (1845), he omitted the original first paragraph, which included references to phrenology, a system by which an analysis of the intellectual faculties can allegedly be made by studying the shape and protuberances of the skull. Stauffer remarks that modern readers are bothered by the length of the four remaining paragraphs about the powers of analysis and their relation to the imagination. It is interesting to note in this regard that Valéry found this part of Poe's tale most fascinating. In a lecture given before members of a book club in Paris ("la Maison des Amis des Livres") in 1922 Valéry read *verbatim* from Baudelaire's translation three long paragraphs from the beginning of "The Murders in the Rue Morgue." See Lawler, *Edgar Poe et les poètes français* 96–99.

8. This text is not included in *Oeuvres*. See CW 6: 167.

9. Baudelaire translated "resolvent" with the word *"analytique."* This image of a double Dupin—creative and analytical—fascinated Valéry.

10. Valéry must have had Poe's tale "The Balloon Hoax" on his mind when he described Teste's capacity for memory and imagination:

    > Certainly his singular memory must have retained for him almost solely those impressions which our imagination, by itself, is powerless to construct. If we imagine an ascent in a balloon, we may with shrewdness and force produce many of the probable sensations of an aeronaut; but there will always remain something peculiar to the real ascent, and that difference from what we imagine expresses the value of the methods of an Edmond Teste. (CW 6: 11; O 2: 18)

11. *Lettres à quelques-uns* 231.

12. A collection of references to Teste taken from the *Notebooks* and translated into English are found in CW 6: 83–153.

13. After Valéry's death, four more pieces were added to the "Teste Cycle" and published together with the earlier ones in 1946: "A Walk with Monsieur Teste" ("Promenade avec Monsieur Teste"); "Dialogue; Sketches for a Portrait of Monsieur Teste" ("Pour un Portrait de Monsieur Teste"); "A Few of Monsieur Teste's Thoughts" ("Quelques Pensées de Monsieur Teste"); and "End of Monsieur Teste" ("Fin de Monsieur Teste"). These are all included in O 2: 57–75 and CW 6: 60–80.

14. *Correspondance Gide-Valéry* 426–27.

15. See Chapter 2, Note 8.

16. Agathe Rouart-Valéry published the piece in an edition that was limited to 190 copies. The text is included in the Notes to O 2: 1388–92 but is missing thirty lines of the 1956 version because of a printing error, a mistake that was repeated in the translation, CW 2: 205–12. The most accessible, complete version is found in Jean Levaillant's *La Jeune Parque, L'Ange, Agathe, Histoires brisées*. The missing lines, pages 46–47 in the Le-

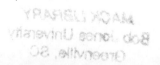

vaillant edition, should be inserted in the paragraph beginning "Sur cette ombre sans preuve . . ." O 2: 1389 following "Si, une fois je les presse et surpasse la vitesse de leur mort . . ." In the English translation the missing lines belong on page 206 in the paragraph beginning "Upon this sophistical shadow . . ." continuing the sentence "Yes, but once I have hurried and harried them to their deaths . . ." For the importance of these lines in our comparison with Poe's tale, see Note 25.

17. *Correspondance Gide-Valéry* 309–10.
18. *Correspondance Gide-Valéry* 370; 374. In the October 19, 1900 letter (p. 370) Valéry commented: "I rarely write or rewrite a sentence from the beginning of 'Agathe.'"
19. *Correspondance Valéry-Fourment* 160. Letter dated January 12, 1901.
20. *Correspondance Valéry-Fourment* 161. Letter dated January 12, 1901.
21. Two excellent studies on "Agatha" in English by Ursula Franklin deal with the intellectual theme and the poetic prose aspects: "The White Night of 'Agathe': A Fragment by Paul Valéry," *Essays in French Literature* 12 (1975) 37–58 and "Toward the Prose Fragment in Mallarmé and Valéry: *Igitur* and *Agathe*," *The French Review* 49.4 (1976) 536–48. The most complete study to date is Nicole Celeyrette-Pietri's "*Agathe*" *ou* "*Le Manuscrit trouvé dans une cervelle*" *de Valéry*," which bears the subtitle "genesis and exegesis of a tale of understanding." It is interesting to note that the author includes the original title linking the text to Poe, "Manuscript Found in a Brain," although her analysis does not deal directly with Poe's tale.
22. Franklin, "Toward the Prose Fragment" 543.
23. Originally given as a lecture at the Library of Congress on May 4, 1959, Wilbur's text is reprinted in Carlson, *Recognition* 259–60.
24. At the age of twenty-two Valéry was fascinated by the idea of visiting Batavia, probably because the reference in Poe's tale excited his imagination. In a letter to Gide, dated December 8, 1893, Valéry describes a conversation with Eugène Kolbassine, a philosophy professor and admired friend to whom Valéry dedicated *The Evening with Monsieur Teste*. Valéry relates the conversation to Gide:

> Kolbassine insists that we go to Batavia. He describes the island as if he had made it or simply as if he had been there. All those details. I am tempted. I am convinced that over there one is closer, not to nature, but to the Cosmos, than anywhere else. There are earthquakes, cyclones, the sky, etc. The unfortunate thing is that neither of us has a cent. (*Correspondance Gide-Valéry* 193)

Four months later Valéry still has the idea on his mind when he writes again to Gide: "Kolbassine is right: Batavia and a chess board" (*Correspondance Gide-Valéry* 202; letter dated March 19, 1894).
25. There is a striking similarity between Poe's description of the narrator's solitude among the phantoms on board the ship and Valéry's descrip-

tion of Agatha in the thirty lines that are missing from "Agathe" in *Oeuvres* and from the translation in *The Collected Works*. As Agatha slips into reverie she remarks: "There, lost as I am, but without horror and mysteriously new, the monotonous loss of thought prolongs me and forgets me. These idols which are developing, through an imperceptible deformation carry me away. Unique, my astonishment vanishes, among so many phantoms who are unaware of each other" (my translation). Original source, Levaillant, *La Jeune Parque* 46–47: "Là, perdu que je suis, mais sans horreur et nouveau mystérieusement, la perte monotone de pensée me prolonge, et m'oublie. Ces idoles qui se développent, par une déformation insensible me transportent. Unique, mon étonnement s'éloigne, parmi tant de fantômes qui s'ignorent entre eux."

26. P. 23.
27. P. 24.
28. See Chapter 4, Note 24.
29. See Chapter 2, Note 13.

4. Poe, Valéry, and Modern Criticism

1. *Correspondance Gide-Valéry* 229.
2. Valéry makes another specific reference to Poe earlier in his essay. Exploring the relationship between the mind and a given object, Valéry mentions the "faculty of identification" and adds the following footnote: Edgar Allan Poe, "On Shakespeare" (*Marginalia*) (CW 8: 26; O 1: 1170). Unable to find this reference in Burton Pollin's *The Brevities*, I wrote to Professor Pollin to find out whether Valéry had imagined the reference. Pollin pursued the matter with characteristic thoroughness, arriving at a plausible answer. The 1875 Ingram edition of Poe's works (published in Edinburgh) contains the Shakespeare reference included in an "Addenda" to the *Marginalia*. Valéry's familiarity with Poe's comments most likely came from this source. In a review of William Hazlitt's book on Shakespeare, Poe develops the idea of "faculty of identification" from Hazlitt's Preface. As Pollin points out in his letter to me, the idea passed from Hazlitt to Poe to Valéry, who incorporated it into his Leonardo essay.
3. Valéry wrote four essays on Descartes. See CW 9: 6–71; O 1: 787–844. In his essay titled "Descartes," first given as a speech at the Sorbonne for the Ninth International Conference on Philosophy in 1937, Valéry proposes a study of the drama of the intellect similar to his approach to Leonardo. The student of the mind, remarks Valéry,

> may go so far as to claim that no poetic material in the world is richer than this, that the life of the intelligence offers an incomparable lyrical universe, a whole theater in which neither

adventure, passion, suffering of a very particular kind, nor com-
edy, nor anything human is lacking. (CW 9: 18; O 1: 796)
For a discussion of the role of Descartes in Valéry's critical approach, see
Ralph Freedman's essay "Paul Valéry: Protean Critic" in Simon, *Modern
French Criticism* 8–17, and Bémol's chapter on Descartes in *La Méthode cri-
tique de Paul Valéry* 47–53.

4. Wellek, *A History of Modern Criticism* 4: 27–35.

5. Wellek does not devote a chapter to Sainte-Beuve in his *History of Modern
Criticism*, a rather curious omission, considering the preponderate role
the critic played during the period of French criticism covered by
Wellek in volume four. One of the best studies of the critic in English is
Chadbourne's *Charles-Augustin Sainte-Beuve*, in which the author claims
that Sainte-Beuve is "one of the few authors in any language to have
achieved major stature on the basis of his criticism alone" (7). One of
Chadbourne's goals is to rectify the "Beuve-bashing" of Valéry and especially Proust, whose essays included under the title *Against Sainte-Beuve*
give a very negative view of the critic. Although Proust's manuscript
was not published until 1954, Valéry would have been a sympathetic
reader.

6. See Wellek, *A History of Modern Criticism* 4: 61.

7. Wellek, *A History of Modern Criticism* 4: 65.

8. Lawler, *Edgar Poe et les poètes français* 87–123.

9. Valéry did not like several aspects of Poe's *Eureka*, which will be discussed in Chapter 6.

10. Lawler, *Edgar Poe et les poètes français* 100.

11. Lawler, *Edgar Poe et les poètes français* 101.

12. Valéry's lecture "Reflections on Art" is not included in *Oeuvres*. See
notes, CW 13: 292.

13. This essay was first presented as a talk before the Société Française de
Philosophie, Jan. 28, 1928. It is not included in *Oeuvres*. See CW 13: 291.

14. Valéry is describing here how "The Graveyard by the Sea" first came to
him, a subject he treats again in his essay "Concerning 'Le Cimetière
marin'" (CW 7: 150; O 1: 1505–6).

15. This lecture was published later. See Gustave Cohen, *Essai d'explication
du "Cimetière marin."*

16. See "Commentaries on *Charmes*" (CW 7: 153–58; O 1: 1507–12).

17. The English translation of this essay is in Bann and Bowlt, *Russian
Formalism* 41–47.

18. "The Theory of the 'Formal Method'" in Lemon and Reis, *Russian
Formalist Criticism* 103.

19. In his essay "The Theory of the 'Formalist Method'" Boris Eichenbaum
quotes Roman Jakobson, crediting him with having formulated this
view with perfect clarity:

> The object of the science of literature is not literature, but liter-
> ariness—that is, that which makes a given work a work of lit-

erature. . . . The literary historians used everything—anthropology, psychology, politics, philosophy. Instead of a science of literature, they created a conglomeration of homespun disciplines. (Jakobson quoted by Eichenbaum in Lemon and Reis, *Russian Formalist Criticism* 107.)

20. Viktor Shklovsky's essay "On the connection between devices of *Syuzhet* construction and general stylistic devices" (1919) in Bann and Bowlt, *Russian Formalism* 48.

21. Valéry uses this analogy again in his essay "Concerning 'Le Cimetière marin'":

> In the art of the Dance, the state of the dancer (or that of the lover of ballet) being the object of that art, the movements and displacements of the bodies have no limit in *space*—no visible aim, no *thing* which, being reached, annuls them; and it never occurs to anyone to impose on choreographic actions the law of *nonpoetic* but *useful* acts, which is: to be accomplished *with the greatest possible economy of effort* and *in the shortest possible way*. (CW 7: 146–47; O 1: 1502)

22. Wellek, "Paul Valéry" in *Four Critics* 35.

23. Brooks, *The Well Wrought Urn* 203.

24. Wimsatt, *The Verbal Icon* 149.

25. In a *Notebook* reference Valéry explains his understanding of Poe's use of the word *consistency:*

> Poe talks about "consistency." I think he meant by it the quality of a thing or a system conceived or existing in such a way that its parts are in symmetrical relation with one another. If A is the cause of B, B is also the cause of A. If A requires B, B requires A, so that every analysis of a particular system is convertible into any other, exactly as an equation may be solved by any one of its letters. . . . In works of art, the *semblance* of consistency must be sought. The study of form may come to this. (CW 8: 356; C 7: 830)

26. See Bucher's chapter "Valéry: Précurseur de la critique formaliste ou structuraliste" in *La Situation de Paul Valéry critique.* Christine Crow gives an excellent discussion of the subject in English in the "Introduction" to her *Paul Valéry and the Poetry of Voice.*

27. *Yale French Studies* 44 (1970) 65–71.

28. Todorov, "Valéry's Poetics" 66.

29. Todorov quotes from Valéry, "The Opening Lecture of the Course in Poetics" (CW 13: 89–116; O 1: 1340–61). This lecture will be discussed in my next chapter.

30. See Emily Zants' "Valéry and the Modern French Novel." For Valéry, psychological time was more "real" than chronological time, an important point for the New Novelists. Referring to the chronological disorder in a collection of texts titled "Mixture" ("Mélange"), Valéry remarked: "One thing was written nearly fifty years ago. Another dates from the

day before yesterday. . . . This quantity of time signifies nothing in matters of the mind's production" (O 1: 286).

31. This text is not included in *Oeuvres;* see CW 7: 337 for details on original
source.

32. As Maurice Bémol points out in his excellent study, *La Méthode critique
de Paul Valéry,* Valéry's interest in literary criticism was inspired by a desire to understand how his own mind functions; in this sense it is a personal approach that also seeks universal answers.

5. *Poetics and Poetry*

1. Fifty-five of these essays are included in CW 10, where they are divided
into the following categories: I. Mind, World, and History; II. Reflections on Politics; III. Women and Politics; IV. The Idea of Europe; V.
The League of Nations; VI. The Far East; VII. France; and VIII. The
Second World War.

2. Valéry describes his return to writing poetry in "Memoirs of a Poem"
(CW 7: 100–132; O 1: 1464–91). In "The Prince and *La Jeune Parque*"
(CW 7: 133–39; O 1: 1491–96) he recalls reaching an impasse while writ-
ing the poem; he found his way again upon reading an article in *Le
Temps.*

3. The English translation is printed with the original on facing pages in
CW 1: 68–105.

4. English translation in CW 13: 83–88 (O 1: 1438–43) along with "The
Opening Lecture of the Course in *Poetics*" (CW 13: 89–111; O 1: 1340–58).

5. *Yggdrasill* was an international poetry review published in Paris from
April 1936 to April 1940. Georges Le Breton's notes on Valéry's lectures
were published in *Yggdrasill* as follows: Lesson 1: 9 (25 Dec. 1937): 141–
46; Lessons 2, 3, 4: 10 (25 Jan. 1938): 153–56; Lessons 5, 6, 7: 11 (25 Feb.
1938): 170–72; Lessons 8, 9: 12 (25 March 1938): 185–87; Lessons 10, 11: 1
(25 April 1938): 2–4; Lesson 12: 2 (25 May 1938): 26–27; Lesson 13: 3 (25
June 1938): 40–42; Lessons 14, 15: 5–6 (25 Aug.–25 Sept. 1938): 70–73;
Lesson 16: 30 (25 Oct. 1938): 102–3; Lesson 17: 32 (25 Dec. 1938): 139–40;
Lesson 18: 34 (25 Feb. 1939): 167–68. The whole collection of *Yggdrasill*
can be found at the Vanderbilt University Library.

6. "Edgar Poe et Valéry" in *Trois essais sur Paul Valéry.*

7. "Edgar Poe et Valéry" in *Trois essais sur Paul Valéry* 137. All subsequent
reference to Cain are from this essay.

8. Cain, 137.

9. Cain, 138.

10. Cain, 138.

11. Ince, *The Poetic Theory of Paul Valéry* 69.

12. Ince, *The Poetic Theory of Paul Valéry* 8.

13. "A Foreword" in CW 7: 39–51; O 1: 1269–80.

14. The French text of this essay was published in *Figaro*, May 22, 1925, and has not been republished; see CW 7: 336.
15. Bremond, *La Poésie pure* 16.
16. Bremond, *La Poésie pure* 22. Bremond's remark about trying to square the circle is a reference to Valéry's opening paragraph in "A Foreword":
    > About forty years ago a doubt was lifted from our minds. Conclusive proof dismissed as an illusion the ancient ambition of squaring the circle. How fortunate the geometricians, who can from time to time resolve this kind of nebula in their system; but the poets are less fortunate; they are not yet assured of the impossibility of *squaring* every thought in a poetic form.
    > (CW 7: 39; O 1: 1269)

    Valéry was probably thinking about the work of the German mathematician Ferdinand Lindemann (1852–1939) who in 1882 succeeded in proving unequivocally that the quadrature of the circle was impossible. William Dunham gives a synopsis of how Lindemann resolved this age-old question in *Journey through Genius: The Great Theorems of Mathematics* 23–26.
17. Bremond, *La Poésie pure* 26.
18. Bremond, *La Poésie pure* 16.
19. Bremond, *La Poésie pure* 27.
20. "La Poésie pure," *Le Temps*, Oct. 26, 1925, 1.
21. These articles are included in Bremond's book *La Poésie pure.*
22. All quotations from this article are from p. 9.
23. Bremond quoted by Arnold, *Paul Valéry and His Critics* 219.
24. "Modulation and Movement in Valéry's Verse" in *Poetic Principles and Practice* 254–69.
25. Stimpson, *Paul Valéry and Music* 261.
26. Stimpson, *Paul Valéry and Music* 142.
27. Stimpson, *Paul Valéry and Music* 148.
28. Stimpson, *Paul Valéry and Music* 169.
29. *Cours de Poétique*, Lesson 6. *Yggdrasill* 11 (Feb. 25, 1938) 171.
30. James Lawler found this comment on a page headed "Orphisme" among Valéry's notes for the poem "Orpheus" (CW 1: 436).
31. For a full-length study in English of Valéry's poetry, see Christine Crow's *Paul Valéry and the Poetry of Voice.* See also Suzanne Nash's *Paul Valéry's Album de vers anciens,* a study of his earlier poems.
32. These details are from Lawler's notes on the poem in CW 1: 467–68. He also wrote an exegesis of the poem, "Je vois le Christ . . ." published in his book *The Poet as Analyst, Essays on Paul Valéry.*
33. This poem is included in O 1: 301–2. The original French is printed opposite the translation in CW 1: 240–41.
34. The translation of this poem and others in the *Collected Works* are by David Paul.
35. Lawler quoting Poe in *The Poet as Analyst* 27 (note 32).

36. Lawler, *The Poet as Analyst* 32.
37. Lawler, *The Poet as Analyst* 33. Florence de Lussy in her recent study of Valéry's manuscripts does not connect this poem with Valéry's crisis of 1892. She believes the inspiration was Valéry's anguish at the bedside of his wife, who was gravely ill from 1908–14. De Lussy's opinion is based on letters exchanged between Valéry and Gide during this period. She mentions that Valéry did not like the poem and decided to eliminate it from his collection *Charmes*. De Lussy, *"Charmes" d'après les manuscrits de Paul Valéry: histoire d'une métamorphose* I, 138–39.
38. Repr. in Carlson, *Recognition* 215.
39. "From Poe to Valéry." Repr. in Carlson, *Recognition* 219.

6. *"On Poe's* Eureka *"*

1. Editions d'art Edouard Pelletan, Paris: Helleu et Sergent, 1921.
2. Lloyd, *Selected Letters of Charles Baudelaire* 201; *Correspondance* 2: 342.
3. In a letter thanking Judith Gautier for the review, Baudelaire wrote: "I felt an emotion that is difficult to describe, half pleasure at being so well understood, half joy at seeing that one of my oldest and dearest friends had a daughter who was truly worthy of him." Lloyd, *Selected Letters of Charles Baudelaire* 202; *Correspondance* 2: 353.
4. *Correspondance Gide-Valéry* 150. Letter dated March 3, 1892.
5. Lefèvre, *Entretiens avec Paul Valéry* 34.
6. In 1900 Valéry became the administrative assistant of Edouard Lebey, director of Agence Havas, the French press association. He worked for Lebey until the latter's death in 1922.
7. Valéry is probably referring to the article he intended to write for *Le Centaure* in 1896.
8. *Correspondance Gide-Valéry* 383.
9. Richard P. Benton points out in his Preface to *Eureka: A Prose Poem* that critical studies on *Eureka* in English began in the 1950s. He credits Valéry with being among the first to take the work seriously. Benton gives a bibliography of studies on *Eureka,* pp. 1–6.
10. Photocopies of this edition are presented in two books edited by Richard P. Benton: *Eureka: A Prose Poem* and *Poe as Literary Cosmologer: Studies on Eureka, A Symposium.*
11. Ostrom, *The Letters of Edgar Allan Poe* 2: 452. Letter dated July 7, 1849.
12. Quoted by Burton R. Pollin, "Contemporary Reviews of *Eureka*: A Checklist" in Benton, *Poe as Literary Cosmologer* 29.
13. *Eureka: A Prose Poem,* ed. Richard P. Benton. Henceforth, all references will be to this volume, indicated in the text as B. The page numbers refer to the Putnam edition photocopied two pages per page in Benton's book.

14. Valéry describes the mind of Edmond Teste as a "mechanical sieve" capable of separating the essential from the non-essential.
15. Lefèvre, *Entretiens avec Paul Valéry* 20.
16. L. Pearce Williams. *Michael Faraday: A Biography* 443.
17. For a detailed study, see Reino Virtanen's *Scientific Analogies of Paul Valéry*.
18. The phases in *The Young Fate* are based on Jacques Duchesne-Guillemin's analysis in *Etudes pour un Paul Valéry* 225–29.

Conclusion: Unity of Effect

1. *Lettres à quelques-uns* 98.
2. "From Poe to Valéry." Repr. in Carlson, *Recognition* 214–19.

Afterword: Poe in France since 1945

1. *Cahier: Edgar Allan Poe* (Paris: Herne, 1974).
2. *Lettres américaines* (Aix-en-Provence: Alinea, 1987).
3. All of the relevant texts in this debate have been brought together in one volume, *The Purloined Poe*, edited by Muller and Richardson. My quote is from Johnson's essay "The Frame of Reference: Poe, Lacan, Derrida" included in the volume, pp. 213–51.
4. See Maurice J. Bennett, "The Detective Fiction of Poe and Borges" and "The Infamy and the Ecstasy."
5. Borges, "Valéry as Symbol" in *Labyrinths* 198.

Selected Bibliography

Paul Valéry

A. BIBLIOGRAPHIES

Arnold, A. James. *Paul Valéry and His Critics, A Bibliography of French-Language Criticism 1890–1927.* Charlottesville: U of Virginia P, 1970.
Karaiskakis, Georges, and François Chapon. *Bibliographie des oeuvres de Paul Valéry publiées de 1889 à 1965.* Preface by Lucienne Julien Cain. Paris: Librairie Auguste Blaizot, 1976.

B. WORKS IN FRENCH, ENGLISH TRANSLATION, CORRESPONDENCE, AND NOTEBOOKS

Valéry, Paul. *Oeuvres.* 2 vols. Ed. Jean Hytier, coll. Pléiade. Paris: Gallimard, 1957, 1960.
———. *The Collected Works of Paul Valéry.* 15 vols. Ed. Jackson Mathews. Bollingen Series, Princeton, NJ: Princeton UP, 1956–75.
———. *Cahiers.* 29 vols. Paris: Centre National de la Recherche Scientifique, 1957–61.
———. *Cahiers.* 2 vols. Ed. Judith Robinson. Paris: Gallimard, 1973, 1974.
Correspondance d'André Gide et de Paul Valéry. Preface and notes by Robert Mallet. Paris: Gallimard, 1955.
Correspondance de Paul Valéry-Gustave Fourment. Intro. and notes by Octave Nadal. Paris: Gallimard, 1957.
Lettres à quelques-uns. Paris: Gallimard, 1952.

C. BOOKS AND ARTICLES ON VALÉRY

Austin, Lloyd. *Poetic Principles and Practice, Occasional Papers on Baudelaire, Mallarmé and Valéry.* Cambridge: Cambridge UP, 1987.

Barbier, Carl B. "Valéry et Mallarmé jusqu'en 1898." *Colloque Paul Valéry: Amitiés et jeunesse. Influences-lectures.* University of Edinburgh, Nov. 1976. Paris: Nizet, 1978.

Bémol, Maurice. *Paul Valéry.* Clermont-Ferrand: G. de Bussac, 1949.

———. *La Méthode critique de Paul Valéry.* Paris: Nizet, 1952.

Berne-Joffroy, André. *Présence de Valéry.* Paris: Plon, 1944.

———. *Valéry.* Paris: Gallimard, 1960.

Bolle, Louis. *Paul Valéry.* Fribourg, Switzerland: Egloff, 1944.

Borges, Jorge Luis. "Valéry as Symbol." *Labyrinths.* New York: New Directions, 1964, 198–99.

Bremond, Henri. *La Poésie pure.* Paris: Grasset, 1926.

Bucher, Jean. *La Situation de Paul Valéry critique.* Brussels: La Renaissance du Livre, 1976.

Cain, Lucienne Julien. *Trois essais sur Paul Valéry.* Paris: Gallimard, 1958.

Celeyrette-Pietri, Nicole. *Valéry et le moi.* Paris: Klincksieck, 1979.

———. *"Agathe" ou "Le Manuscrit trouvé dans une cervelle" de Valéry.* Paris: Lettres Modernes, 1981.

Charpier, Jacques. *Essai sur Paul Valéry.* Paris: Seghers, 1956.

Cioran, E. M. *Valéry face à ses idoles.* Paris: L'Herne, 1970.

Cohen, Gustave. *Essai d'explication du "Cimetière marin."* 8th ed. Paris: Gallimard, 1958.

Crow, Christine M. *Paul Valéry: Consciousness and Nature.* Cambridge: Cambridge UP, 1972.

———. *Paul Valéry and the Poetry of Voice.* Cambridge: Cambridge UP, 1982.

De Lussy, Florence. *"Charmes" d'après les manuscrits de Paul Valéry: histoire d'une métamorphose.* 2 vols. Paris: Minard, 1990.

Doisy, Marcel. *Paul Valéry, intelligence et poésie.* Paris: Cercle du livre, 1952.

Duchesne-Guillemin, Jacques. *Etudes pour un Paul Valéry.* Neuchâtel: La Baconnière, 1964.

Eliot, T. S. "From Poe to Valéry." *Hudson Review* 2 (1949): 327–42. Repr. in Carlson, *Recognition,* 205–19.

Fernandat, René. *Autour de Paul Valéry.* Grenoble: B. Arthaud, 1933.

Franklin, Ursula. "The White Night of 'Agathe': A Fragment by Paul Valéry." *Essays in French Literature* 12 (1975): 37–58.

———. "Toward the Prose Fragment in Mallarmé and Valéry: *Igitur* and *Agathe.*" *The French Review* 49.4 (1976): 536–48.

———. *The Rhetoric of Valéry's Prose Aubades.* Toronto: U of Toronto P, 1979.

———. *The Broken Angel: Myth and Method in Valéry.* Chapel Hill: North Carolina Studies in the Romance Languages and Literatures, 1984.

Freedman, Ralph. "Valéry: Protean Critic." *Modern French Criticism.* Ed. John K. Simon. Chicago: U of Chicago P, 1972, 1–40.

Gheorghe, Ion. *Les Images du poète et de la poésie dans l'oeuvre de Valéry.* Paris: Minard, 1977.

Gide, André. *Paul Valéry.* Paris: Domat, 1947.

Grubbs, Henry A. *Paul Valéry.* New York: Twayne Publishers, 1968.

Hytier, Jean. *La Poétique de Valéry*. Paris: Armand Colin, 1953.
————. *The Poetics of Paul Valéry*. Trans. Richard Howard. Garden City, NY: Doubleday, 1966.
Ince, Walter. *The Poetic Theory of Paul Valéry*. Leicester: Leicester UP, 1961.
Jallat, Jeannine. *Introduction aux figures valéryennes: imaginaire et théorie*. Pisa: Pacini Editore, 1982.
Jones, Rhys S. "The Influence of Edgar Allan Poe on Paul Valéry Prior to 1900." *Comparative Literature Studies* (Fall 1946): 10–15.
La Rochefoucauld, Edmée de. *Paul Valéry*. Paris: Editions Universitaires, 1954.
————. *En lisant les cahiers de Paul Valéry*. 3 vols. Paris: Editions Universitaires, 1964, 1966, 1967.
Latour, Jean de. *Examen de Valéry*. Paris: Gallimard, 1935.
Laurenti, Huguette. *Paul Valéry et le théâtre*. Paris: Gallimard, 1973.
Lawler, James R. *Lecture de Valéry: une étude de "Charmes."* Paris: P.U.F., 1963.
————. *The Poet as Analyst: Essays on Paul Valéry*. Berkeley: U California P, 1974.
————. *Edgar Poe et les poètes français*. Paris: Julliard, 1989.
Lefèvre, Frédéric. *Entretiens avec Paul Valéry*. Paris: Flammarion, 1926.
Levaillant, Jean. *La Jeune Parque, L'Ange, Agathe, Histoires brisées*. Paris: Gallimard, 1974.
Loubère, Joyce A. E. "Balzac: le grand absent de chez Teste." *The French Review* 47.6 (1974): 82–91.
MacKay, Agnes Ethel. *The Universal Self: A Study of Paul Valéry*. Toronto: U of Toronto P, 1961.
Maurois, André. *Introduction à la méthode de Paul Valéry*. Paris: Grasset, 1933.
Mondor, Henri. *Précocité de Valéry*. Paris: Gallimard, 1957.
————. *Propos familiers de Paul Valéry*. Paris: Grasset, 1957.
Nash, Suzanne. *Paul Valéry's Album de vers anciens: A Past Transfigured*. Princeton, NJ: Princeton UP, 1983.
Noulet, Emilie. *Paul Valéry*. Brussels: La Renaissance du Livre, 1951.
Oster, Daniel. *Monsieur Valéry: Essai*. Paris: Editions du Seuil, 1981.
Perche, Louis. *Valéry, les limites de l'humain*. Paris: Editions du Centurion, 1965.
Pistorius, Georges. "Le problème de l'influence selon Paul Valéry." *International Comparative Literature Association. Proceedings of the Congress*. 1966.
Pommier, Jean. *Paul Valéry et la création littéraire*. Paris: Editions de l'Encyclopédie française, 1946.
Porche, François. *Paul Valéry et la poésie pure*. Paris: M. Lesage, 1926.
Raymond, Marcel. *Paul Valéry et la tentation de l'esprit*. Neuchâtel: La Baconnière, 1946.
Robinson, Judith. *L'Analyse de l'esprit dans les "Cahiers" de Valéry*. Paris: José Corti, 1963.
Scarfe, Francis. *The Art of Paul Valéry: A Study in Dramatic Monologue*. London: William Heinemann, 1954.

Sewell, Elizabeth. *Paul Valéry.* New Haven: Yale UP, 1952.

Souday, Paul. "La Poésie pure." *Le Temps,* Oct. 26, 1925, 1.

Stimpson, Brian. *Paul Valéry and Music: A Study of the Techniques of Composition in Valéry's Poetry.* Cambridge: Cambridge UP, 1984.

Suckling, Norman. *Paul Valéry and the Civilized Mind.* Oxford: Oxford UP, 1954.

Thibaudet, Albert. *Paul Valéry.* Paris: Grasset, 1923.

Todorov, Tzvetan. "Valéry's Poetics." *Yale French Studies* 44 (1970): 65–71.

Virtanen, Reino. "Paul Valery's Scientific Education." *Symposium* 27 (1973): 362–78.

———. *The Scientific Analogies of Paul Valéry.* Lincoln: U of Nebraska P, 1974.

Whiting, Charles. *Valéry, jeune poète.* Paris: P.U.F., 1960.

———. *Paul Valéry.* London: The Athlone Press, 1978.

Yeschua, Silvio. *Valéry, le roman et l'oeuvre à faire.* Paris: Minard, 1976.

Zants, Emily. "Valéry and the Modern French Novel." *L'Esprit Créateur* 7.2 (1967): 81–90.

Edgar Allan Poe

A. BIBLIOGRAPHIES

Dameron, J. Lasley, and Irby B. Cauthen, Jr. *Edgar Allan Poe: A Bibliography of Criticism 1827–1967.* Charlottesville: UP of Virginia, 1974.

Hyneman, Ester. *Edgar Allan Poe: An Annotated Bibliography of Books and Articles in English 1827–1973.* Boston: G. K. Hall, 1974.

B. WORKS IN ENGLISH AND FRENCH TRANSLATION

The Brevities: Pinakidia, Marginalia, Fifty Suggestions, and Other Works. Ed. with Introduction and Notes by Burton R. Pollin. New York: Gordian Press, 1985.

Collected Works of Edgar Allan Poe. 3 vols. Ed. Thomas Ollive Mabbott. Cambridge, MA, and London: The Belknap Press of Harvard UP, 1969, 1978.

Edgar Allan Poe, Essays and Reviews. Comp. G. R. Thompson. New York: Literary Classics of the United States, 1984.

Eureka: A Prose Poem. Ed. Richard P. Benton. Hartford, CT: Transcendental Books, 1973.

The Letters of Edgar Allan Poe. 2 vols. Ed. John Ward Ostrom. Cambridge, MA: Harvard UP, 1948.

Oeuvres en prose d'Edgar Allan Poe. Trans. Charles Baudelaire; Notes by Y.-G. le Dantec, coll. Pléiade. Paris: Gallimard, 1951.

C. BOOKS AND ARTICLES ON POE

Alexander, Jean. *Affidavits of Genius: Edgar Allan Poe and the French Critics, 1847–1924.* Port Washington, NY: Kennikat Press, 1971.

Bandy, William Thomas. "New Light on Baudelaire and Poe." *Yale French Studies* 10 (1952): 65–69.

————. *The Influence and Reputation of Edgar Allan Poe in Europe.* Baltimore: Cimino, 1962.

————. "Mallarmé's Sonnet to Poe: The First Text?" *Revue de Littérature Comparée* (jan.–mars 1963): 100–101.

————. "Who was Monsieur Dupin?" *PMLA* 79 (1964): 509–10.

————. *Edgar Allan Poe: Sa vie et ses ouvrages.* Toronto: U of Toronto P, 1973.

————. "Huysmans and Poe." *Romance Notes* 17 (1977): 270–71.

Bennett, Maurice J. "The Detective Fiction of Poe and Borges." *Comparative Literature* 35.3 (1983): 262–75.

————. "The Infamy and the Ecstasy: Crime, Art, and Metaphysics in Edgar Allan Poe's 'William Wilson' and Jorge Luis Borges's 'Deutsches Requiem.'" Repr. in Fisher, 107–23.

Benton, Richard P., ed. *Poe as Literary Cosmologer: Studies on Eureka, A Symposium.* Hartford: Transcendental Books, 1975.

Bolle, Jacques. *La poésie du cauchemar, la vie hallucinante d'Edgar Poe.* Neuchâtel: La Baconnière, 1946.

Bonaparte, Marie. *Edgar Poe: Sa vie, son oeuvre—Etude psychanalytique.* Paris: Denoël et Steele, 1933.

————. *The Life and Works of Edgar Allan Poe: A Psycho-Analytic Interpretation.* Trans. John Rodker. London: The Hogarth Press, 1949.

Buranelli, Vincent. *Edgar Allan Poe.* New York: G. K. Hall, 1977.

Cabau, Jacques. *Edgar Poe par lui-même.* Paris: Editions du Seuil, 1960.

Cambiaire, Célestin Pierre. *The Influence of Edgar Allan Poe in France.* New York: Stechert, 1927. Rpt. New York, 1970.

Campbell, Killis. *The Mind of Poe and Other Studies.* New York: Russell and Russell, 1962.

Carlson, Eric W., ed. *The Recognition of Edgar Allan Poe.* Ann Arbor: U Michigan P, 1966.

————, ed. *Critical Essays on Edgar Allan Poe.* Boston: G. K. Hall, 1987.

Cevasco, G. A. "*A Rebours* and Poe's Reputation in France." *Romance Notes* 13 (1971): 255–61.

Chiari, Joseph. *Symbolisme from Poe to Mallarmé.* New York: Gordian Press, 1970.

Defosse, Marcel. *La Méthode intellectuelle d'Edgar Poe.* Paris: Editions de Minuit, 1952.

Fisher, Benjamin Franklin IV, ed. *Poe and Our Times: Influences and Affinities.* Baltimore: The Edgar Allan Poe Society, 1986.

Forclaz, Roger. *Le Monde d'Edgar Poe.* Bern: Herbert Lang, 1974.

————. "Edgar Poe and France: Toward the End of a Myth?" Trans. J. Kelly Morris. Repr. in Fisher, 9–17.

French, John C. *Poe in Foreign Lands and Tongues.* Baltimore: Johns Hopkins UP, 1941.

Harrison, Michael. *The Exploits of the Chevalier Dupin.* Sauk City, WI: Mycroft and Moran, 1968.

Hennequin, Emile. *Ecrivains francisés.* Paris: Perrin et Cie, 1885.

Hutcherson, Dudley R. "Poe's Reputation in England and America 1850–1909." *American Literature* 14.1 (1942): 211–33.

Hyslop, Lois, and Francis E. Hyslop, Jr., eds. and trans. *Baudelaire on Poe.* State College, PA: Bald Eagle Press, 1952.

Jones, Buford, and Kent Ljungquist. "Monsieur Dupin: Further Details on the Reality behind the Legend." *Southern Literary Journal* 9 (1976): 70–77.

Kennedy, J. Gerald. *Poe, Death, and the Life of Writing.* New Haven: Yale UP, 1987.

Lemonnier, Léon. *Edgar Poe et la critique française.* Paris: P.U.F., 1928.

————. *Edgar Poe et les poètes français.* Paris: Editions de la Nouvelle Revue Critique, 1932.

Lombardo, Patrizia. *Edgar Poe et la modernité.* Birmingham, AL: Summa Publications, 1985.

Mauclair, Camille. *Le Génie d'Edgard [sic] Poe.* Paris: A. Michel, 1925.

————. *Princes de l'esprit.* Paris: A. Michel, 1930.

Muller, John P., and William J. Richardson, eds. *The Purloined Poe: Lacan, Derrida & Psychoanalytic Reading.* Baltimore: Johns Hopkins UP, 1988.

Patterson, Arthur S. *L'Influence d'Edgar Poe sur Charles Baudelaire.* Grenoble: Allier, 1903.

Pinto, Eveline. *Edgar Poe et l'art d'inventer.* Paris: Klincksieck, 1983.

Quinn, Patrick F. *The French Face of Edgar Poe.* Carbondale: Southern Illinois UP, 1957.

————. *Poe and France: The Last Twenty Years.* Baltimore: Enoch Pratt Free Library, 1970.

Richard, Claude. *Cahier: Edgar Allan Poe.* Paris: Herne, 1974.

————. *Poe: journaliste et critique.* Paris: Klincksieck, 1978.

————. *Lettres américaines.* Aix-en-Provence: Alinea, 1987.

Seylaz, Louis. *Edgar Poe et les premiers symbolistes français.* Lausanne: Imprimerie La Concorde, 1923.

Stauffer, Donald Barlow. "Poe as Phrenologist: The Example of Monsieur Dupin." *Papers on Poe.* Repr. in Veler, 113–25.

Thomas, Dwight, and David Jackson. *The Poe Log.* Boston: G. K. Hall, 1987.

Veler, Richard P., ed. *Papers on Poe.* Springfield, OH: Chantry Music Press, 1972.

Wetherill, Peter M. "Edgar Allan Poe and Madame Sabatier." *Modern Language Quarterly* 20 (1959): 344–54.

————. *Charles Baudelaire et la poésie d'Edgar Allan Poe.* Paris: Nizet, 1962.

Wilbur, Richard. "The House of Poe." Repr. in Carlson, *Recognition,* 255–77.

Zayed, Georges. *The Genius of Edgar Allan Poe.* Cambridge, MA: Schenkman Publishing, 1984.

Other Works Cited

Bann, Stephen, and John E. Bowlt, eds. *Russian Formalism.* Edinburgh: Scottish Academic Press, 1973.

Baudelaire, Charles. *Correspondance.* 2 vols. Texte établi, présenté et annoté par Claude Pichois avec la collaboration de Jean Ziegler, coll. Pléiade. Paris: Gallimard, 1973.

———. *Oeuvres complètes.* 2 vols. Texte établi, présenté et annoté par Claude Pichois, coll. Pléiade. Paris: Gallimard, 1976.

Borges, Jorge Luis. "Valéry as Symbol." *Labyrinths.* New York: New Directions, 1964, 198–99.

Brooks, Cleanth. *The Well Wrought Urn.* New York: Harcourt Brace, 1947.

Chadbourne, Richard M. *Charles-Augustin Sainte-Beuve.* Boston: Twayne, 1977.

Dunham, William. *Journey through Genius: The Great Theorems of Mathematics.* New York: Wiley, 1990.

Fowlie, Wallace. *Mallarmé.* Chicago: U of Chicago P, 1953.

Gilman, Margaret. *Baudelaire the Critic.* New York: Octagon Books, 1971.

Huxley, Aldous. "Vulgarity in Literature." *Saturday Review of Literature,* Sept. 27, 1930, 158.

Huysmans, Joris-Karl. *Against the Grain.* Trans. Havelock Ellis. New York: Dover, 1969.

Lemon, Lee T., and Marion J. Reis, eds. *Russian Formalist Criticism, Four Essays.* Lincoln: U of Nebraska P, 1965.

Lloyd, Rosemary. *Baudelaire's Literary Criticism.* Cambridge: Cambridge UP, 1981.

———. *Selected Letters of Baudelaire, The Conquest of Solitude.* Chicago: U of Chicago P, 1986.

Mallarmé, Stéphane. *Thèmes anglais.* Paris: Gallimard, 1937.

———. *Correspondance 1862–1871.* Eds. Henri Mondor and Jean-Pierre Richard. Paris: Gallimard, 1959.

———. *Oeuvres complètes.* Eds. Henri Mondor and G. Jean-Aubry, coll. Pléiade. Paris: Gallimard, 1961.

———. *Stéphane Mallarmé, Selected Poetry and Prose.* Ed. Mary Ann Caws. New York: New Directions, 1982.

Proust, Marcel. *Against Sainte-Beuve and Other Essays.* Trans., intro, and notes John Sturrock. London: Penguin Classics, 1988.

Ransom, John Crowe. *The New Criticism.* Norfolk, CT: New Directions, 1941.

Simon, John K., ed. *Modern French Criticism.* Chicago: U of Chicago P, 1972.

Starkie, Enid. *Baudelaire.* Norfolk, CT: New Directions, 1958.

Wellek, René. *A History of Modern Criticism: 1750–1950.* Vol. 4. New Haven: Yale UP, 1966.

————. *Four Critics: Croce, Valéry, Lukács, and Ingarden.* Seattle: U of Washington P, 1981.

Williams, L. Pearce. *Michael Faraday: A Biography.* New York: Basic Books, 1965.

Wimsatt, W. K., Jr. *The Verbal Icon.* Lexington: U of Kentucky P, 1954.

Index

Académie Française, 142, 143
Adam, Juliette, 106
Aeneid, 141
Agence Havas, 75, 201n.6
Alain (pseudonym of Emile-
  Auguste Chartier), 119, 124
Alcoholism, 18
Alembert, Jean Le Rond d', 165
Allan, John, 19
Allan, Mrs. John, 18
Ampère, André Marie, 49, 165
Architecture: Valéry's interest in,
  47
Aristotle, 162
Arnold, Elizabeth, 18
Art: as a machine, 5, 26, 109–10,
  117, 128, 139, 145, 152, 191n.7;
  combined with scientific analysis,
  17, 107, 110
Asselineau, Charles, 23
Austin, Lloyd J., 147

Bacon, Francis, 18, 162
Balzac, Honoré de, 17, 113
Bandy, W. T., 12, 13, 186n.2,
  187n.8, 188n.17, 189n.44, 191n.5,
  193n.6
Barbey d'Aurevilly, Jules, 28–29
Baudelaire, Charles: discovered
  Poe's stories, 1, 12; and influence
  of Poe on Valéry, 2; interest in
  Poe's work and life, 14–16, 42;

references to America, 17; Taine
  misjudges his work, 113;
  translator of Poe, 15, 26–27, 159–
  60; Works by: "Edgar Allan Poe,
  His Life and Works," 14–16; "Le
  Flambeau vivant," 21; "The
  Flowers of Evil," 2, 15, 20, 29, 40;
  Histoires extraordinaires, 32; "Salon
  of 1845," 15; "Salon of 1846," 15,
  26
Benton, Richard P., 201n.9
"Biographical fallacy," 113, 120
Borges, Jorge Luis, 183–84
Bremond, Henri, 142–45
Brooks, Cleanth, 122, 123
Brunetière, Ferdinand, 112, 113,
  114, 120
Bucher, Jean, 124, 198n.26
Byron, George Gordon, Lord,
  188n.15
Byronic hero, 16

Cain, Lucienne Julien, 134, 187n.14
Cambiaire, Célestin Pierre, 185n.1
Carlyle, Thomas, 70
Caws, Mary Ann, 36
Cazalis, Henri, 31, 32
Celeyrette-Pietri, Nicole, 192n.19,
  195n.21
Centaure, Le, 77, 78, 130, 201n.7
Champollion, Jean François, 163
Chiari, Joseph, 34

About the Author

LOIS DAVIS VINES (Ph.D., Georgetown University) is Professor of French at Ohio University, where she has taught twentieth-century literature for the past two decades.